WESTMAR COLLEGE LIBRARY

W9-BOA-132

CLASSROOM GROUPING
FOR TEACHABILITY

CLASSROOM GROUPING FOR TEACHABILITY

Herbert A. Thelen

With the assistance of:

Henry Peterson
Alan Oppenheim
William Hoock
Stephen Perls
Anne Brody

John Wiley & Sons, Inc.   New York · London · Sydney

371.255
T379

LB
3061
.T45

COPYRIGHT © 1967 BY JOHN WILEY & SONS, INC.

All Rights Reserved

This book or any part thereof must not be reproduced in
any form without the written permission of the publisher.

Library of Congress Catalog Card Number: 66-28763

Printed in the United States of America

71466

PREFACE

This is the account of a research investigation which began in the spring of 1957 and ended, except for treatment of the data, in June 1960. The question that began the investigation was: How can the "resources" of teachers and students be utilized more effectively for educational purposes in the classroom?

This first year was devoted to exploring how classroom activities in three school subjects could become experiences of inquiry. With a group of fifty sophomores in the Laboratory School at the University of Chicago, three of the school's teachers, Mr. Robert Boyd, Mr. Paul Moulton, and Mr. "Hutch" Gordon (with the consultation of H. A. Thelen, the administrative facilitation of Mr. Robert Ohm and Dr. Herbert Schooling, and the departmental encouragement of Professor Francis S. Chase), attempted to apply the whole gamut of tools and techniques—team teaching, closed circuit TV, feedback panels, telephones, etc.

By the spring of 1958, it was apparent that the truth of any of our statements would depend upon whom we were talking about. In other words, any comment about educational method would have a different kind of "truth" from one teacher to the next, and from one student to the next. We became convinced that the nature of classroom teaching and learning depends very much on the particular combination of students and teacher. And that until this combination could be specified, we could not know, with any accuracy, what outcomes to expect from various concepts or methods of teaching. This directed us toward the problem of "grouping"—placement of students in the classes of particular teachers. During the last two months of the Sophomore Project, we began experimenting with a wide variety of instruments that might clarify this problem.

In June 1958 we happily received a grant from the Cooperative Research Branch of the U. S. Office of Education. The proposal was to investigate "The Development of Educational Methods for Different Types of Students" (Project 428). This book reports the activities and findings of the project.

The year 1958–1959 was spent in developing instruments and in making arrangements for the next year's experiments in schools. The research team consisted of Alan Oppenheim, Henry Peterson, William Hoock, Stephen Perls, and Anne Brody, under the supervision of Herbert A. Thelen. Each researcher was responsible for the development and validation of at least one of the instruments in the assessment battery. Meanwhile, contacts and arrangements with schools were going forward with the assistance of another group in the Department of Education, the School Improvement Program. Messrs. Gilbert, Schlagle, Seager, McCarty, Downey, Holcombe, Evenson, Anderson, and Cunningham were working with a large panel of schools in the area around Chicago, and they were chiefly responsible for helping us to find cooperating schools and then to establish and maintain working relationships with them.

In January 1959, the Assessment Battery was tried out in Skokie, Forest Road, Cossitt, Congress Park (all in Illinois), and Asa Mercer (Seattle) junior high schools; and in Mishawaka (Indiana), New Trier (Illinois), Nicolet (Wisconsin), Bloom (Illinois), and University of Chicago high schools.

By June 1959, with the assistance of the administrators in the various schools, and through the special efforts of Donald Cawelti who worked with the research team for six months, 15 teachers were actively cooperating to prepare the way for experiments involving their own classes: Miss Joan Peterson and Mr. Louis Rubidoux at Arlington Heights Junior High School (Illinois); Mrs. Charlotte Zinke at Forest Road Junior High School (Illinois); Mrs. Theresa Barnes and Mr. Jonas Lashmet at Lincolnway High School (Illinois); Miss Janice Swanson and Mr. Robert Borich at Rich Township High School (Illinois); Mr. Henry Abram and Mr. Bruce Sandberg at Niles Township High School (Illinois); Mr. Dawn Neil, Mr. Richard Sherman, and Mr. Raymond Anderson at Bloom Township High School (Illinois); Mr. Vincent Brunner and Mr. Robert Herold at Nicolet High School (Wisconsin); and Mr. Richard Arndt at Mishawaka High School (Indiana). To these teachers, who tolerated our observing, administered many of our tests, and passed on to us their many valuable impressions, we are deeply grateful.

At the many stages of data processing and treatment we received great help from the staff of the Operations Analysis Laboratory (Univac), Shirley Golden of the Board of Examinations Office, and a number of consultants: Professors Benjamin Bloom, Robert Hess, Dorothy Stock, Desmond Cartwright, John Butler, Benjamin Wright, and William

Kruskal at the University of Chicago; and Ivan Scheier and Kern Dickman at the University of Illinois.

Hard work, both creative and routine, was the lot of the research assistants who worked as a loyal team from July 1958 to December 1960. And, with the assistance of Professor Francis Chase, in the absence of the principal investigator, they worked through a pilot project (Chapter 9) for the purpose of developing methodology for assessing the changes that occurred in the social-psychological relationships within the classrooms.

The technical report was written at the Center for Advanced Study in the Behavioral Sciences, with the assistance of the Center, the Department of Education, Mr. Henry Peterson, and a wonderfully able secretary, Mrs. Julie Raventos. The technical report was completed and bundled off to the Cooperative Research Branch, U. S. Office of Education, in July, 1961. The 300 copies had soon been distributed. Since 1963, the only account available to the public has been a short summary article which appeared in *Theory into Practice*, **2**, No. 2, April, 1963.

While these events were gradually unwinding, some extraordinary forces were at work in the big outside world. Grouping became a prominent issue for whole communities, and Admiral Rickover, Ex-President Conant of Harvard, Professor Bestor the Historian, and many others entered the discussion. Behind the scenes, excellent and well-nigh conclusive studies of homogeneous ability grouping were being conducted by Elizabeth Drews, Walter Borg, Harry Passow, and associates. Across the ocean, England was becoming fed up with its "track system," and in Stockholm, Husen and his associates were trying to work out sensible compromises.

In November 1964, this ferment came to a head in a Conference on Grouping which was set up by Torsten Husen of Sweden, Benjamin Bloom of Chicago, Harry Passow of New York, and Neville Postlethwaite of the Unesco Institute of Education in Hamburg, Germany, with the support of the U. S. Office of Education. (This conference is described in Chapter 1.) Scholars from 11 countries prepared working papers describing the forms of grouping used in the schools of their countries; Postelethwaite, Passow, and a team headed by Douglas Pidgeon, from National Foundation for Educational Research in London, prepared and circulated abstracts of fifty of the better studies out of the several hundred that have been conducted over the last half-century. Under the Chairmanship of Gustav Ögren, the Conference shared evaluations, surveyed research and practices, and drafted a book that describes and evaluates grouping practices, puts them in a social-political context, and summarizes the major studies of grouping. *Grouping and Education,* edited by A. Yates, appeared in 1966.

As a participant in the Conference, I found support for many ideas that our study of Teachability Grouping had been directing me toward and, thus heartened, I resolved not only to tell the story of the experiment but also to place it in the context of societal and educational events of the last thirty years. Chapter 1 is a result of the Hamburg discussion and should be dedicated to the Conference participants, all men of good will. Chapter 2 reports the doctoral study of Henry Peterson which he has recently completed from data collected during the experiment; it serves as a model for us to consider what kind of contributions scientific research should be expected to make to practical decisions about grouping. For the rest, while rewriting the technical report, I tried to improve its substance and, bleeding every step of the way, shortened the appendix by 39 tables. Researchers, administrators, and theorists will, I hope, find parts of the book useful. The decision to try to present the "whole picture"—even in simple fashion—was made deliberately, for the rapprochement between behavioral science and educational practice is long overdue.

Herbert A. Thelen

December 1966

CONTENTS

Appendices

CLASSROOM GROUPING
FOR TEACHABILITY

Chapter One

CONTEXT: Social Issues and Educational Alternatives

The Common Sense of Classroom Grouping · A Bit of Quasi-History · The Legacy from the Past · Grouping Under Various Educational Approaches · Strategy and Prospectus for Grouping

THE COMMON SENSE OF CLASSROOM GROUPING

At first, the grouping of students into classrooms appears to be a relatively trivial technical affair. If there are 200 children and ten teachers, why not just divide the students into ten groups of 20, and give one group to each teacher? This would make grouping a matter of random choice and it would certainly be fair to all concerned. In practice, grouping has to be more complicated because there are certain constraints, for example, boys usually do not take physical education with girls and some students take Spanish, whereas others take Russian, Fortran, or some other language. Also, teachers are not interchangeable, and several or even most of them may have specific combinations of subjects they can teach. Thus simple division gets mixed up with scheduling difficulties, and procedures that seemed trivial and obvious become quite elaborate—so elaborate, in fact, that the vice principal spends the first month of each summer merely trying to schedule everyone into next semester's classes. For the past several years, computers have entered the field, and many school systems now schedule their students electronically, so to speak.

It does not take much nudging to see that the necessity of grouping for mechanical reasons can become a virtue for other reasons. For example, a teacher can take the computer read-out and note that his prospective class looks fairly good except for Joe Villain whom the teacher cannot tolerate. So why not make a small shift, and swap Joe for Mary Saint who is presently earmarked for a different teacher's class that meets at the same hour? Although teachers do not usually

1

engage directly in such trading, they can in many schools make their wishes known to a counselor—who is likely to have some ideas of his own—and, within limits, certain sensible adjustments can be made. How seriously this corrective maneuvering is undertaken depends on the interpersonal interests of the teachers and also how easily students can be shifted after the semester gets under way. However it is done, there is little doubt that some students and teachers should be kept apart or put together for the good of both. The practical question is not whether this sort of screening should occur, but when and how and on the basis of what information.

In addition to more or less distinctive, even possibly harmful, combinations of a particular teacher with certain students who seem to mobilize both his anxiety and his anger, certain combinations are commonly found to make life difficult for most teachers; in this case, the difficulty would be attributed mostly to the students alone, rather than to the particular combinations of students and teachers. For example, many teachers feel that both "fast" and "slow" students make teaching more complicated, and they therefore regard such students as "difficult." Yet the source of difficulty is the method of instruction which actually creates "fast" and "slow" students. Thus if there is a certain amount of ground ("content," pages, number of experiments) to be covered, and if the task is defined the same way for all students, then children with greater capacity, drive, or skill are noticed because they habitually finish the work first. At the other extreme, slow students stand out because they are still busy working, while others who have finished are looking around the room. It seems entirely reasonable to put the fast students together and the slow students together, and thus to produce groups that are more or less "homogeneous" with respect to the *rate* at which the individuals "cover the ground."

The usual alternative to homogenization by *ability* (which may or may not be the same thing as *rate*) is "enrichment," by which is meant giving the more able or rapid students more work so that the time element for completing assignments will be the same as for slower students. But this simple device, of punishing students for being fast, does not eliminate their tendency to catch the point of a discussion more quickly and thus to spoil the developmental sequence the teacher had in mind. And it does tend to make quite clear that there are actual differences in roles, participation, constructiveness, prestige, etc., among students during class discussion—a painful thought for dyed-in-the-wool egalitarians. Speed tends to be associated mentally with a general characteristic called "brightness," an attribute thought to be possessed by properly brought up, intelligent, moral, white, college-bound persons.

Slow students, on the other hand, are thought to come from "under-privileged" homes, never read a book, be predominantly Negro, and live an indolent life because of some deficiency (possibly genetic) in their character.

One suspects that there may be many reasons, some of them having little to do with education, for grouping students homogeneously "by ability." If we read the newspapers, listen to people, and add up all our information, the suspicion becomes a certainty.

Decisions about how to group children into classrooms are over-loaded and overheated by emotions similar to those involved in deci-sions about who shall have a key to the executive washroom; how "horizontally" to integrate hotels, armies, and labor unions; to whom and under what conditions political favors will be dispensed; and, in general, how seriously, in a million settings, we shall subscribe to that grand old phrase "without qualification by race, creed, or color"—and, more invidiously, by social position or "socioeconomic status."

A BIT OF QUASI-HISTORY

There is a close connection between the state of affairs in the larger society of the nation and the smaller society of the community or even of the school. This is understandable because the smaller segments are part and parcel of the larger; dialogue at the level of national govern-ment is animated by the same attitudes, prejudices, and values that nourish local dialogue. The words at the two levels may be about differ-ent topics, but the emotional dynamics are the same.

What this means in practice is that successful innovations of new practices in schools have to satisfy not only the criterion of educational plausibility or soundness; they must also catch the mood of the public. For example, teaching machines are currently failures because they do not teach the "higher mental processes" such as critical thinking—but the public is willing to buy them. At the same time, "self-directed study," which can be valuable for the child's education, has been driven underground by the national drive toward standardization, automation, and routine-teaching procedures applicable to everyone. The purpose of this book is to demonstrate the soundness of another proposed innova-tion, "teachability grouping," but its success in the schools will depend to a considerable degree on the mood of the community when the change is attempted.

One way to demonstrate the connection between national affairs and school practices is to show that as one changes so does the other. A brief historical excursion through the last 35 years will disclose that the mood of the Nation, as it faced, in turn, depression, World War II, the cold war, Sputnik (etc.), has been faithfully reflected in school practices. By this is meant that the common denominator among such changes is largely explainable by shifts in the national thinking. Within the last decade, the connection between national affairs and school practices has become extraordinarily close: most changes at present are the direct result of federal legislation, and "local control" has come to be "gate-keeping" which decides which of the national initiations will be resisted or accepted in the local schools.[1] The autonomous community, effectively striving toward its own self-determined goals, portrays a far less accurate image than the community that reflects national and even international issues.

Depression

Thirty years ago, then, we were in the midst of the Great Depression whose tremendous impact resulted from two characteristics of our society. First, a very large part of the citizenry seriously questioned whether the American way of life, with its brand of democracy, could survive. Was the productive society in its present form finished, and would some other form, such as socialism-communism take over? Second, the "wrong" people were suddenly poor. We have always had marginal groups who are the last to have money when things go well and the first to be broke whenever the economic applecart is upset. These are the "poor" as in the phrase "the poor are always with us." But the top-hatted financier jumping out the skyscraper window accurately cartooned the facts of a new kind of poverty, one that touched the leaders and the educated as well as Mr. Roosevelt's "common man."

Educationally, the Depression opened the door to the emergent curriculum, to teacher-pupil planning, to active inquiry by students in high schools. The adult attitude that made these activities possible was humility. The sad state of affairs in the nation eloquently testified that what we had taught or the way we had taught must have been seriously at fault. The fact that well-educated persons were suddenly poor and helpless made the educated man of the time somewhat more modest in thinking of himself or his way of life as a model to be emulated by the upcoming generation of high school students. High school commencement speeches offered the hope, uttered with a degree of fervor previously unmatched, that the new generation now entering adulthood would "find the way." Youth was taken seriously; we had during this period the first large-scale studies of high school-aged citizens, such as the study by Leonard Koos in 1932. We had the first national provisions for youth welfare: the Civilian Conservation Corps and the job-providing National Youth Administration. High schools, which had remained aloof from the liberalizing manual training, Herbartian, and child-centered movements that began in the elementary schools during the 1890's now began to go "progressive." The traditional goals, confined to learning school subjects and preparing for a trade or for college seemed trivial compared to the development of each student's own "unique potentials," whatever they might be. In short, high schools tended to look for their goals less in the established society that was crumbling all around them and more in the developable creativity, capacity, and commitments of the citizens to be.

It seemed obvious that the potentials could make themselves known and be realized only as the students worked in many different roles on problems that were "real" and "meaningful" to them. Hence the schools emphasized such things as teacher-pupil planning, student self-government, collapse of the distinction between curriculum and extra-curriculum, development of measures to appraise sophisticated skills of problem solving, and development of "fused" courses which invited the student to use the skills of English to investigate the substance of Social Studies.

Collaboration with students was the order of the day, and the usual loneliness of teachers—a loneliness which veers rather readily into punitiveness—was noticeably lacking. Many look back on the middle thirties as a golden age in schools, a time when the extent to which one was able to challenge serious thought by students seemed far more important than how much "content" was covered. (And this was right, too, for the Eight-Year Study of graduates from thirty progressive schools and thirty matched "regular" schools showed that success in college was correlated less with what school "subjects" the student "took" than with how rigorous the thinking required in whatever subjects he did take.)[2]

Hot War

Any period of decent relationships between strong and weak, whether it be boss and employee or adult and youth, is set by the attitudes of the stronger party. The attitude of humility, which made educational practice in the thirties a real dialogue between adults and youth, evaporated as the nation began in 1939 to mobilize for war. There was a job to be done, and our goals were suddenly clear. War may be hell, but in those days, at least, we knew who the enemy was and therefore could fight the enemy rather than ourselves. There were some educational casualties, such as the "life-adjustment" movement, but most aspects of education were not much affected by the war. A vast training enterprise was developed within the armed forces and contracts were written with universities and extension divisions to take over certain limited training chores. We could suppose the major new educational concept bequeathed to us from the war years was the notion of the "crash" educational program. This was the idea that by putting enough money, time, manpower, and ingenuity into a course we could accomplish virtual miracles such as preparing young men to navigate in a foreign, non-English speaking country in three months. The sneaking suspicion that teaching is entirely a rational matter, whose success is contingent on materials, time, and money, has, as we shall see, persisted to the present.

McCarthy

In 1946, something new was ushered in: a condition of diffuse anxiety about which nothing could be done. The war was over, and we were the victors, and there began a cold war, an extraordinarily frustrating affair in which we have to make all the preparations for a hot war without any of the relief-bringing outlets for action. There is no bold coup, no clear-cut strategy which will enable us to break out into an open field for decision. We no longer feel there are genuine alternatives open to us. There is a lessening of freedom of choice and, therefore, of intelligence because intelligence is useful only when alternatives can be formulated and weighed.

Two events capture the flavor of this period. The first was the rise of Senator Joseph McCarthy and a host of lesser demagogues; the second was the election of Dwight Eisenhower. Both of these were reactions to the national mood of frustration. McCarthy mobilized and channeled our aggressions. Since we could not see the enemy ourselves, we supported someone who thought he could—a classic illustration of Bion's observations that under certain conditions a group may elevate a paranoid to leadership. Eisenhower was elected, not because "generals make good (or bad?) presidents" but he had ended the war in Europe and reduced our anxieties. As a candidate, he promised, personally, to end the tense stalemate in Korea. Thus our rather worrisome tendency to run away from it all suddenly became legitimate, we were leaving it all to Father.

The McCarthy legacy is peculiarly important for our understanding of adult concern for grouping of all sorts, for McCarthy moved interpersonal associations and friendships out of the private and into the public realm. For the first time, and in the very teeth of our Anglo-Saxon legal tradition which says that a man can be punished only if he engages in illegal, overt *behavior,* whom you associated with suddenly became a matter of public interest. In short, you could be damned, not for anything you did wrong, but because you were a member of an organization which certain authorities decided was "subversive." (I don't know about you, but it is only during the last two or three years that I have freely signed any petition I wished without wondering whether some day, under changed societal conditions, my signature might be used against me.)

The legacy from the McCarthy period is fear. Community-school relationships in most systems became a public relations activity, designed to placate, smooth, and sweep under the rug all signs of controversy, for even local bickering could escalate into a McCarthy TV spectacular. School administrators became "managers" rather than prophets encouraging youths to build a new society, and the schools became defenseless against Rickover, Bestor, the fundamentalist groups, the Birchers, and anyone else who wanted, for whatever reason, to take a poke at the schools. Fearful persons can only defend, not cooperate. The average tenure of school superintendents in the nation as a whole is even now a little more than two years. The weakness, regardless of its justification, of the head man sets the tone for the rest of an organization. Teachers found that they would receive little protection or support from most administrators if some noisy minority got sore at their mentioning communism or suggesting that any question, while it may have only one side, can at least be examined from several points of view. This was the period of the loyalty oath, a period in which men who would have seemed decent enough a decade earlier now openly acted against their consciences (and good sense) and explained there was nothing else they could do. Professors discovered that academic freedom must include responsibility not only to speak the truth but to protect their profession as a distinguishable group in society.

McCarthy, of course, got his support from somewhere: us. He was a product of our anxieties—he was made by them. That within ourselves we were revolted by him only underscores the kind of ambivalence that makes action impossible. But, during the Army-McCarthy hearing of 1954, the submerged side of our ambivalence suddenly created a new national hero, Attorney Welch. We participated via television in a national morality play, with dark, beetle-browed, profusely sweating ponderous evil in face-to-face combat with wit, sophistication, and just plain old-fashioned good. Exit McCarthy. Now things that had been too risky or could not get a hearing while the nation was so preoccupied suddenly began to blossom. Those who had felt immobilized now began to move, to think about the future. In education we saw the beginning of the new national curriculum movements in science, the NDEA education acts, the provision of federal funds for educational research, etc. These were small beginnings, but they were constructive and forward looking, and they caused us to work on problems as our enemy rather than on each other. This period, from 1954 to 1957, was short-lived, but it did bring temporary surcease from the cold war and its domestic manifestations.

Sputnik

In 1957 a team of German-trained Russians launched Sputnik and all the cold war uneasiness suddenly focused on the schools—of all places. Within weeks after the Russians sent off their rocket, school boards all over the country were requiring one more course in science or mathematics as a prerequisite for graduation. (And N. Khrushev became an *ex officio* member of every school board.) We now had a new theory that the Cold War would be won by the country with the most scientists, and, since scientists are trained by schools, the schools suddenly became instruments of national defence. Their mission since 1957 has been to prepare the manpower needed to maintain and prosper the economic, military, and technological establishment in this country. The war cry became: Automation, Standardization, Authorization, Nationalization and Dehumanization. The reasoning was simple. (*a*) We need more chemists (allegedly). (*b*) There are certain things all chemists should know, and today's top chemists know what they are; (*c*) therefore, obtain the "better" chemists to write the curriculum in chemistry; (*d*) select the students who can do the work; (*e*) give them all the same experiences; (*f*) give them all the same tests; (*g*) gear every resource of machinery, computer know-how, and manipulative psychology (?) to turning out these identical chemists; (*h*) and finally, let the school become the best manpower factory possible.

And so we had the national curriculum committees deciding what ought to be taught. By their very prestige and cornering of resources, these committees pushed debate from the local level to the national level, with consequent inhibition of local initiative; the establishment of the national external examination system in which the same tests are used all over the nation to assess achievement; the advocacy of "tracks" which are more-or-less restricted range (homogeneous) groupings by ability to "achieve" in each major subject; the development of counseling primarily to persuade high IQ students to continue into college; the Merit Scholarship Board, to make sure money does not stand in the way of academic advancement of high achievers within standardized courses; the tremendous development of teaching machines, learning programs, and visual aids of all sorts (including an airplane circling over seven states and spraying them with televised lessons in most subjects). The dehumanization of the schools was part of the dehumanization of a society in which the technologists gained the upper hand over the managers, who had at least been somewhat responsive to individual workmen. It became clear that unskilled and even semiskilled occupations were going to evaporate—that the kind of production not requiring a high school diploma of a worker would soon be taken over by machines. (If we had not had so many unemployed we might have had a higher estimate of the capabilities of at least some nongraduates.)

It became evident that in spite of all the neat distinctions that sociologists and anthropologists make, we have two basic societies in this country, productive (affluent) and nonproductive (poverty). These societies have different cultures, different ways of life, different traditions, different attitudes toward themselves and each other. The nonproductive society was differentiated from the productive society by an employability criterion, just as the lower tracks in high school were separated from the upper tracks by the criterion of academic learnability. And we can now see the close relationship between the two—the learnability of students in the lower tracks indicated they would be unemployable; learnability in the upper tracks indicated that these students would constitute the productive dominant society. This learning includes more than school subjects—it includes the attitudes and expectations of a student regarding his own personal worth, his prospects for the future, his influence on others, his associates, his autonomy, his opportunities. Maintenance of the Establishment became broadened to include not only manning the computers and reactors but also affirming the existing structure of society—for example, keeping power in the hands that presently hold it.

By 1960 the pendulum had swung about as far as it could away from the humanistic listen-to-the-kids attitudes of the middle thirties. And something had happened to all those involved. The teachers were making fewer professional decisions about what to teach and how to teach it. Teachers unions, affiliated with AFL, emerged to challenge the more professionally oriented NEA; although teachers still talked as if they identified with doctors or lawyers, they organized like tradesmen. The high school curriculum, which in the thirties had meant the sequence of planned learning experiences set up both in and outside of class, came to mean simply the syllabus and materials for teaching a subject. The conception of courses as *experiences* having certain qualities of meaningfulness, rigor, imaginativeness, etc., simply disappeared. It is doubtful that a single study was done on teacher-pupil planning during 1957 to 1962, although this had been a highly popular subject during the thirties and early forties.

As for the students, especially those in high school, what happened to them is shameful. The increasing content standardization in courses and examinations produced, as the first condition of academic survival, conformity to a detailed set of specifications fixed by outsiders who did not know the children, the community, or the school situation. The criterion of "meaningfulness for each individual" became a phrase to be mouthed only on ceremonial occasions. A simple proposition of logic was discovered: the more detailed the set of specifications, the more persons will be found who do not fit them. A great number of "deviates" was discovered and "ability tracks" and personnel services of all types were developed to "adjust" them.

Meanwhile, the baby boom just after World War II had begun to hit the colleges, and they could now afford to tighten their entrance requirements (thus adding luster to the new definition that the mission of schools was to select rather than to educate). High prestige colleges became unbelievably particular, for they were deluged by applications from a middle-class clientele increasingly oriented to the Establishment. In some cases, over 90% of the applicants were rejected. Students, who a decade ago would have had nothing to worry about, have become almost unnerved worrying about whether they can get into the college of their choice.

The dominance of the manpower goal over the goal of individual development biased education in all its aspects: toward reduction of the possibilities of exploration and discovery necessary in meaningful study; toward teaching the student that his role is to conform to patterns he had no choice in setting up, thus helping create the "organization man"; toward the technical concept that maladjustment should be dealt with by making special adjustments for a variety of groups (created for the purpose) rather than by setting conditions so that each person can learn to act on his own behalf; toward making the passing of exams and pleasing teacher the goal of education, rather than learning to cope more adequately with the world; toward the agonizing perception by youth that there is no place in the world for them except whatever place adults condescend to give them; and finally, toward turning schools into prison, creating "pushouts" or dropouts in large numbers, and changing the role of teacher from a profession to a trade.

Protest

The latest phase was clearly recognizable by 1962; its sign was the large number of civil rights demonstrations of college students in the Midwest and the South. It has taken three years for the pattern to become clear—the riots on the Berkeley campus, the marches in the South, the sudden development of groups like SWAP at Chicago, in which college students tutor the "culturally deprived." The entire community of youth is involved in various ways: in addition to the tough gangs, who have always expressed their inadequacy and lack of place by taking it out on the surrounding society and on each other, there emerged on the scene the passive ineffectuals withdrawing into a world of their own which features beards and private incantations; the lower average college kids who become submissive, identify with their captors, and suppress their resentment as they support the system; the more adequate college students who create activities where they cooperate with the persons they most closely identify with, namely underprivileged Negroes, who like themselves see a better life around them but feel a strong denial of liberty, autonomy, and opportunity to be part of this better life; and finally the "upper crust," who maintain the correct rituals of disagreement and find relief as much in the consciousness of themselves following the traditional ways of rebellion as in any reorientation that occurs in the process.

In viewing these activities, we can see that the more adequate students and, to some extent, youth in general, through their various forms of protest, are demanding "civil" or human rights for themselves. There have always been more or less picturesque low status groups of adolescent protesters, but the scene is different today because the disaffected and alienated now include a high percentage of the leaders—not the misfits. These are the prophets who speak in valid tongue for something universal, international, and highly significant. We have created this group in reaction to the manpower concept of education—and to all the inhumane techniques and attitudes we assume such a concept requires.

THE LEGACY FROM THE PAST

The legacy from the past is an embarrassment of riches. The richness is of sensitivity, attitude, and emotion because our past has ranged through the incredible gamut of depression, war, affluence, hysteria, technical determinism, and political-ideological conflict. During each period, individuals have had to redefine their place in society as a response to events that "others" have brewed for them. The task of most adults has been to accommodate to "happenings," hopefully in an enlightened way. Today's adults suppose that their children will encounter their same agonies and anxieties of adjustment in the classrooms. To some extent and in some ways adults relive their fears and hopes by seeing them repeated in the lives of their children. In short, we have discovered what it means to have to remake our place in society every few years, and we identify with children, who, we think, must have the same problem because schools and classrooms too are societies.

But that is only half the legacy of adult involvement in the child's social experience in the classroom. The other half is far less sentimental, more objective, and, supposedly, quite awkward. In short, although we identify with the social plight of our own child, we also lump all children together into one group, a peer or youth society, and build a barrier around it. We learned earlier to distinguish the good guys from the bad guys, the communists from the noncommunists, the bright from the dull, the productive from the nonproductive. Although we have always known that there are some differences between children and adults, it is only recently that we have tended to endow them with a society of their own in which we have no place. Having no place, we wall them off, we feel excluded by jargon we cannot understand, by enthusiasms we cannot applaud, by activities that seem to have no purpose beyond celebrating activity in its own right, and by attitudes toward us that we find decidedly uncomfortable. There is, after all, an adult side to the "alienation" of youth. We feel as alienated by youth as they do by us. The child of today is the citizen of tomorrow, and we want to make quite sure that that citizen will protect us in our old age. High school students must be made to work hard so they can get into the college of our choice—I mean of their choice (don't I?). They must work hard so our country can be strong. They must learn to do distasteful, required things because that is our image of our own lot in society.

All this adds up to considerable ambivalence on our part. Regarding children as an alien group, adults tend to pour the work on, make arbitrary demands, and treat children like raw materials to be processed by an impersonal machine. This makes the children tense and rebellious and unhappy, and most of us are sorry about that because, we tell ourselves, "we love our children." I suppose the rationalization is that what is done against students is done "for their own good" and "more in sorrow than in anger"—exactly the way we see ourselves being treated by authorities in the adult (over-age) world.

A further legacy is a variety of concepts about the goals and methods of education.

1. *From the Depression.* The classroom group is an interactive milieu within which each individual must discover and develop his own potentials. Furthermore, these potentials must be developed in a socially constructive manner. In short, more adequate persons must be developed in order to have a more adequate society.

The classroom group is a place for dialogue, controversy, challenge, compromise, reality testing: in other words, a place for all those things men do in order to strengthen their powers.

The basis of decisions by the group is its own tested experience, and the more heterogeneous the resources and backgrounds of students, the wider the range of experiences is to build on and the more capable the group's discussions.

2. *From the war years.* The classroom group remains an interactive milieu to support individual learning and to carry out activities. But it loses its importance in reality as a tester of attitudes and insights by which pupils would later build a more adequate society. Educational attention shifts to crash programs of indoctrination and skill training; that is, to nationwide curricula, required to support, sustain, and improve the total war effort. The target here is not the unique individual but rather the roles of citizen or warrior, and producer—offices, not personalities. The social psychology of manipulation of groups becomes increasingly relevant as the old progressive educational ideas, now carried out routinely and perfunctorily, gradually lose their thrust.

The new conception of the group is that it consists of citizens who are to be trained for the same patriotic roles; and the fact that each citizen is also an individual must be acknowledged and then circumvented but not catered to.

3. *From the McCarthy period.* Society is divided into "good guys" and "bad guys," and the "bad guys" are not entitled to any rights at all. Whom you associate with is more important than what you do, and all members of a group obviously have identical beliefs and goals. The educated individual, seeking to follow dictates of conscience, searching for the truth through open examination of experiences, is an egghead, probably misguided and therefore untrustworthy. Behavior must reflect such sensitivities as fear of the mob, guilt by association, demands of conformity, distrust of higher thought processes, and ridicule of civilized aspirations. The argument of *ad hominem* is substituted for the authority of law and it becomes the criterion for validity of proposals. (These assumptions incidentally, still exist among the proponents of the extreme right—assumptions which make us timid when it comes to applying social common sense to the organization of learning in schools.)

4. *From the Sputnik-manpower period.* The classroom group is a device for putting social pressure on students to engage in tasks which are not meaningful enough to elicit their voluntary involvement. Rewards for learning—and punishments—are extrinsic, having little to do with the nature of the task and a great deal to do with belongingness, prestige, and social skill within the group. The norms of the classroom group, the methods of teaching, and even the programming of materials are all

calculated to reinforce a large number of specified behaviors rather than to develop insights through which appropriate specific behaviors would be created. The prevailing conception of instruction is that first the teacher must "manage" the group, then he can teach it. The prime function of grouping is to make the group "manageable," not educable.

5. *From the present period, the Age of Protest:* we have youth desperately eager to be deeply involved in something important to themselves, to have commitments by which to navigate, to identify with worthy aspects of the productive society, to abate their sickening sense of alienation from the practically totalitarian world of schools. As this is written, the need of youth for identity seems especially to be revealed in their uncanny sensitivity to those adult behaviors which are anti-thetical to freedom. Adults who study the plight of all youth vis-a-vis modern society are fairly well agreed on what is required. The classes of today should be resourceful, adventurous groups which capitalize on a wide range of talents and, in so doing, develop them further. Any seg-regation (for example, by race or IQ) must be justified on educational grounds, and in the absence of strongly confirming evidence, classes should be composed heterogeneously with respect to all such socially significant but educationally irrelevant factors as race, religion, ethnic origin, and social class.

At various periods in the past, different ideas about the goals and means of education have prevailed, and today these views are still very much alive. Certain views are characteristic not only of individuals but of groups and organizations, and, in a way, a person's educational "philosophy" betrays a good deal about his location in our pluralistic society. All views of education must consider the same ingredients: subject matter to be taught, activities through which it will be taught, methods for determining which activities to use and in what sequence, norms and values by which to judge effectiveness and make selections, climate of interpersonal influences with characteristic degrees of free-dom, responsibility, and identification with teacher and others, and, finally, provision of community and parental support outside the class-room. Each of these elements may be the starting point, the most essential "given" factor from which all else follows. We can find rationales for education which begin by defining content, activities, method, value-orientation, climate, and roles of parents, counselors, etc. Which element will be considered next, and how cursorily, differs from one rationale to the next.

Students may, of course, be grouped in many different ways, both with respect to each other and the teacher. Grouping is a means, a malleable variable, and a contributing factor to education; the various rationales (and the persons subscribing to them) differ not only in their awareness of the importance of grouping but also in the kind of grouping deemed most appropriate to the point of view. It follows that there is no right way to group "in general." Any discussion of grouping remains vague until we define what we consider the aims and methods of education to be. Judging by this proposition, a vast amount of today's discussion of grouping is unintelligible as educational discourse, however valuable it may be as an occasion for striking postures face-to-face with the larger society.

Let us now consider several rationales of education, each having a different starting point and each having quite different implications for classroom grouping.

Education as the Learning of Specified Content

The fundamentalist view of education is that there are certain things that all students ought to learn, and these things comprise education's basic "content." Content includes specific items of information, principles which explain common phenomena, and certain skills (for example, the three R's). All adults should have mastered this content, and so everyone knows what this is. "Covering" this content is of highest priority in our schools, and all else is "frills" or luxury. Learning this subject matter is the obligation of the student, and it is not required that he like it or even understand why it is important. The teacher's job is to see that the student learns the material, and any teacher who is not willfully incompetent can teach it. The techniques of teaching seem obvious to the fundamentalists who seldom discuss the nature of the activities or methods; they tend to ignore everything about the teacher except his character: if his character is good, he will teach things all citizens should know; if it is bad he will subvert society by raising incompetents (who will have to be taken care of by those who *did* learn the basic materials provided by education).

When we compare this position with others, we become aware that there is a great deal more to it that is not made explicit by its proponents. And this additional part, being inexplicit and even denied, is in some ways the most influential part. Reference is made to (*a*) how much of the content of education is to be considered "fundamental"; and (*b*) what attitudes and world views undergird the position which are probably communicated to the student by it.

The information, principles, and skills that everyone needs to know in modern society include reading to the point of understanding directions, becoming acquainted with the issues and controversies of the day, and finding enjoyment; writing competently for official purposes and documents and for personal correspondence; arithmetic sufficient to keep track of one's money, to estimate costs and carrying charges, to purchase the amounts and sizes of materials needed. Required information would be about civic services we use, about foods, clothes, cars, appliances, recreational possibilities, reasons why the values of the society are as they are, and facts about ways of life different from ours that exist in our country and must be dealt with. Fundamentalist or not, we all agree on these requirements. It seems that these requirements make up the core of a civilized way of life, a core that is noncontroversial. The controversies and accusations that erupt from time to time really have nothing to do with these basic needs and beliefs.

The underlying disagreements stem from attitudes. To the fundamentalist, the concepts comprising the core are more numerous than noted. They are likely to include all the beliefs, attitudes, rationales, and values of the fundamentalist groups—who are not notorious for recognizing that there are viable alternatives held by other groups in our pluralistic society. Alternatives cannot be accepted as legitimate because the alternatives are not only different but morally wrong. The attitudes that are implicit in the fundamentalist position follow: (*a*) their beliefs are right and other beliefs are wrong; (*b*) the authority by which they are right is a traditional one, that is, it remains unexamined and is usually supported only by citing personal experience; (*c*) everyone should conform to the fundamentalist's unexamined authoritarian position; (*d*) although there is certainly no objection to being pleasant, harshness and punitiveness are justifiable "for the student's own good." The attitudes are intolerant, conforming, univocal (black or white), simple, and traditional.

The methods of teaching emerging from this position tend to approximate the kind of socializing that goes on in a firm, authoritarian household. The student is not expected to have any say about what he is to learn or how he is to learn it; he is too inexperienced to have any worthwhile opinion on these scores. Drill, repetition, and recitation; reward and punishment; consistency of attitude; frequent explanation of what is right and wrong; moral training rather than insight—these are characteristic of the fundamentalist's procedures.

The teacher has two functions: teaching and management. Teaching is engagement in drill, recitation, examination, etc. Management includes all the things that must be done to make the students go along with the teaching. The "good" child gladly does what he is told to do; other children must be corrected, cajoled, scared, persuaded, or otherwise induced. When a fundamentalist objects that "Johnny simply will not learn," the most unacceptable thing you can suggest is that he must try to make the work more interesting and meaningful to Johnny. What is wanted instead is some simple threat, some easy kind of extrinsic reward, some kind of sugar-coating (possibly) to make Johnny stop resisting. In recent years some who maintain this position have been attracted to something they call "group dynamics" because they see that under certain conditions groups do indeed pressure their own members into conforming with required standards and performances.[3]

With respect to grouping, the teaching function is indifferent. Everyone must go through the same wringer and participate in the same experiences for the same rewards. But with respect to the management function, differences can be recognized. There are good and bad children, meaning that some are slow, resistant, rebellious, curious, creative, skeptical, energetic, social, or may have other traits difficult to cope with. Generally speaking, the groupings advocated by fundamentalists differ along a continuum of "superior" to "inferior," meaning "cooperative and submissive" to "unresponsive or rebellious" or, possibly, "having our authoritarian orientation to the world" to "having some other orientation."

We shall see that some of these same elements, but in milder form and with different sorts of justification, are part of other positions which we now discuss.

Education as Participation in Classroom Activities

This starting point can lead us in several different directions. The fundamental recognition is that what a child does in class is "participate" in activities set up, for one reason or another, by the teacher. If he participates appropriately, his education is being furthered; if inappropriate, his education suffers. Unlike the fundamentalists, who use tests to check learning and relegate participating to management, the activity-oriented teacher assesses the participation as a direct indicator of learning in progress.

Teachers have an image in their minds of what a class looks like when it is "learning." It tends to be orderly, attentive, responsive, cooperative, respectful, good-natured or it is enthusiastic, hard-working, full of interesting ideas, noisy at times, encouraging of individual opinions, etc. These patterns of participatory behavior and attitudes are perceived by the teacher. When the class fails to resemble the image the teacher has in mind, he takes steps. He may change the activity, rebuke an individual, break the class into subgroups or individual work, make a joke, make clarifications, request an examination of what is going on, etc.[4]

In all classrooms, there are at least two types of activity. One maintains the classroom group as a society and the student's role is that of a citizen or group member. The qualities of participation that count are cooperation, consideration, sharing of knowledge and skill, controlled competitiveness, taking turns, offering support to the teacher, exerting a modicum of discreet leadership. To the extent that one regards socialization as important, learning to be a "good citizen" is important; this learning is of habits that will, presumably, carry on through life and help maintain an orderly society. For the student who comes from a typical (if such exists) middle-class educated family, this aspect of classroom participation is more or less automatic; for the very large numbers of students who have not had these "advantages," it is difficult; many of these students do not learn "better," they learn only that there is no place for them in school.

The other type or aspect of activity places the student in the role of "learner"—one in which he deals with the content that is being taught. In this role he reads textbooks, works exercises, writes in his notebook, studies for tests, discusses ideas previously studied, makes applications, offers examples, etc. His participation is examined to see if he expresses sound ideas, corrects mistakes, remembers accurately, works efficiently and neatly, formulates shrewd questions, takes an interest in "learning."

An activity-centered rationale assumes that the student must participate in certain activities in order to learn what is expected. The content is not as rigidly specified as in the fundamentalist position; minor choices but not major substitutions are possible. The key conception is of "readiness." Ability and attitude, as general traits, are more or less meaningless. Readiness is specific to activities, and the practical question for the teacher is "What activity is this child ready to engage in with profit right now?" The teacher decides this with tests, student testimony, and any other aid he can; then he forms subgroups of the students who are ready for the same activity. The teacher believes that sooner or later all the students will participate in the same or similar activities, but they will not all be ready for the same activity at the same time, and they may differ in the time they need to spend on each.

The clearest practical example of this sort of activity-orientation is the subgroupings in reading classes provided they are reconstituted at frequent intervals.[5] Although these subgroups are often formed on the basis of "ability" rather than of readiness, the abilities are specific to the activities and, given the strong pressures to learn to read, become rough measures of readiness. The clearest theoretical example is the "ungraded" classroom in which readiness is paramount.[6] It is there assumed that maturity, sophistication, and readiness to engage in any given activity are attributes more of individuals than of age groups; and subgroups may be formed from a class whose ages span three or even more years.

Grouping under the activity-dominated approach is thus *ad hoc* with respect to activities, changed frequently, and draws on a class which is heterogeneous with respect to age and, probably, also with respect to attitudes and abilities. It is psychologically sound in that this approach judges students for what they can do at any given time, not on who they are or how *generally* "able" they are. The child is known by his behavior and behavior is to some extent under his own control; thus he has the opportunity to develop at least some autonomy. This is encouraged by the teacher who has learning objectives in mind but can be completely flexible in his constitution of groups and partly flexible in his creation of activities as a means to the ends.

Education as Engagement in Inquiry

This view gives attention to content, to activities, and to methods of study and investigation. It is the most comprehensive educational rationale and, because it takes account of more factors and tries to explicate their relationships, it should also have better educational results. On the other hand, its very complexity and sophistication work against its understanding and acceptance by the public and by a large part of the teaching profession.

The concept of education as inquiry took hold in the high schools during the thirties because it geared classroom procedures to individual needs and potentials of imminent citizens.[7] As society and, as a consequence, education changed during the next two decades with increasing emphasis on specific content, orthodox activities, and standardized examinations, inquiry fell into disrepute. Some of the ideas (in watered-down form) are of interest to the national curriculum committees[8] which began in 1955; as the Age of Protest develops, let us hope to see a resurgence of inquiry. One especially encouraging new reality in the sixties is the interest of behavioral scientists, for they tend to value purposiveness, individual autonomy, and a rational society. That is, their implicit view of human nature is for the most part consonant with the assumptions held by those who view learning as a form of inquiry.[9]

The "inquiry" view holds that the student learns most effectively when he is actively seeking a goal which is known to him and to which he is committed. Under these conditions, the student captains himself; he seeks information, he listens to relevant opinions of the teacher and of other students, he knows when he is making progress; he not only acts, he thinks about what he is doing. He is actor and observer at the same time. He gets "feedback" from his own behavior and he uses this to correct or plot next steps. He is absorbed in the work and therefore unselfconscious and spontaneous; he risks failure and therefore savors success all the more; he has emotional highs and lows; he is fully alive, fully functioning.

How may this formidable array of values be achieved in the classroom? The rationale of teaching includes at least four cardinal points. First, content is not specified as an organized body of information even though an organized body of information will be learned; content instead is specified as certain basic principles to be made one's own and certain basic types of problems in which the utilization of these principles is exemplified. It is postulated that life is a series of challenges to be met; that these challenges will take on all sorts of specific unforeseeable forms and guises; that, at the same time, the challenges will be of a finite number of types. Knowledge, it is assumed, was developed by men in order to meet these challenges; it was developed for human purposes that may be manifested in different ways in each decade but which live on through the centuries. The development of knowledge is a continuous record of man's striving, and the knowledge of most worth is not answers but questions. Principles (content) are the salient ideas asked for in such questions as: What is justice and how can it be secured? What responsibilities does a man have for other men, and how do these depend on circumstances? What determines whether a chemical reaction will go to completion? What universal qualities are found in great art, and how are they achieved? How may the past be reconstructed and its events reenacted? What is the nature of conflict within individuals, and how can it be recognized and dealt with? The specific answers to these questions change, but the questions themselves and the approaches to their answers are the very heart of the disciplines of knowledge. It is these questions that the educated man struggles with and so develops personal worth and adaptability to changing conditions.[10]

Second, although some of the same activities emerge each year, there is always something unique about them: the expectations held by the class, the materials used, the purposes in which they are imbedded, the phenomena they direct attention to. Activities are to be planned, to be purposive, form a sequence of investigation, thought about, decided upon, and followed up. They result from asking questions of various phenomena; and from deciding what question to ask next of what phenomenon. Generally, each activity develops imperatives for the next. For example, if one is confronted by an unusual event, he "just naturally" wants to talk it over with a friend; if he and his friend come up with several possible explanations, he "just naturally" wants to see if they can be used in another situation, etc. A major contribution from the behavioral sciences could be an understanding of these natural tendencies and the circumstances under which they tend to occur.[11]

Third, the activities should "make sense" to each student. The reason they can is that they are a result of the student's own experience as testified in class; they are thoroughly anticipated and their purposes are clear before they are undertaken; other students and the teacher are seen to value them; they provide opportunity for personal and private rewards. In short, activities are decided upon by the teacher and class together, and conflicting suggestions are resolved or compromised by agreements to the demands implied by the shared purposes (rather than resorting to the teacher's undemonstrated opinion). Usually a variety of activities are planned and the students decide which one they would like to be involved in because of the activity itself or a desire to be with friends. Activities should make sense because they are tailor-made by actual questions and interests. If the students do not have any questions, the teacher sets up a new confrontation which will, hopefully, provoke questions, interests, and, at times, anxieties.

Fourth, the most striking feature of inquiry is, in my opinion, its emergent character. It is guided by feedback, and it is therefore self-corrective. The only failure possible is the lack of recognition of perhaps unrealistic expectations for the inquiry. It is a teaching method that deliberately plans to reveal the things that must be taken account of as it goes along. It focuses attention always on behavior which occurs in specific defined situations. It teaches a way of life characterized by making choices, noting their consequences, and formulating new choices in the situation. It has a basic rhythmn of discovery and dialogue: one explores and solves problems on his own; discusses them with the class, the teacher, and (in effect) with authorities represented in books; and develops readiness for new discoveries and further subsequent dialogue.[12]

The inquiry method is of special interest when it comes to grouping, for it is best suited for a heterogeneous group—in contrast to those methods which, as we saw, begin in the specification of required "content" or "activity" and then "adjust" students to them, the inquiry method starts with reactions of the children, whoever they are, to a confronting phenomenon or artifact. And the activities from then on are those that make most sense to the group and to the educationally oriented teacher. Success of teaching depends more on the adequacy of the inquiry method than on the selection of children. Nevertheless, engagement in inquiry (or any other method for that matter) is a different experience for each child, and there are some combinations of children that tend to exploit the greater freedom of the inquiry situation. Normally and within limits, the question of how effectively the class is inquiring is itself a legitimate question to ask and investigate; that is, developing the conditions under which inquiry can be effective is part of what it means to inquire. In this sense, the method of inquiry merges teaching and management functions within a single rationale of education.[13]

Education as Socialization for a Position in Society

We have considered three approaches to education through specification of its content, its activities, and its method. Let us now consider a rather different starting point: the pupil combination. Theoretically there are a number of ways pupils could be combined. They could be chosen, for example, to complement each other's resources; or they could be chosen to be alike in some respect such as speed, attitude, friendship, sex, or occupational plans, or the group could be built around a couple of strong individuals. I wish to consider here the most frequent way of combining pupils: by placing together those whose IQ and achievement measures fall within a narrow range, for example, the middle 20% of the distribution. Such groups are generally called homogeneous ability groups.

The process of selecting students for class begins long before the teacher actually encounters his students. There are four points at which selection occurs. The first selection determines which school-age children in the community will go to school. With younger children, social and economic selection is relatively ineffective. Most of them are in school. But with each added year in age, social economic factors exert stronger pressure. Their influence is obvious in the schools of a large city. In Chicago, for example, the rate of turnover—that is, drop-out and replacement of students—ranges from 1 or 2% to close to 300% during a single school year. The way school-district boundaries are drawn may have a marked influence on the nature of the student body in a particular school. Maximum heterogeneity is obtained when a large central high school serves an entire metropolitan area; maximum homogeneity results when several smaller high schools serve relatively homogeneous neighborhoods.

The second point of selection is the division of the total school enrollment into large subdivisions. The most common division is by grade, which is roughly a separation by age with some modification, depending on promotion and performance. The division into various curricular tracks is also common, and division by ability seems to be increasingly popular. Another possibility is the division of a large school into several smaller schools, each with several hundred students and its own core group of teachers. It is possible to imagine a school that has no subdivisions, a school in which the staff studies the entire student population in search of children who would profit from a particular classroom.

The third point of selection is the formation of classes. Typically, a class is a group of about 25 to 35 students assigned to one teacher for instruction in a subject. A class could be a collection of 50 students assigned to three teachers for instruction in several subjects. Or a class could consist of any other combination of teachers and students. In this sense, a class is an administrative unit, marked off by the assignment of responsibility to particular adults.

The fourth selection occurs when the actual instructional group within the class is formed. The instructional group is the particular set of students with whom the teacher is working at any particular time. This group may be, and too often is, identical with the administrative class; however, many kinds of subgroups can be formed to obtain a better organization of effort in various learning activities.

Recently, for example, 50 sophomores were assigned to three teachers for instruction in three subjects in the Laboratory School of the University of Chicago. Yet all 50 students were hardly ever brought together for instructional purposes. The instructional group seldom exceeded 17. During most of the time, the students were working alone, in groups of 2 to 4, in project committees of 5 to 12, or in small classes (with the teacher present) of 16 or 17. The entire group was assembled only when the students were to be an audience for the presentation of information, for stimulation by participation in a dramatic affair, or for participation in "town meetings" to consider the state of the sophomore project.

These, then, are the kinds of selections whose cumulative and successive impacts determine the group toward which the teacher directs his educational efforts. In the following, however, we are concerned primarily with processes of selecting students for classes, not subgroups.

Homogeneous ability grouping has a long history, both as a practice and as an object of research. Even so, the case for ability grouping is by no means proved. Let us examine its history, using Harry Passow's article[14] as an authoritative source. We learn that age-grading began in the Quincy Grammar School in Boston in the 1840's, and the first segregation by ability is generally conceded to have occurred in St. Louis in 1867. Other places and dates are Elizabeth, New Jersey, 1886; Pueblo, Colorado, 1888; then Cambridge, Massachusetts and Portland, Oregon; Santa Barbara, California, 1898, etc. Although ability grouping was already popular in the nineties, its peak was during

1920 to 1930, and its coincides with the introduction of intelligence tests into the schools. In 1929, two-thirds of the elementary school systems with enrollments between 2500 and 25,000 reported they were using some form of homogenous ability grouping.

In 1936, Edward Reisner wrote in the NSSE Yearbook that the challenge posed by the urban inmigration of students from nongraded rural schools to graded city schools could be met "only as we succeed more and more completely in getting the right children together to follow those experiences that are adapted to their abilities and economic future."

Ability grouping fell into disfavor in elementary schools and, using existence of special classes or schools for the gifted as an index, it was found that such provisions existed in only 15 of the 3203 cities with populations over 2500 during 1938 to 1948. Continuing with Passow's study, homogeneous grouping at this time was almost an "anathema" to elementary teachers. But in the 1950's the practice began to evolve due to "shortages of trained specialized manpower and the pressures of the cold war together with critical appraisals of educational quality."

Passow does not report actual percentages of high schools using ability grouping, but he tells us that a survey in 1960 found that 81% of "large" secondary schools reported an increase in ability grouping during the preceding five years. The Establishment's present professional opinion about ability grouping is well represented in James B. Conant, *The American High School Today*.[15] Most salient for our purposes are the following excerpts from his Recommendations:

"It should be the policy of the school that every student has an individualized program; there would be no classification of students according to clearly defined and labeled programs or tracks such as "college preparatory," "vocational," "commercial." (*Recommendation II*)

"In the required subjects and those elected by students with a wide range of ability, the students should be grouped according to ability, subject by subject. For example, in English, American History, ninth grade Algebra, Biology, and Physical Science, there should be at least three types of classes—one for the more able in the subject, another for the larger group whose ability is about average, and another for the very slow readers who should be handled by special teachers. The middle group might be divided into two or three sections, according to the students' abilities in the subject in question. This type of grouping is not to be confused with across the board grouping according to which a given student is placed in a particular section in *all* courses. Under the scheme here recommended, for example, a student may be in the top section in English, but the middle section in History or ninth grade algebra." (*Recommendation IV*)

"It will turn out that many students of similar ability and vocational interest will have almost identical programs but a student who has elected an academic sequence may shift to a vocational sequence and vice versa." (*Recommendation II*)

Referring to vocational education:

"Furthermore, efforts should be made to prevent isolation (of vocational students) from other students. Homerooms may be an effective means to this end." (*Recommendation VII*)

"For the purpose of developing an understanding between students of different levels of academic ability and vocational goals, homerooms should be organized in such a way as to make them significant social units within the school. To this end, students should be kept together in one homeroom for the entire senior high school course (3 or 4 years), and care should be taken to have each homeroom a cross section of the school in terms of ability and vocational interest. . . . Sufficient time should be allotted to the homeroom so that students may use this period to develop a sense of community interest and to have practice in a small way with representative government. The homeroom should elect one or two representatives to the student council and these representatives should report back after each meeting of the council; they should listen to the opinions of their constituents and be guided by their opinions in voting on matters before the student council." (*Recommendation XX*)

Additional recommendations include provisions for special classes for honors and emotionally or mentally retarded students; heterogeneous grouping in Senior Social Studies; counselors to work with parents and students to plan their course programs.

Mr. Conant's ideas and statements are straightforward enough. In courses whose purpose is the acquisition of knowledge or skill, students should be separated by ability, so that they can all profit from the same materials, and participate effectively in discussion, and other class work. In Senior Social Studies, where opinion, attitude, and value are important content, let the group be heterogeneous so that the students can see other points of view and learn as adults do, from engagement in controversy. Use homerooms and student government as a way to maintain a sense of community and common purpose throughout the school; and make diversity of background visible, respectable, and useful to the community.

It is assumed that children learn better or are more easily taught when they are segregated by ability; but that there is a danger, however, that students may become isolated and segregated, *de facto,* in academic or vocational sequences. Such segregation is undesirable because it may create a stratified prestige or "class" structure from which students will learn to think of themselves as inferior or superior in general rather than with respect to accurately appraised specific skills. Homerooms and student government, in which participation is not necessarily correlated with academic ability will, it is hoped, redress the balance as well as demonstrate that all students, as citizens, do have equal political rights regardless of special talents.

The dangers Mr. Conant wishes to avoid of having students classified, stratified, and segregated are exactly what Admiral Rickover would embrace. In the *Chicago Sun-Times* of August 21, 1960, the Father of the nuclear powered submarine wants segregation in separate schools. He writes:

"What good would it do the dullards to be admitted to a school where they would just sit around and understand nothing? . . . What is Democratic about penalizing God-given talent by letting it go to waste so average children won't feel a sense of inferiority? It may be beguiling in theory to think of all our children going to sch6ol together, but will it really serve their best interests to send them to schools where the child with an IQ of 70 sits beside one of 170, and where the morally weak child freely associates with the child who has been carefully raised to distinguish between right and wrong and to conduct himself responsibly? This makes no sense to me. Obviously no child will receive an education best suited to his abilities and vocational aims in such a school; nor will the bright child develop admiration and respect for the dullard, or the potential young delinquent profit from associating with well brought-up children. It is far more likely that the dullard will be frustrated, the bright child bored, the average child never challenged mentally, the good child corrupted by the young ne'er-do-well, and everyone's manners and mores downgraded to a dead level of mediocrity."

The Admiral need not worry about separate *schools*. Separate *tracks* do very well. The large high school near my home has five tracks, and its student body is about 90% Negroes who come from a fairly broad range of socioeconomic class levels. The 10% whites come from mostly average or "higher" class homes. Of the students in the top two tracks, preponderantly middle class, about 85% graduate from high school; of the students in the bottom two tracks, preponderantly lower class, about 65% drop out and do not graduate. The suggestion that ability grouping is also socioeconomic-class grouping crops up wherever the matter is studied. In England, for example, "streaming" (separation in homogeneous ability tracks) has long been commonly practiced and, more recently, exhaustively studied.[16] Jackson[17] compared the socioeconomic family status of the pupils with which ability groups they were in. He found that over 73% of the children in the upper ability classes were also in the upper socioeconomic brackets, and 79% of the children in the lower ability classes were also in the lower socioeconomic brackets. Another investigator, Willig,[18] found Mr. Conant's fears to be thoroughly justified. He reports that with respect to social "adjustment" (roughly mental health) "the evidence emphasizes the social advantages of mixed-ability grouping over streaming by academic attainment." (This latter finding is not consistently supported by other studies in this country.)

The possibility that ability grouping may be attractive as a way to achieve segregation of other sorts is well anticipated by Eash,[19] as a result of his study of reports on grouping researches conducted in the United States prior to 1961. One of his nine concluding generalizations is:

"Pressures to institute certain grouping practices in our schools represent pervasive social problems in our culture. Educators need to be doubly alert that the schools are not utilizing grouping practices which assist in maintaining and promoting social and racial biases which militate against the general education objectives, equal educational opportunity and the development of each person as an individual."

The situation then, would appear to be about as follows:

1. Homogeneous ability grouping is expected to result in more learning or more effective teaching in skill and conceptual subjects.

2. Homogeneous ability grouping roughly approximates socioeconomic class grouping and therefore may produce social stratification of the student body.

3. A person with high ability in one subject may be of low ability in another, and, if so, he may escape being pegged or stereotyped in any particular level of social status.

4. If social stratification were to result from homogeneous ability grouping in academic subjects, its "undemocratic" consequences could

still be vitiated or ameliorated by having the school operate as a self-governing community with political rights guaranteed for all.

Let us consider these four propositions. We begin by noting that the first is the most fundamental in the sense that the other three would not be required if the first were not held. That is, homogeneous ability grouping is urged primarily for better achievement, and two of the other three propositions are ways of reducing possible undesirable social side effects. But are these propositions true? And, particularly, what about the first one? Granted that separation by ability seems obviously useful to increase achievement, but what are the facts?

There have been several examinations of all published studies in which achievement of students when grouped homogeneously by ability was compared with achievement when students are left in unselected or heterogeneous ability groups. In 1932 Billett[20] reviewed the studies between 1917 and 1928; in 1931 Turney[21] made his independent survey of the studies; Wyndham,[22] an Australian, similarly, in 1934; Otto[23] reviewed the studies in 1941 for the *Encyclopedia* of *Educational Research;* Goodlad,[24] similarly, for the 1960 edition; Ekstrom[25] a fresh analysis in 1959; Passow,[26] made several surveys and studies between 1958 and 1965. In addition to these reviews of all previous research, several recent experiments, conducted with much more adequate scientific designs have attempted to pinpoint the effects of homogeneous ability grouping on a large number of specific cognitive and attitudinal learnings. Of these, mention can be made of studies by Elizabeth Drews[27] at Michigan State, Miriam L. Goldberg and Harry Passow[28] and associates at Teachers College, Walter Borg[29] at the University of Utah, and The National Foundation for Educational Research,[30] which is carrying on a study of "streaming in primary schools" of England and Wales. From several countries of Europe various scholars have tried, mostly with little rigorous research backing, to "pull together" their country's experiences: Visalberghi at the University of Rome, Mme Delepine at the Institut Superieur de Pedagogie, Morlanwelz, Belgium; Barker, Daniels, Pidgeon, and Yates in England; Husen and his group in Sweden, Norway and Denmark; Pause from Germany; M. Ortar, Israel, and Passow and Thelen, United States. These people plus the surveys mentioned previously in addition to abstracts of 48 of the better studies, were brought together for an international conference on grouping held at the Unesco Institute for Education in Hamburg,[31] Germany, in November 1964. The job of the conference was to review what is known about grouping, primarily by ability, and see what recommendations could be made concerning the various grouping practices. Their report is currently in press; the editor of their book[32] is Alfred Yates of Oxford University.

In general the findings are clear: grouping either homogeneously or heterogeneously by ability produces almost the same result. When it comes to school achievement in the various subjects as measured usually by tests, the evidence fails to support the hypothesis that children will learn more when they are separated by ability. (In several studies they seemed to learn more during the first one or two years, but these differences ironed out later). When, say, 32 specific scores for gains in achievement are collected, it is usually found that perhaps a quarter of them show statistically significant differences between the two forms of grouping, and the differences between them are equally favorable. Moreover, to make matters even more interesting, there seems to be no rhyme or reason in the particular patterns of superiority and, as noted, they may be reversed the following year.

When it comes to noncognitive outcomes, such as self-perception, feelings of inferiority, mental health, etc., the evidence is scantier except in England where the *unstreamed* classes (heterogeneous) are consistently superior.[33] Goldberg and Passow found that "the effects of narrowing the range or separating the extreme levels (of ability) was to raise the self assessment of the slow pupils, lower the initially high self rating of the gifted, and leave the intermediate levels largely unaffected." Self attitude was the only nonacademic variable on which grouping had any consistent effects.[28]

Perhaps it will be possible now to examine homogeneous ability grouping from a pedagogical point of view. In the first place, if grouping is for the purpose of urging students to learn more, then the factor by which they are grouped ought to be one which is very influential on learning. If the process of learning is participation in learning activities (and it is), then the factor ought to be one which determines the success of the child's participation. Is IQ such a factor? IQ tests are timed, presented in words, and require certain associations in a fund of informational specifics; that is, speed, verbal fluency and available knowledge are the components of IQ which are measured and used for ability grouping. Are these also important factors determining how effectively a student can participate in classroom learning activities? The answer may be different from one teacher to the next, but so far not one teacher has been found who would admit that these factors were significant in his classroom. (They certainly are not in the author's!) So why should we suppose that separation by IQ (along with achievement tests which usually correlate 0.5 or better with IQ) would make any sense? The reason has just been given: IQ tests do correlate fairly strongly with achievement *tests*. The intelligent child does tend to do better on achievement tests. But this would merely lead us to suppose that students with high IQ would get better test scores, *regardless* of whether they were grouped homogeneously or heterogeneously and regardless of the course of study—which is exactly the case. Our common sense error is in assuming that the ability that predicts success in taking tests will also predict success in very different activities like assimilating ideas presented by the teacher, doing workbook problems, engaging in subcommittees, doing homework of all sorts, and so on.

The first pedagogical argument against homogeneous ability grouping is that the ability factor has little demonstrable relation to effective participation (and learning) in "learning" activities—even though it has a fair relationship to achievement test scores.

The second argument poses the question: Why are the results of homogeneous grouping inconsistent? Why are there significant differences? As a matter of logic, if a factor is influential only sometimes, we are justified in concluding that this factor is irrelevant, and that this difference is due to another cause. In other words, the significant differences are accidental as far as grouping is concerned. What, then, *really* accounts for the results? The various scholars mentioned previously have come up with one or two possible answers: either the teacher knows what to do with a bright class (or a dull class) or the methods and materials of instruction are especially appropriate to the particular class. In short, any type of grouping affects only the capabilities of the group; but to obtain any better results from these capabilities we must capitalize on them in some way. Given a class of very bright children, what would you do with them that you could not do equally well if they were in a mixed group? We are a long way from knowing in what ways a bright child should be taught differently from a dull child so that he can learn better. The usual hunches are that bright children have a special aptitude or need for self-direction or independent work, have more intense interest to be satisfied in school subjects, and need or want to work harder. But these common assumptions on which courses for the bright are based have so far found no foundation in scientific study. It is unfortunate that much of what is done for segregated bright students is more exploitative than educative.

Before concluding this section, let us identify what may well be the most persuasive reasons for ability grouping.

If we think of homogeneous ability groups as socioeconomic class groups, and if we agree that the grouping cannot be justified for better school achievement, then what is the educational relevance, if any, of the grouping? It is in the socialization mission of the school. In short, students at each socioeconomic level are taught what to expect of themselves and of each other as denizens of that place in society. They are also trained for some degree of tolerance or sympathy toward groups at other levels. The reason for separating bright children is to indoctrinate them to expect that they will go to a university; hold top jobs in industry, research, or business; live in the suburbs; belong to clubs suitable to that level of society; cultivate the right taste in liquor and women, etc. This is what can be done more effectively in homogeneous ability groups than in heterogeneous groups. This is what parents of the upper class groups probably desire—a reinforcement of family expectations for the child. (Lower class parents do not come to school, so their voices are not heard.)

It seems that this concept corresponds well with recent history of schools and of society. The status quo within the structure of society is best maintained by teaching each child to recognize and accept his position and to live as full a life as possible. The school makes no attempt to effect social changes, because it is too busy turning out masses of technicians, teachers, and welfare clients to fit existing slots.

Assuming that this is a realistic view of what is special about the unique opportunities provided by homogeneous "ability" groups, then vigorous reservations must be expressed. The first reservation is pedagogical: the method of learning is training, conditioning, or reinforcing expectations which do not have to be made explicit because they are not controversial. The danger is that children will be raised into a particular way of life, without understanding alternatives and without finding out what is common to all ways of life. This is definitely miseducative in our modern pluralistic society. It also sells short the distinctive mission of the school, which is to help children learn to live more effectively through their utilization of knowledge. In this respect, a method of learning is educative to the extent that it involves inquiry; and inquiry means, among other things, formulating alternatives and weighing their pros and cons. The alternatives emerge from the diverse attitudes and opinions of persons, and a heterogeneous or unselected group will have much greater opportunity to engage in effective inquiry and dialogue than a homogeneous group.

Mr. Conant's proposals, incidentally, recognize this: he provides specifically for a senior social studies course to be pursued in a heterogeneous group. To relegate the whole inquiry into a student's expected position in life to one course at the end of high school seems very definitely too little and too late. The student is a member of a society in every one of his classrooms, and regardless of subject matter, each class should examine those aspects of its organization, expectations, and system of rewards that are relevant to engagement in productive work, that is, inquiry.

Another major difficulty with social indoctrination in homogeneous ability groups is one which Europeans are more sensitive to than we are: the problem of judging who the group members should be. Here the situation is especially acute because the tendency is to have the child in the same "stream" throughout all his subjects. In the United States, the decision tends to be made individually for each subject, but it is still doubtful whether this results in any real diversity for each child. In any case, the British are facing a true educational crisis because it is clear that when a student is earmarked for one group or another at an early age and then indoctrinated into a specific way of life, his whole future—colleges, jobs, associates—is determined. It is an awesome responsibility to make that sort of judgment about a child who is only eleven years old or even younger; even if an accurate assessment could be made, it would fail to take account of the very drastic "growth" that often occurs up into the twenties. One recourse would be to allow a student to shift "streams" if it became evident that he was misplaced. But most of the misplaced students are not, in fact, shifted. Dr. Daniels' findings, reveal that teachers under the system habitually overestimate by 400% the amount of shifting that really occurs.[34] The Swedish also have the same educational procedure, and they attempt to ameliorate the possible unfairness of the system by getting each child to choose his own "stream" or track at regular intervals; parents and counselors are also involved in the choice.[35] But what a lot of bother for a system that has no demonstrable educational advantages!

Even more tragic for our country is the indoctrination received by the lower groups—that there is no place for them in the productive society. About half of them get the message quite early and drop out of school. The Job Corp and Anti-Poverty programs, commendably concerned about these youths, try with little success to "unteach" at fantastic expense an unfortunate lesson that the schools should never have taught these youths. For the fortunate children, indoctrination to accept without question their better position in life may not be detrimental, even though it makes it unnecessary for them to develop potentials desperately needed by society. But for the "disadvantaged" child, indoctrinating him to accept without question his oppressed condition is doing a very severe disservice to him, the community, and the country. There are many commendable innovations going on in schools today, but they are confined for the most part to gaining academic efficiency, and they do not begin to touch the fundamental inadequacy of indoctrination as the process through which students learn and accept their place in society. Our problem, of course, is that we cannot make up our mind whether maintaining the social order and the Establishment in status quo is more important than educating children and thus doing something effective about the problems of our society.

Education as an Interpersonal Transaction with the Teacher

We have considered educational positions that start with different assumptions: specified content, activities, methods, and reinforcement of value-communalities among students. There is another assumption in the classroom, and it is more fundamental than the four we have considered so far because it determines how successful they will be. This factor is not incomensurate with any of the preceding ones. It is complementary and, as far as most psychologists are concerned, it is also far more fundamental because it respects the subterranean world of hidden needs and values which we subconsciously act on rather than consciously voice. We are referring to those processes within and between persons that are in the domain of personality and interpersonal dynamics. The observation that makes this consideration necessary (even if not sufficient) is that every teacher teaches some students more effectively than others. The observation of differences in teachability could suggest simply that some students are more "teachable" than others; but the disagreement among teachers as to which students are the most and least teachable suggests that "teachability" results from interaction between teachers and student. In short, a class teachable for one teacher might not be for another.

Just how vital the teacher–pupil relationship is depends on how the teacher conducts the class. The relationship is least evident when the teacher simply stands before the class and lectures. In this case it matters not whether the students listen or understand, and their overt responses are limited to gestures, shifts in posture, and occasional outbursts of laughter or groans. We might say that in this situation the role of the teacher is completely independent of the student and that of the students is that of a passive listener.

Teacher-pupil relationships are at their height when the roles of teacher and student are highly interdependent. For example, a teacher who is at his best answering questions raised by students is at a disadvantage if no questions are asked. A student whose success until now has stemmed from his enthusiastically doing whatever he was told will have a bad time if the teacher becomes permissive. Any valid conception of education today proposes that learning is an active experiential process; that it is the student who learns, and that the teacher attempts, by arranging conditions, making demands, and consulting with the student, to keep the learning at a high pitch. This is obviously a situation of interdependence, and the roles are usually determined and defined by negotiation over a period of a few weeks or months. Much of this negotiation takes place subconsciously with neither the teacher nor his students aware of its processes. For the negotiation is primarily with respect to psychological conditions of threat, security, and trust, which together constitute the climate [36] of the classroom.

There is a quality of identification from which the teacher acquires whatever influence the children are willing to concede. Children have no legal right to nominate and elect a teacher. However, the teacher cannot guide children unless they accept his leadership, for learning is a process that goes on inside the child where the teacher cannot always reach. The teacher with whom the child identifies is someone who is meaningful to him, whose style or way of life is in some respects desired by the child, whose approval is important to the child, and who is imitated by the child without being aware of it. Even in a straight lecture situation, these psychological interpersonal influences are at work, and probably largely determine what a student will "get out of" a lecture. The interpersonal relationship between teacher and student has a good deal to do with the child's "openness" to ideas, his acceptance of suggestions, his perseverance, his motivation to learn. Every student somehow profits more from some teachers than from others. Even the student who gets A's in all his courses and also the one who apparently gets very little from any course finds some classes more "meaningful" or rewarding or less punishing than other classes. It is true that the content, activities, methods, and other students are more attractive in one class than in another, but they have to be experienced to have any meaning at all. The nature of this experience is strongly colored and, for most students, largely determined by their reactions to the attitudes, enthusiasms, aversions, interests, public goals, and private purposes of the teacher. Since no two students are identical, their reactions and, therefore, their experiences are not identical. The same student will have different experiences under different teachers, who in turn will affect students with varying degrees of impact.

All teachers know this. If you ask a teacher what change would be most beneficial to his teaching, he is quite likely to reply "Get Johnny and George out of my class." Certain combinations of student and teacher are simply destructive, with each playing on the other's anxieties or weaknesses—these situations are far too common to argue about. The further concept that each teacher has his "favorites" or at least tends to count more on some students than others when it comes to guiding the class also has considerable merit, although some teachers will deny it. There have been many instances, usually not reported in the literature, in which the teachers sit down toward the end of the school year to suggest which pupils ought to be shifted to certain teachers for next year's classes. Thus for many years, the kindergarten teachers in the Laboratory School at the University of Chicago made recommendations as to which first grade teacher each child should be assigned. Frequently, counselors in the school make similar recommendations.

All of the foregoing is so well recognized by teachers, students, and parents—who, by the way, often take heroic measures to get their students under certain teachers and away from others—it amazes us that little or no present grouping considers the fit between student and teacher. But when we consider the possibilities within any existing school, we see that there are severe practical difficulties that would have to be overcome; the difficulties are so severe that the idea, while conceded to have merit, is dismissed as practically impossible to work out. The obstacles are instructive, for they constitute an excellent catalog of generally accepted conditions which militate against the school being an educative organization.

The first obstacle is profound hypocrisy. It is the official belief that all teachers ought to be able to be effective with all students; and if a teacher is not, he is performing poorly. (The one exception to this is that when a particular student is dramatically and drastically impossible in a class, the school psychologist may be called in to gather evidence to prove that it is the child's rather than the teacher's fault.) Student teachers are taught this hypocrisy. Principals often tell teachers that if a student is troublesome he should be sent to the Principal, but most teachers are made to feel, after the first couple of referrals, that the proposal is a good deal less than whole-hearted. To deliberately and openly select students to "fit" teachers would, in the eyes of many teachers and administrators, be tantamount to an admission that teachers are incompetent.

The second obstacle, similar to the first, is that there must be one right way to teach—if one could only find it. It is this feeling which accounts for the notable lack of professional discussion among teachers. Teachers, especially in the elementary school, will gossip endlessly about individual children (as Jackson[37] points out): their parents, home life, dramatic misbehavior, etc.; but teachers are notably reticent with each other when it comes to describing (except in vague and general terms) what they actually do in class. For no one knows what the "right way" is, and whatever you do there are valid arguments against it. If the teacher talks about giving the children opportunities to help plan the work, he may be accused of being "permissive" and "soft"; if he decribes an ingenious sequence of activities through which he guides the children, he may be accused of being "authoritarian," or "anti-democratic." To the social psychologist, this state of affairs shows that whatever the common purpose is that binds the faculty together as a group, it is not the development of educational methods.

The notion that there is some one right way to teach (and each person thinks he has it and others do not; or that nobody has it and it cannot be found, so why talk about it?) is like the notion that all teachers ought to be able to deal with all individuals in that it denies the differences in teacher personalities and resources.

The third obstacle is concerned with teacher "homogeneity," and it is basically the hidden argument for homogeneous groups (for purposes of socialization and cohesiveness) moved up a step. The Principal would like a nice "family" group of teachers who hold the same values (his) and have the same manners and morals.[38]. But to capitalize on the idea of "fitting" students to teachers, we should have a faculty which is very heterogeneous in its outlook, opinions, and personal goals so that a wide range of student orientations and personalities could be accommodated. In such a school, the faculty would have a common purpose in that each teacher was working to develop to the hilt his own individual resources and style as a teacher, and faculty discussion would be motivated by controversy, legitimate and exciting, over the nature of teaching. Such conversation does occur in some teaching teams,[39] and is a sufficient justification for them. But for the reasons just noted, this is not the common purpose of the faculty; rather it is to exist as a comfortably pleasant group, cohesively united to present a solid front to the "public." Thus the required heterogeneity of the faculty not only does not exist, it is strongly resisted.

The fourth obstacle is entirely practical. There is no point in talking about the "fit" between students and teachers unless there is a choice among teachers in the various subjects. If only one teacher teaches tenth-grade English, all the students must take tenth-grade English from him. Choice is possible only under three conditions: (1) The school is large enough to have at least two teachers for each subject. (2) Each teacher teaches several subjects. In other words, if the school is in the great middle range, having two or three classes in each subject, let each class be taught by a different teacher. But this would require each teacher to work up several different "preparations" each day, and the disadvantages in increased "fatigue" and "inefficiency" cannot be ignored. Possibility (3) is that teaching of each class be assigned to a team of teachers, with subgroups of students selected for the immediate supervision of each teacher. There is room here for experimenting with apprentices and "adjunct" personnel in the classroom as a way of obtaining variety.

The fifth obstacle is even more practical. Even with the help of computers, it is no mean feat to schedule each child into the courses he wants. The introduction of the teacher's choices would complicate scheduling even more. It would be like trying to solve an algebra problem in which there were more unknowns than equations!

These obstacles are presented partly in order to sympathize with them, partly to acknowledge them so that our subsequent discussion of what happens when students and teachers are fitted to each other may be less contaminated with practical reservations that block communication, and partly (but incidentally) to illustrate a general principle about improvement of education. The principle is that any genuine shift in basic policies, in this case having to do with grouping, will require a vast array of further changes and accommodations throughout the school; therefore the changes that are most likely to be made (and have been made) tend to be confined to trivial procedures rather than to more powerful understandings needed to improve the educational quality of the school.

Education as Ego Strengthening Outside the Classroom

Awareness of the profound importance of interpersonal relationships for the maturation of the child has generated still a further position about educative process, and it is appended here as a kind of footnote. This view of education is attractive to some counselors and psychiatrically (and noneducationally) oriented persons. As with all the other views presented so far, this view has some merit; the puzzle is to know just how to give it its due. The idea is that, although each person has greater adequacy in some situations than in others, there is nevertheless a general adequacy factor (that is, "ego-strength") which makes the child educable. Anything that can be done to strengthen this factor will help the child accommodate better and more productively to the classroom demands. This help might come within the classroom or outside of it, as in the family, in informal peer groups, in youth-serving agencies, in group-therapy meetings, in "adjustment" camps, or anywhere else within the formal and informal structure of the child's social relationships.

When a child's general adequacy is so low that he has a long record of strife and failure in classrooms, it seems reasonable to assume that there is little point in hoping that his adaptability will be better in the next classroom. It would seem far better to get help for him, intensively, directly, and professionally. But what about the more usual student who is able to get by, or even the talented student whose resources for coping are unlikely to grow because they are not sufficiently challenged? Is not the enhancement of "general adequacy" a part of general education? If we agree that it is, rather than being salient only for the "maladapted," then what? We can take either of two positions. First, adequacy-development is part of the educational mission of the classroom, and if we think the classrooms are failing the child, then we had better go to work on teachers, methods, and curricula. We must help teachers to see that their job is to cooperate with the child in his own, personally important inquiries, for knowledge assists adequacy-development only when it serves meaningful purposes for the child. This is the view that makes much of the conceptualizing and inquiry methods of the thirties seem salient and exciting today, and it emphasizes one aspect of education as engagement in inquiry.

The second position is that the teaching profession is of such a nature that it cannot assume responsibility for adequacy in general, but only for developing cognitive "skills" in certain limited classes which are most directly illuminated by "subject matter" as it is now organized in courses of study.

To go beyond this, we would have to consider extra-class possibilities, still, however, within the school. One possibility centers on the role of counselor or psychologist. For example, eleven years ago the suggestion was made[40] that counselors ought to give a modified form of group "therapy" to all students; this would amount to adding a new course to the curriculum. A growing body of experimentation with "T-Groups"[41] (also called human-relations training groups, laboratory groups, social work groups, sensitivity training groups) for adolescents shows that with volunteers, at least, these treatments work quite well for enhancement of the personal adequacy of normal children. There is surely a place for such experiences for almost every student at some time in his life, but this place has yet to be demonstrated and translated into educational policy.

Personal experiences with running T-groups (mostly with adults) lead to considering this possibility: such groups are an excellent place for the *teacher* to learn how to conduct meaningful inquiry, and many a teacher has gained much useful insight into how to develop adequacy better within his classroom. We are on safe ground in regarding these special group experiences as tremendously valuable in-service or pre-service training aids for at least some teachers. In addition, when the child has clear-cut needs, as the development of leadership skills needed by an officer in the student government, he will probably profit greatly from T-group or equivalent experience.[42] Therefore it does seem reasonable to assume that T-group or other self-discovery experience would be available within the school, but it may be that students should be subjected to it only when they recognize their clear need for it.

Lying somewhere between the development of self-discovery and self-insight in the inquiry-oriented classroom and the special quasi-therapeutic group outside the classroom, is, in theory at least, a type of job experience. It has been increasingly recognized that the experience of working in the productive adult world stimulates many children to mature more quickly. Such experiences are ordinarily set up in college for a period of two or three months, alternating with campus experiences. In high schools, the student is usually engaged in work during part of the school day. In either case, the student is invited to anticipate being part of the functioning society and various sensitizing activities may be used to prepare him for his future role of worker and citizen.

It is fair to judge that in very few schools and colleges have the growth-producing or educational potentials of work experience been realized. But enough is known to suggest that it can salvage some students who would otherwise be drop-outs. It can significantly help other students with their problems of identity and goal under the following sorts of conditions. First, the work situation is chosen for each student in order to provide the sort of interactive milieu he needs in order to reality-test and resolve ambivalences and doubts about the persistent problems and directions he is currently facing. In this sense it can be conceptualized as a species of "milieu therapy." Second, the work supervisor (whether a boss or adult co-worker) talks with the student, his counselor (or school adviser), and his parents about what they all expect from the work experience. Third, a person skilled in counseling and not part of the work situation, is available as a "third party" to talk with the student quite candidly about his perceptions of the situation, and to help him set up small experiments with new ways of behaving. Fourth, several students, all of whom are having work experience at the same time, meet regularly and informally to exchange experiences and perceptions. Fifth, there are channels of communication to the school through which any proposals or issues the students identify can be "fed back" for better guidance and development of the work experience program. And sixth, at the end of the experience, another conference is held with the student, his counselor, his parents, and whoever has been on the job with him in order to clarify changes in the student's goals, attitudes, and self-assessments.[43]

It seems probable that every student at some time or times during his educational career could profit greatly from work experience, but we still have a great deal to learn about how to determine when the best time would be.

A further variation of the plan would be to broaden work experience to cover a wide range of activities set up and supervised by groups of youths within the community. The notion is appealing because the problem of developing identity and finding roles in the "outside" world will be best solved by youths themselves, with enabling legislation and consultative services available from sensitive adults. It is but a small further extension of the plan to have it include some genuinely cooperative community problem-solving with adults, and to have some aspects of this experience serve to stimulate changes within the school itself.

In summary, we can see that a variety of experiences outside the classroom may, under certain conditions, enhance the student's self-esteem, "strengthen his ego," help him find commitment to goals, and enrich his experiential background. These are not trivial gains, and they would greatly contribute to his educability within the classroom.

STRATEGY AND PROSPECTUS FOR GROUPING

Each of these approaches, positions, views, or aspects has a point to make. Each is supported by men of goodwill, and each contains one or more germs of truth. None is either right or wrong, but each has a certain usefulness. The problem, then, is not one of deciding among alternatives but rather of combining the various insights. When it comes to grouping, the following rationale is offered in a series of propositions:

1. We live in a pluralistic society which includes various ways of life. Each person must find his identity through development of his own way of life and through his acceptance of reference groups which help him maintain and improve it. He must also be able to work and live together with persons who are oriented differently to life and, therefore, hold other values, for it is only through cooperation, driven by the dynamics of controversy, that society can remain viable.

Therefore all schools in some or all their classrooms should incorporate the pluralism of the larger society *and* should make this pluralism, as it demonstrably influences the classroom society, an object of study. In order to insure cultural heterogeneity in the classroom, school districts must include a variety of neighborhood ways of life.

2. Our experience of our cultural pluralism over the last thirty years has accentuated anxiety and uneasiness about human rights, feeling of belonging, justice, individual recourse, and freedom of association. In the face of this anxiety our goals have become confused. Is it more essential to do a good job of productive work or to rely on knowing the right people or to give up striving in the hope that the welfare state will take over? These are questions that complicate the quest for personal autonomy and self-expression in the larger society; and they are hidden agendas, draining energy and attention away from learning in the classroom.

Therefore these problems should be explicitly discussed and reality-tested when their disturbing influences are felt in the classroom. There are two requirements. One is that students be with teachers they can trust and identify with; that they be in "teachable groups" selected for each teacher. The other is that teachers themselves, through T-groups or other equivalent experience, gain the sensitivities and skills they need to help the class work out such problems.

3. Within each class, a variety of activities should be planned with the class and students should be subgrouped with respect to their readiness for the activity. These subgroups would be reconstituted every time the class embarked on a new set of activities.

4. The entire class would meet as a legislative body hearing testimony from subgroups and individuals and agreeing on goals for the next round of learning activities, organized as individual or subgroup work. Each subgroup would be expected to appraise its own progress and determine how to be more productive and rewarding the next time. Having been divided into subgroups, teams, or individuals in order to do the work, consummatory activities within the class as a whole would enable each working party (whether it be an individual or subgroup) to make its contribution to the class as a whole, and effectiveness of the consummatory activity would be diagnosed as the basis for establishing the next group of activities.

Note that classes are "teachable" groups, selected for each teacher and that they will be quite heterogeneous in most respects.

The change to "teachability" grouping will not be brought about easily; it will take possibly ten years of continuous effort and thought to accomplish it in any school. In order to maintain such an effort, we must be first convinced of its worth, and we must understand full well the educational relevance and value of the goal. Such understandings develop from careful study and assessment of experimental efforts made in working out the scheme—this is what the remaining chapters are concerned with.[44]

NOTES

1. Campbell, Roald F. and Robert A. Bunnell (Eds.), *Nationalizing Influences on Secondary Education,* Midwest Administration Center, University of Chicago, 1963. "With the increases of international tensions following the official cessation of hostilities (of World War II), an emphasis on national solutions has continued. Education is one of our institutions that is no longer to be taken for granted but has come to be seen as contributing to, as well as being a part of the remedy for the uncertainties that we face as a nation. Thus, the demand for national solutions to educational problems has led to the creation of influential programs unknown to previous generations." (Page iii)

2. Chamberlin, D., E. S. Chamberlin, W. E. Drought, and W. E. Scott, *Did They Succeed in College?*, Harper and Row, 1942.

3. Bany, Mary A. and Lois V. Johnson, *Classroom Group Behavior*, Macmillan, 1964. A good exposition of "group dynamics" as related to the management function quite apart from the educational function.

4. Thelen, H. A., *Dynamics of Groups at Work*, University of Chicago Press, 1954, Chapter 2. A variety of classroom images apparently held by teachers.

5. Robinson, Helen M. (Ed.), "Reading Instructions in Various Patterns of Grouping," *Supplementary Education Monograph No. 89* (December 1959), University of Chicago Press. See especially, Clymer, Theodore, "Criteria for Grouping for Reading Instruction."

6. Goodlad, John I., and Robert H. Anderson, *The Nongraded Elementary School*, Harcourt Brace and World, 1959.

7. Dewey, John, *Experience and Education*, Macmillan, 1939; *Science in General Education*, "Report of the Committee on the Functions of Science in General Education, Progressive Education Association," Appleton-Century-Crofts, 1938. Two classical expositions of this position in the thirties.

8. Schwab, Joseph, "Invitations to Inquiry," *Biology Teacher's Handbook*, John Wiley and Sons, 1963. A very sophisticated modern treatment.

9. Bruner, Jerome S., *The Process of Education*, Harvard University Press, 1960. The best known exegesis by a psychologist-turned-educator.

10. Hutchins, Robert M., *Education For Freedom*, Louisiana State University Press, 1943. One influential spokesman for this position.

11. Thelen, H. A., "Some Classroom Quiddities for People Oriented Teachers," *Journal of Applied Behavioral Science*, **1**, No. 3 (July–September 1965), pp. 270–285; "Reading for Inquiry" in Helen Robinson (Ed.), *Controversial Issues in Reading and Promising Solutions*, *Supplementary Education Monograph No. 91*, University of Chicago Press, 1961. Further speculations about "natural tendencies."

12. Ausubel, David P., *The Psychology of Meaningful Verbal Learning*, Grune and Stratton, 1963. An attempted refutation of the position discussed in our text as unrealistic.

13. Thelen, *op. cit.*, Note 4, Chapter 5. A didactic case study demonstrating what is involved.

14. Passow, Harry A., "The Maze of Research on Ability Grouping." *Educational Forum*, **26**, pp. 281–288, March 1962.

15. Conant, James B., *The American High School Today*, McGraw Hill, 1959.

16. Barker, J. C., J. C. Daniels, D. A. Pidgeon, and A. Yates, "Grouping in Education: England and Wales," *Mimeographed working paper S 46/10*, UNESCO Hamburg Institute for Education, 1964.

17. Jackson, Brian, *Streaming: Education System in Miniature*, Routledge, Keegan, and Paul, London, 1965.

18. Willig, C. J., "Social Implications of Streaming in Junior Schools." *Educational Research*, **2**, 1963.

19. Eash, Maurice J., "Grouping: What Have We Learned?" *Educational Leadership*, **18**, April, 1961, pp. 429–434.

20. Billet, Roy O., "Provisions for Individual Differences, Marking, and Promotion," *National Survey of Education Monograph No. 13*, U. S. Government Printing Office, 1933.

21. Turney, Austin H., "The Status of Ability Grouping," *Educational Administration and Supervision*, **17**, (January and February, 1931), pp. 21–42 and 110–127.

22. Wyndham, Harold S., *Ability Grouping*, Melbourne (Australia) University Press, 1934.

23. Otto, Henry J., "Elementary Education III. Organization and Administration," in Walter S. Monroe (Ed.)., *Encyclopedia of Educational Research*, Macmillan, 1950.

24. Goodlad, John I., "Classroom Organization" in Chester W. Harris (Ed.), *Encyclopedia of Educational Research*, Macmillan, 1960.
25. Ekstrom, Ruth B., *Experimental Studies of Homogeneous Grouping: A Review of the Literature*, Educational Testing Service (Princeton, N. J.) 1959.
26. Harry Possow has a distinguished career in research and utilization of various forms of grouping. His analysis of the pros and cons of homogeneous ability grouping is given in "Enrichment of Education for the Gifted," in *Education for the Gifted*, Part II of the fifty-seventh yearbook of the National Society for the Study of Education edited by Nelson Henry (University of Chicago Press, 1958).

    His most recent study is *The Effects of Ability Grouping*, by Goldberg, M. L., Passow, A. H., Justman, J., and Hage, G. Teachers College Press, 1966. Passow was a member of the steering committee which set up the Hamburg Conference which we referred to in the text.
27. Drews, Elizabeth, *Student Abilities, Grouping Patterns, and Classroom Interaction*, Office of Research and Publications, Michigan State College, East Lansing, Michigan 1963.
28. Goldberg, Passow, Justman, and Hage, *op. cit.*, Note 26.
29. Borg, Walter R., *An Evaluation of Ability Grouping*, Utah State University, 1964.
30. The National Foundation for Educational Research in England and Wales is an independent educational research agency. One of its current projects is a study of "streaming" in primary schools. The address is N.F.E.R., *The Mere*, Upton Park Road, Slough, Bucks, England.
31. Each of these persons prepared a working paper, mimeographed by the Institute, describing all types of grouping practiced in his country.
32. The book is in two parts. The first part presents analysis and conclusions. The second contains abstracts and surveys of the reported researches in countries all over the world. This book will be as conclusive as the present research allows. Because this book will be available by the time this book is published, I suggest that interested persons read it rather than being content with the cursory discussion possible in this chapter.
33. Reported in the English working paper by Barker, J. C., J. C. Daniels, D. A. Pidgeon, and A. Yates, *op. cit.*, Note 16.
34. Daniels, J. C., "The Effects of Streaming in the Primary School. Part I, What Teachers Believe," *British Journal of Educational Psychology* 31, 1961, pp. 69–78.
35. Reported in the Scandinavian working paper, prepared by I. Johannesson, S. Marklund, N. E. Svensson and T. Husen.
36. The concept of climate began as "atmosphere" in the classical study by Lippitt and White under the direction of the late great Kurt Lewin. This study has been rewritten, and appeared in 1960 as *Autocracy and Democracy*, White, R. and L. Lippitt, Harpers. An excellent survey of studies on climate is Withall's chapter in Gage, N., *Handbook of Research on Teaching*, Rand McNally.
37. In conversation with Professor Philip Jackson, University of Chicago.
38. Gross, Neal, and Robert Herriott, *Staff Leadership in Public Schools: A Sociological Inquiry*, John Wiley and Sons, 1965, p. 152. "If principals must work with newly appointed teachers whose educational beliefs are contrary to their own, or those of others on the staff, or whose personal characteristics hamper cooperation, strain and tension may ensue between principals and teachers, which may erode the principals' professional leadership."
39. Shaplin, Judson and Olds, Henry F., *Team Teaching*, Harper and Row, 1964. In his chapter in this book, Joseph C. Grannis points out that in team teaching a great many more decisions have to be made explicitly—and justified with reasons—than in teaching

by a single teacher. He explains that "The teachers in teaching must revise their curriculum because, more often than not, they have hitherto not perceived in it the texture of intentions which they now require in order to rationalize their decisions." (page 130).

40. Lund, Kenneth, "Student Personnel Services in the High School," *The High School in a New Era,* Chase, F. S., and H. Anderson, (Eds.), University of Chicago Press, 1958.

41. Bradford, L. P., Jack R. Gibb, and K. D. Benne., *T-Group Theory and Laboratory Method,* John Wiley and Sons, 1964.

42. Professor Ronald Lippitt has run T-groups for student officers and has reported the experience and findings in a mimeographed document issued by the Institute for Social Research, University of Michigan, Ann Arbor.

43. This idea is presented at some length as the essence of "Personal Inquiry," Chapter 6 in Thelen, H. A., *Education and the Human Quest,* Harper, 1960.

44. Thelen, H. A., "Grouping for Teachability" *Theory Into Practice,* **2,** 1963, pp. 81–89. A summary of the experiment discussed in this text.

Chapter Two

KNOWLEDGE: Scientific Research and Educational Practice

Psychological and Sociological Views · A Research Study: Work and Work-Avoidant Groupings · Experimental Findings in Relation to Grouping Policies

PSYCHOLOGICAL AND SOCIOLOGICAL VIEWS

If teachers were all alike it would be foolish to talk about "fitting" students to each individually. The students whom one teacher could teach best would also be the students that each of the others could teach best; and a student who could not learn in one class could not learn in any class. Under these conditions one would soon find himself grading students by using such categories as "choice," "prime," "commercial," etc., like so much dead government-inspected beef. And you would be classifying some students as superior and others as not belonging in the school at all. This, of course, is exactly what happens under the "track" system. But it is completely wrong in two ways: First, it is not true that all teachers are alike even as teachers (let alone as human beings), and the assumption is both false and self-proving (as Jackson's study of the gradual equalizing of teacher personality with age illustrates). Second, branding each child as inferior or superior is simply unfair, a denial of personality; its consequence is a waste of human potentials which remain undiscovered and therefore undeveloped.

In teachability grouping, the assumption is that teachers are completely different from each other, and that the child who is classified as teachable by one teacher may be classified as unteachable by another. This is respecting the teacher's personality with a vengeance. At the same time, the children are fitted into certain categories, which might be called "Teacher A Prone," "Teacher B Poison," etc. The number of categories of students depends on the number of teachers from which to choose for a particular subject. If there are four teachers of tenth grade English, then there are four "types" of students, namely those who ought to be assigned to Teacher A, to Teacher B, etc. Some of these types will be more vividly recognized than others. In practice, however the matching of students with teachers is made, it will be very clear that Joe, say, should go to Miss A; but with Mary, accord with one of the available teachers may be less obvious; Tom, as far as one can tell, might possibly be suited for any of the available teachers. Under these conditions, it is hard to see how any child could be branded. The pattern of characteristics that determined the assigning of children to any particular teacher would be complex, and it could not be condensed into a single dimension of social superiority or value; moreover, the extent to which the child fitted the pattern (whatever it might be) could range from being very close to merely indicative. Thus in teachability grouping, the personality of the child as well as that of the teacher would have to be recognized as a unique one. These conditions obviously are most coherent within a rationale of education that values individual meaning, difference, and potential; one that regards society as pluralistic, flexible, and with infinite variations in its productive roles.

These two positions about educational practice could be supported if certain factors were present. For example, the first position would be arrived at if it were true that teachers are all alike and that "learnability" is truly a single dimension or ability. Since neither of these is true, the first position is not justified by the facts and must therefore find its support (if any) either in fantasies or in determining to change these existing facts. The second position would be arrived at (and was arrived at) from the fact that the achievement of the child is very strongly dependent on his relationship with the teacher; further, that this relationship is unique with each combination of child and teacher. But what sort of validity or truth do these two generalizations have? To the psychologist or novelist these statements are axiomatic, for these social investigators are concerned with individuality and are aware of it; if not, they have to keep digging until they find it. They deal with specific persons, events, groups, and their job is to define what the qualities are that make these specifics distinguishable.

To the sociologist or anthropologist, however, these generalizations are irrelevant, for these scholars do not look at individuals (except by way of illustration, perhaps). They deal with groups, types, categories, classes—with tendencies that are true of collectivities rather than with consistent qualities unique to individuals. If we want to compare "lower class" persons with "middle class" persons, then we seek the help of a sociologist rather than a psychologist. If we wish to compare a primitive tribal culture with a complex urban culture, we go to an anthropologist, and we adopt his vocabulary and his purposes as we make the comparison. These researchers, along with political scientists and econo- mists, are students of *society,* not of individuals. And since the com- munity, the school, and the classroom are all societies, the concepts of the various social scientists can be applied to them, and, it might be added, with intriguing results. All of Chapter 1 is an exercise in societal science.

But when the generalizations of the sociologist are used to make psychological decisions, trouble ensues, which goes by the name of stereotyping or prejudice. Suppose, for example, we compare 1000 five- year-olds raised in slums with 1000 five-year-olds raised in the "nice" part of town. Differences, would be found between the average scores of these two groups with respect to verbal fluency, complexity of sen- tence structure, language uses, knowledge of objects in the environ- ment, emotional reaction to stress, attitudes toward policemen, etc. (These differences might be quite slight, even though consistently found. To be made more "reliable," the size of the groups should be increased to 2000 or 10,000.) This all sounds reasonable—sociologists are entitled to make a living too. What is not reasonable occurs when someone asks Johnny where he lives, notes that the address is in a slum neighbor- hood, and then assumes that Johnny lacks verbal fluency, speaks in a "restricted" language code, uses language only as a substitute for point- ing, is ignorant about much of the world, is overimpulsive in his emo- tional expression, and hates policemen. It may be that not a single tendency which *in general* distinguishes persons living in his locality from persons living elsewhere is correct about Johnny himself. All that can be said is that it is more likely to be true about Johnny than about his contemporary across the tracks, but how likely is more likely? The like- lihood is different for each tendency, ranging from 0 to 100%, and the only way to know how well the group tendency fits Johnny is to study Johnny as an individual as a psychologist might. If, instead, one sup- poses that whatever he thinks is true of Johnny's group must also be true of Johnny, then he is prejudiced.

Let us bring this a bit closer to home. Suppose a teacher gives an intelligence test and an achievement test to a large population of stu- dents. All the students who cannot read are bound to flunk both tests; all the students who mark them both at random are likely to get at least a "chance" score; all the superior readers are likely to do the best on both tests. On this basis, both intelligence and achievements tests are merely measures of the ability to read.

Furthermore, the relationship between the measures will depend on the shrewdness in selecting the students tested. To get a very high correlation, take 50 nursery school children, 50 fifth graders, and 50 college students. For this highly artificial population, the correlation between "intelligence" and "achievement" scores should be inordinately high. But now suppose you limit the population to 150 fifth graders. Their reading scores will (probably) range from the level of a second grader to that of a tenth grader, but the great bulk of them will probably lie within a reading range of three years. Under these conditions, the gross abilities to read will be relatively less influential because many other factors in addition to reading will affect the performances: whether the student likes one test and tries harder on it than on the other; whether he is more or less sophisticated in his understanding of the tasks on the two tests, and whether one test is more threatening to him than the other. Taking all these "accidental" or "randomly distributed uncontrolled factors" into account, the correlation between intelligence and achievement will be about 0.4 or 0.5 (within a possible range from 0 to 1.0). But note that this comparison is of the whole array of 150 intelligence test scores as compared to the other array of 150 achievement test scores; it is a group relationship, and the bigger the group the more certain the relationship. But what if the group contains only one individual? In that case, the accidental factors have no chance to average out, and the probable relationship, instead of being represented by a correlation of 0.4 or 0.5, would be best represented by the square of these numbers, 0.16 or 0.25. The interpretation of this statistic, which is our best guess in the absence of other information, is that 16 or 25% of the determination of achievement can be attributed to intelligence. This leaves 84 or 75% of the determination of achievement due to other "accidental" factors. Conclusion: given two children of the same intelligence, they may both achieve equally well, one may be a spectacular success and the other an equally spectacular failure, or any possibility in between. This is the sort of reasoning that has led many investigators to doubt that "homogeneous" ability groups are in fact appreciably more homogeneously teachable than any unselected group.

What we seem to be saying is that the sociologist studying societies can find general tendencies and estimate their strength; that these tendencies may be suggestive as hypotheses or expectations for individuals; that the best estimate of the tendency when applied to the individual is considerably lower than the estimate for the original groups. In knowing something about a society, we also know to a lesser degree what to expect from its members; how directly the two kinds of knowledge conform to each other is itself a further characteristic of the society.

Thus we seem to have arrived at the possibilities of grouping children on a basis different from ability or personality, namely in terms of some property of the classroom society. A general term for the most salient property of the classroom society is *its way of life*. And the "types" of students that can be found are those that go along with this way of life, those who accept it but modify it to suit themselves, those who fight it, and those who withdraw from it. The congruence between the way of life demanded in the classroom and the way of life the child actually lives decides how much and which of his potentials will be realized. According to recent evidence collected by Thomas Hawkes,* the extent to which the child goes along with classroom expectations is as influential as his IQ on his achievement. Expectation *meeting* correlates 0.4 with achievement; IQ correlates 0.4 with achievement; and IQ correlates only 0.2 with expectation meeting. In general, a child who is both able and a "good citizen" will achieve most in school—either characteristic by itself counts toward achievement; and yet being able and being a good citizen are not at all closely related to each other.

Here then, is another factor, which we shall temporarily call "citizenship," that makes as much difference as IQ in the child's achievement. And, if you must group "homogeneously," grouping by "citizenship" is at least as sound an idea as grouping by IQ. But at this point, we are much more interested in the light thrown by these findings on the nature of the classroom, especially with regard to relationships among the dramatis personae.

A RESEARCH STUDY: WORK AND WORK-AVOIDANT GROUPINGS

As a part of the larger study of teachability grouping which is investigated in our later chapters, Henry Peterson† studied the social-anthropological "types" of students to whom we referred previously. He reasoned that there are certain behaviors almost universally expected and demanded in our classrooms, and there are others that are not. The student who "goes along" would exhibit the demanded ("work") behaviors and not the verboten ("work-avoidant") behaviors. (Peterson labeled these students "adaptive-academic.") Another set of students would present the demanded behaviors and also some of the disallowed behaviors, meeting expectations but adapting the situations to their own interests (adaptive-social). A third group would show little or no behavior, would be essentially nonparticipant, or overtly withdrawn

---

* Ph.D. research now in progress, Department of Education, The University of Chicago.

† Peterson, Henry A., *Teacher and Student Reactions to Overt Work and Work-Avoidant Behavior in Secondary School Classrooms*, Unpublished PhD dissertation, Department of Education, University of Chicago, 1963.

(maladaptive-passive). And finally as a fourth possibility, there would be those students who fought it, showing only the verboten behaviors and none of the expected behaviors (maladaptive-active or aggressive). The two lists of behaviors which Peterson observed and used to select each type of student are:

Work Behaviors

1. Raises hand.
2. Volunteers an answer.
3. Called on by teacher for an answer.
4. Impulsive answers given by speaking without teacher recognition.
5. Lesson participation other than to questions asked by teacher.
6. Questions asked by student.
7. Relevant comments made by student.

"Work-Avoidance" Behaviors

1. Private play—dodling, combing hair, etc.
2. Study, not related to lesson.
3. Disturbs other people.
4. Blows off to class, impulsive nonwork expression.
5. Behavior causing reprimand from teacher.
6. Whispers, etc. (except when observed to be work oriented).

Two classes of each of some fourteen teachers were observed, a total of approximately 750 students. The classes covered all subjects and touched grades eight through eleven. They were observed three to five times during the school year by a pair of researchers, and each time one of the listed behaviors was spotted, it was tallied for that child on a seating chart. In addition to the observers, the teachers ranked the children on several "work" and "work-avoidant" characteristics, and, through a form of "guess-who" instrument, the students also revealed their perceptions of each other on the same continuum. The top and bottom quarters of the ranks, agreed on by two of the three raters (researcher, teacher, other students) were selected. Thus the adaptive-academic students were those in the top quarter for work and the bottom quarter for work-avoidance; 86 of the 750 students satisfied both criteria applied by two of the three kinds of ratings. Similarly, the adaptive-social were in the top quarter of the ranks for both work and work-avoidance, and 35 students were screened into this category. The maladaptive-passive, in the bottom quarter for both sorts of behavior, amounted to 65 out of the 750; the maladaptive-active, in top quarter for work-avoidance and bottom quarter for work, came to 62.

One interesting immediate finding is that there are different ratios of boys and girls in the four groups. The adaptive-academic split 50-50; the adaptive-social are three boys to each girl; four-fifths of the maladaptive-passives are girls; and four-fifths of the "acting out" maladaptive-actives are boys. It seems quite clear that the two sexes have their characteristic ways of resisting classroom expectations—the girls are withdrawn and the boys are aggressive.

What else can be said about the four types? A great deal. Peterson noted the marks they received, what the teachers thought of them, how well they liked the other groups and the teacher (also, vice versa), and all the differences among the groups revealed by a 405-item comprehensive battery of attitudes toward many aspects of life in the classroom. Table 1 summarizes the more routine information about the four groups.

Table 1. Comparisons among the Four Work- Work-avoidant Groups of 50 Students Each

Characteristic	Adaptive-Academic	Adaptive-Social	Maladaptive-Passive	Maladaptive-Active
Teacher's Marks				
A = 4; F = 0	3.72 (A)	2.54 (C+)	2.60 (B−)	1.38 (D)
Teacher preference: (1 = highest, 5 = lowest)				
"work with"	1.18	2.24	2.08	3.16
"chat with"	1.30	2.02	2.16	2.72
Student preference for teacher—No. of first choices (out of 50) for:				
"work with"	28	28	25	23
"chat with"	25	24	13	13
Classmates preference:				
"work with"	2.33	2.65	2.78	3.19
"chat with"	2.41	2.47	2.76	2.86
No. discriminating items from test battery:				
Positive response	33	6	29	9
Negative response	2	4	12	80
Ratio (No. pluses ÷ no. minuses)	16.5	1.5	2.4	0.11
Acceptance ratios:				
66 teachability items	3.1	1.9	2.6	1.3
152 teacher-agree items	1.8	1.4	1.7	1.1

Table 1 tells an interesting story. On every index the all-work, no-play group is highest and the overtly aggressive ones are lowest. The figures for the highly active group, engaging in largest numbers of both work and work-avoidant behaviors, almost agree with those for the all-girl passive nonparticipant group.

These groups, of course, are extreme representatives of their types. Peterson selected 50 students for each group (he had to squeeze 15 extras for the adaptive-social group). It is well to remember that of the original 750, 550 were *not* selected. These 550 are less extreme and would tend to blur the picture presented by Table 1.

Etched in boldest relief is the fact that the all-work group gets As, whereas the extreme, active work-avoiders get Ds (without regard for IQ). Consonant with these extremes are the attitudes the students have toward class, teacher, and classmates. Down toward the bottom of Table 1, you will find how many items of the 405-item assessment battery discriminated each group from the others, and you will also see the ratio of positive or affirmative responses to negative or hostile or anxious responses. The A students show 16.5 times as many positive as negative responses; the F students cordially hate just about everything, to the tune of 9 times as many negative as positive responses. The other two groups are squarely in the middle, and tend to be a bit more positive than negative.

While we are at the bottom of the table, the next line is also dramatic. The "66 teachability items," which are the subject of Chapter 7, are the ones, culled from the 405-item battery, which best distinguish the whole population of teachable kids from the unteachable kids for all the teachers. We see that the A students give the characteristic "teachable" response to 3.1 times as many items as they give neutral or nonteachable responses to, whereas the corresponding ratio for the D students is only a bit more than one-third as great. Perhaps the most surprising outcome is really the opposite side of the coin: the A students accept 76% of the teachable items, whereas the D students still accept 57%. You would never know it from their behavior, however, and we can already begin to feel sorry for students who have many private attitudes and values in common with A students but somehow feel compelled to behave with unmitigated insolence. We wonder what they think of themselves, and we will examine this later.

When all the teachers took the same battery, the majority of them agreed fairly well in their response to 152 items, thus showing, among other things, that teachers are much more alike than are the students they select as teachable (152 compared to 66 items). Peterson thought it would be interesting to see how much the four groups are like their teachers, and the last line of the table shows that this degree of similarity follows the same trends but in somewhat muted fashion. The ratios of items accepted to items rejected range from 1.8 to 1.1, corresponding to a range of 63% to 51%—a rather narrow range. In short, the A students (especially) are much more like the composite of teachable students than they are like their teachers; but for the D students, the figures are about the same (1.3 and 1.1). Clearly, teacher-similarity provides not as good a prognosis as does similarity to other students whom the teachers consider most teachable.

Somewhat more persuasive—because it reflects the "whole" person rather than a small fraction of items from a large battery—are the judgments the students and teachers make of each other. Let us consider first the feelings the students have for each other. All the students in the 28 classes rated each other on a 5 point scale in reply to the questions: whom would you prefer to work with, and whom would you prefer to chat with? The five ratings ranged from "really would be very pleased" to "would rather not." The average ratings received from their classmates by the four groups are fairly similar for "chat with." The average figure 2.63 for all four groups is about half way between 2 and 3, "would like to" and "would be willing to." To their classmates in general, all four groups are about equally popular for sociability. When asked about "work with" choices, the picture is not much different except for the actively aggressive students who are downgraded from "willing to" to "don't know how I would feel." (People usually have to have intense dislike for someone to state on a questionnaire that they out and out reject him.)

What is perhaps the most interesting trend to discover is that the same one that we have seen consistently in the other data exists when classmates express preferences for each other: the more work-oriented the group, the more it is preferred even in friendship by the others. Peterson explains this with considerable ingenuity. Before, however, delving into this further, let us see what the situation is with respect to the teacher.

It is noteworthy that the teacher tends to make sharper distinctions among the children than they do for each other and that the teacher's ratings are more positive. The teachers "would really be very pleased" to work and chat with the A students, and they are more positive toward the next two groups than are the classmates. Only the fourth group is as strongly disliked by teachers as by their classmates.

How do the students feel about the teachers? The answer is: very favorably—so favorably, in fact, that only the first-choice ratings are discriminating, and then only for the more personal relationship, "chat with." Of the 50 students in each group, about half (23 to 28) "would really be very pleased" to work with the teacher. But what they really feel about the teacher as a *person* rather than as a protector, boss, father, or power figure is revealed in the "chat with" choices. Here the two adaptive groups are almost as favorable to chat with as to work with the teacher; and the two maladapted groups are alike in having only half as much preference for chat as for work. The teacher, as the symbol for and the living embodiment of the adult work-oriented world, is almost equally attractive to all the students—possibly for quite a variety of reasons (including, perhaps, denial of their own hostility); which again reinforces our feeling that even the outwardly aggressive and hostile students know that they ought to grow up. In the imagined voluntary relationship of friendly chatting, however, it is no surprise to find the hostile students showing far less preference: the teacher does not care for them and they reciprocate as heartily as the instrument and the power relationships allow.

The most arresting finding concerns the passive girls. The teachers say they like these girls quite well, but they do not reciprocate; they rate the teacher no higher than do the hostile aggressors. Here we are given a strong clue to their passivity: a sense of personal inadequacy. Observe the pattern! The girls' reactions to the battery are quite similar to teachers and to teachable children in general, with only the A students being higher. In general they are 20 times more "positive" than the active aggressors (2.4 to 0.11). And the teachers like them. It is very hard to believe that these girls keep their distance from the teacher because of dislike for the teacher; it is far more plausible to guess that they are too shy, distressed, or self-doubting to wish risking a personal encounter.

Before pursuing the analysis that will clarify this point, let us consider one more set of ratings: how do the members of the various groups feel about each other? We have been considering the preferences of all their classmates, regardless of what types they represent. Now let us see if classmates of different types respond differently to each other. Since only the students who had classmates in each of the four groups were able to rate each other, there were different numbers of ratings for each type of student and Peterson had to perform some involved statistics to get averages that could legitimately be compared with each other. The evidence is contained in 32 figures, 16 each for "work with" and for "chat with." The findings can be summarized for our purposes rather quickly.

The A students prefer each other on both criteria; next in order are the groups as written: the adaptive socials, the passive girls, the aggressive boys.

The adaptive-social students prefer each other for both working and chatting, and the A students even more so. They have lesser and equal preference for both the passive girls and aggressive boys as work-with companions, and they prefer the aggressive boys to the passive girls for purposes of chatting.

The passive girls prefer each other equally with the A students to work with, and their preference drops for the A students as chat-with companions. They dislike the aggressive boys more than the active-adapted students, and they prefer both of these groups somewhat more to chat with than to work with.

The aggressive boys prefer themselves and the active adaptives about equally to work with, and themselves slightly more to chat with. Next they prefer the A students to work with more than to chat with and the passive girls come in last on both measures.

In short, each group prefers people like themselves to work and chat with, and the A sudents are equal or second choices except by the aggressive boys who place the adaptive-active students (high work coupled with high work-avoidance) second. The two maladapted groups reject each other the most. The passive girls look toward the A students; the aggressive boys look toward the adaptive-actives (this suggests what kind of "pairings" of "strong" (adaptive) and "weak" (maladaptive) students might be most helpful to the bottom two groups).

Finally, we discuss the analysis of the responses of each group to the assessment battery. This is not easy because the items cover a very wide range of relationships and because the items that discriminated for each group varied in number and topics covered. To make comparable analyses on the basis of such differing amounts and kinds of evidence presents problems. Peterson solved these by formulating 11 questions against which to compare the data on each group. He then summarized the pattern made by the 11 answers, and came up with the following, which is quoted from pages 89 and 90 of his doctoral thesis:

"The attitude characteristics distinguishing each of the four behavioral types are remarkable for their degree of consistency with the overt behaviors manifested by these students. Each type gives evidence of perceiving themselves accurately. If consistency between attitudes and overt behavior is a sign of mental health then members of each of these behavioral types are mentally healthy.

The high work-participative adaptive-academic students reveal the most favorable attitudes toward nearly all aspects of the school milieu. In their attitudes they are work-oriented, assertive, socially poised, intellectually confident, contented with the conventional methods and objectives of the schools. In short, they tend to reveal, on the attitude questionnaires employed in this investigation, a set of mental-emotional states that are in harmony with their overt behavior patterns.

In like manner, the adaptive-social students (whose behavior patterns were the most active, erratic, nonconformist and unpredictable of the four types) displayed attitude tendencies that were consistent with their behavioral patterns. They demonstrate their individuality by having little in common with one another, with the result that there are considerably less items distinguishing these students than are found for the other three types. The few items that adaptive-social students do agree upon are concentrated in their concern for active, autonomous behavior. They see themselves as energetic, obtrusive, and adventuresome, all characteristics which parallel their overt-behavior patterns.

The passive-withdrawn, maladaptive students state their preferences for routine, teacher-dominated, unthreatening classroom tasks. They acknowledge their dependency needs, perceiving themselves as shy and helpless. They tend to be work-oriented, but as followers not leaders. They like work activities which are well-structured and routine. They seem to have the mentality of clerks, not managers. Once again these self-expressions of attitudes are all in harmony with the overt-behavior patterns typifying these students.

The maladaptive-active students tend not to fit in the type of work-achievement milieu commonly found in the schools. They dislike the work demands of the classroom. They resent the authority wielded by teachers. They are bored with the learning activities employed in their classes. In general they reflect, in their attitudes toward school, the dissatisfaction and rebellion that is to be seen in their behavior. In addition, the attitudes of these students toward themselves indicate that they feel inadequate in coping with the cognitive, ideational demands of the classroom. They persistently express feelings of discomfort when required to handle ideas. Perhaps this lack of ability and/or confidence to meet the intellectual demands of the classroom is the primary reason for the maladaptive-active students' work-disruptive behavior."

EXPERIMENTAL FINDINGS VERSUS GROUPING POLICIES

The preceding study is an outstanding example of its type. It begins in a set of propositions: that schools are dominated by powerful adults and that these adults enforce a common set of expectations for behavior of students; that students are there to work, not play; that the teacher will dictate and control or guide activities; that the class is to be orderly, respectful, and diligent, and that the "community" accepts and desires that these standards be maintained in the school. Expectations such as these define what Peterson calls the "achievement" culture, supporting a way of life characteristic of the productive adult world. The behaviors demanded in this culture are the "work" behaviors, and we have seen that the A students, the adaptive-academic group, accept this culture, reinforce it, and find satisfaction and reward in it.

Opposed to the adult-achievement culture are ways of life characteristic of children: emotionally impulsive, oriented to interpersonal relationships rather than to tasks, undisciplined. Theirs is a "play" culture, maintaining a way of life whose rewards are immediate rather than deferred, in which activities are engaged in "for their own sake" rather than as calculated means to further ends. In its pure form, the social perspective of this culture would be anarchy. Its chief proponents in school are the maladaptive-active students, the aggressives, who, in order to maintain this culture in the face of the powerful and unrelenting opposition of the teacher, have to muster considerable aggressiveness and antagonism.

Obviously, there are two further possibilities besides accepting the one culture and suppressing the other. Feeling that he cannot choose between them, a person may withdraw completely, taking no active role in either—hence the maladaptive-passives. They are distressed because they think that whatever they contemplate doing will be frowned upon by proponents of one or the other culture. Finally, a highly energetic, active person may refuse to distinguish between the child and adult cultures and simply follow his own bent. The adaptive-actives, average achievers in this study, appeal to the psychologist as being the most autonomous and potentially the most creative of the lot, even though they are unlikely to make it to graduate school.

Thus concludes our presentation of a coherent set of ideas which are supported by carefully designed experimentation, are based on shrewdly developed evidence, and are demonstrated by acceptable canons of scientific research. Is not the implication of this study clear— that we should decide which of the four types each student is and then, through experimentation over time, learn what combinations of types result both in efficient teaching and effective learning? The answer is no.

The following are several reasons why not.

1. These types apply in a clear-cut way to only 200 out of 750 students. What about the other 550?

2. The phenomena the study deals with have no existence. The "groups" of students representing each type never saw each other, have no interaction; they were drawn from 28 classrooms throughout the Midwest. What we are calling one or another type of student is not a

student at all; it is a label given to a very limited number of measurable or countable behaviors, and these type labels resulted from "taking an average." What kind of probability is there that statistical "averages" taken from a widely dispersed population have relevance to any actual, living, interactive group?

3. The "achievement culture" and the "work-behaviors" that define this culture operationally are assumed to be demanded by the 14 teachers and, presumably, by all normal teachers. Unlike the descriptions of types of students which come from averaged actual data, the achievement culture is defined *a priori* as a characteristic of American schools—a generalization that takes in rather considerable territory. It is "in the nature of schools" to be like this. Obviously, any further reasoning that uses this as a starting point must either be confined to an equally vague generalized American school, or it had better take the propositions as hypotheses to be tested. It is evident in our study that at least one teacher rejected the "achievement culture" almost completely, and that it had different meanings for different teachers. American schools are so diverse that there is hardlly anything truthful that can be said about *all* of them beyond the fact that they have teachers and students.

4. As we shall show later on when we consider what happened in 26 actual classrooms, the conceptual restrictions that we must impose to make a piece of research manageable (and possible) mean that any one study, however comprehensive, can encompass but a small part of classroom phenomena. The Peterson study is quite properly limited to ideas that are relevant to the concepts of "achievement" and "play" cultures, and its method of inquiry—again quite properly—is to assert the existence of these "cultures" and then see what light the concepts throw on the persons involved in them. But a great deal is left out, and we have no idea how much or how important it is compared to what is included. The advantage of the study is the finding of many relationships, some of them quite "strong." But it is a mistake, common to be sure but nevertheless a mistake, to assume that because A is strongly related to B that, therefore other possible factors, such as C, D, E, etc., can in practice be disregarded. Thus, the finding of a fairly strong relationship between IQ and achievement was translated into ability grouping without awareness that work-orientation has just as much relationship to achievement; and that predictions of achievement based on IQ could not possibly be accurate unless we could insure that the able students would be at least as work-oriented as the original populations from which the generalization was derived.

In the face of objections such as these, what kind of implications do scientific studies have for practices such as grouping? Will the present great effort to find ways of disseminating research findings to practitioners merely contribute to confusion and further encourage the hope for simplified magic panaceas? What does the virtual abandonment of special laboratory schools in the forties on the grounds that the findings from them did not fit "ordinary" schools suggest about the conditions, if any, under which research efforts may aid educational practice?

The answer to these questions calls for nothing more complicated than making a simple distinction among the different ideas. The simple distinction embodies a paradox, which makes it more interesting, and it is summed up in the most often quoted expression by Kurt Lewin, the great psychologist: "There is nothing so practical as a good theory." Any adequate research activity is the working out of a dialogue between what can be said about a single, specific, particular actual case and a broad category of cases to which the particular case belongs. What Lewin meant was that the more one understands about the nature of the world in general, the more likely one will be able to act intelligently in the next actual concrete situation. (This, of course, is the basic premise of "liberal" education, however antithetical its own methods may be to its goal.)

To the extent that we try to solve practical problems by understanding what is involved in them and then *creating* new action on understanding the specific situation, Lewin was right. But insofar as we try to solve practical problems by translating theory directly into practice or by searching for procedures or cookbook formulas that were developed for somebody else's problems, Lewin's dictum, although not wrong, is irrelevant. Any scientific experiment of the sort considered adequate by reputable researchers today has as its goal the development of theory, that is, understanding of phenomena; if we want to solve problems without first understanding them, research has nothing useful to tell us. Unfortunately, however, researchers also have data, which come from real situations. There is a great tendency on the public's part to regard these data, rather than the theories they support, as the findings of the study and to assume that these findings should somehow represent the facts about other more or less "similar" situations. And if the experimental situation is not reasonably similar to the problem, then clearly the research has no trustworthy implications for it. Laboratory schools, usually containing bright students, well-trained teachers, and enlightened administrators, were discarded because they were not like the run-of-the-mill school; it was argued, anything found out in them would be of no value to ordinary schools. Yet the reason for setting up laboratory schools in the first place was that schools were believed to be unable to engage in good research for the very reason that they were ordinary schools. This "data-transfer" argument assumes that the application of research experience to new situations is solely through constructing analogies rather than through what we have been calling "understanding." Analogous thinking asserts that if School A and School B are alike in certain salient respects, then what happens in School A will also happen in School B and therefore there is no reason to ask why. Obviously the most salient aspects of a school are the brightness of its pupils and the "excellence" of its staff, and if two schools are markedly different in these respects, then it is assumed that the experiences of one cannot possibly throw any light on those of the other. It is precisely because no two schools, individuals, societies, or groups are alike, that all problem solving based on analogy must be viewed with suspicion.

We return now to Peterson's study and the applications it illustrates for grouping. The results of his study indicate that certain ideas seem to be useful in portraying and understanding some relationships among students and between them and their teacher. These ideas are general ones—that the classroom is the place where two cultures interact; that each child must settle the conflict between the cultures as it impinges on him; and that only a limited number of different solutions are logically possible. At this high level of generality, these propositions are the conceptual backbone of many studies and of much practice (for example, psychotherapy, human-relations training, etc.) In fact these propositions, with slight rewording, apply in ethics and religion—in any field of inquiry concerned with the human dilemma. Ideas this broad, which can guide inquiry in many different fields, belong properly to metatheory; perhaps they should be referred to as metasocial science and be regarded as comparable to metaphysics. So Peterson's first finding is that these ideas are indeed useful in a new and original research application.

The second finding is more specific. When two cultures are defined in certain ways, for example, "achievement" and "play," four types of students can be predicted and will in fact be identifiable among actual students. This finding "confirms" the validity of the idea of "achievement" and "play" cultures as factors that impinge on real persons and help explain their conduct. At this point the theoretical idea of the two cultures begins to be rather "practical." It suggests to the educator that maybe it would be worth asking himself what the state of conflict is between the adult and child-dominated cultures in *his* school.

The next finding is even more specific. It refutes the analogy approach. Peterson found that certain attitudes, performances, and relationships distinguished students who engaged mostly in his specified "work" behaviors from those who engaged mostly in his specified "nonwork" behaviors. But how certain can we be that these particular behaviors are, in any of the other schools, good indices of the general orientation to work and nonwork? Among the 14 teachers Peterson dealt with, further study showed that at least one of them accepted most of the *nonwork* behaviors as work behaviors. (He also had his own rather odd definition of "achievement.") Peterson's theories were about the two cultures, *not* about the particular behaviors he counted and summed up as *indices* of these cultures. The behaviors he decided to use fit our image of teachers in general, and they make sense when an average of the 14 teachers was computed. But if the study had been confined to only one teacher's classes, a more specific list could have possibly been drawn up. Thus the finding that these lists of behavior worked as indices of the two cultures is contingent upon circumstances that might very well differ from one school situation to the next, and to reject the more abstract findings because these lists of behaviors are not very appropriate to some other school is ridiculous indeed.

The contribution that might have been made at this level of the study would have been not the specific behaviors but the method of investigation through which these behaviors were defined. It is within the province of a scientific study to offer do-it-yourself routines through which each person can arrive at specific instruments that apply sharply to his particular situation.

Finally, to use these results as an aid to creating better methods of grouping, we need some additional ideas that, quite properly, are not even mentioned in the research report. These ideas, which we may call technological or political rather than scientific, are needed because the purposes of the researcher are not the same as those of the practical problemsolver. The researcher is trying to establish some new ideas about phenomena; the practitioner is seeking more effective ways to shape the phenomena to his own ends. The research report should, at its various "levels," give the reader the guidance he would need to replicate the research in his own different situations; in this case the reader and the original researcher have the same purposes, to check out certain proposed generalized relationships.

However, the practitioner who is on the receiving end of research not only has the problem of translating its concepts to his situation, he also has another difficulty in that his reasons for examining the phenomena are very different from those of the researcher. For example: Peterson found that work-oriented kids tends to get better marks than nonwork oriented ones. Peterson says nothing about whether it is good to get high marks. Such a decision he keeps to himself because it is irrelevant in finding out simply who gets the good marks. Yet this is an important decision for the practitioner. In general he would say that getting good marks is desirable, and that children whose grades are low should, especially if they are "intelligent," be helped to improve them. Having committed himself to seeking ways to help them, the practitioner would probably see the implication that one way to help would be to increase students' work orientation or decrease their play orientation. He might also find further implied a method of changing the orientation through the influence of students on each other. Peterson points out that maybe the maladaptive-actives could be reached through the adaptive-socials and the maladaptive-passives through the adaptive-academics. It would be worth putting these combinations together—if we could discover a way to do it. But the scientific study gives little guidance on this point, although a clinician who studied the assessment items that Peterson found discriminated among the various groups could certainly arrive at some good ideas as to what sort of tasks the combinations could work on effectively, and what sort of social conditions and teacher behaviors should be avoided.

The technological ideas that are needed to supplement the scientific ones are ideas about which factors can be changed or influenced by the practitioner, how this can be done, and realistic ideas about the values and costs of changed procedures. Peterson's study might be useful to a teacher whose teaching technology includes the use of small groups of students interacting with each other. It would be of little or no use to a teacher who never heard of small groups, is wary of them, and would rather not even experiment with them.

The conception of teachability grouping, to which we now turn, asks for someone who is neither a scientist nor a practitioner as these terms have been used above. It calls for an "action researcher." The characteristics the scientist would be most interested in, namely those that generally and predictably make kids "teachable" do not have to be known, although this information is presented in Chapter 5. On the other hand, a positive formula to be followed in all schools is also missing, and in its place we only reveal our goal and the possible ways to reach it—hoping that each school will weigh these and use them as stimuli to develop their own peculiarly appropriate and effective routines.

Chapter three

OBJECTIVE: From Student Types to Teachable Classes

**Classroom Beginnings · Types of Students as Perceived by Teachers ·
Types of Students Resulting from Assessment of Personality ·
Empirically Determined Teachable Types · The Course of the
Investigation · The Report of the Experiment**

CLASSROOM BEGINNINGS

During the year 1957–1958, the author along with three teachers, Robert Boyd, Paul Moulton, and "Hutch" Gordon, and fifty sophomores in the Laboratory School of the University of Chicago, set out to discover the workings of team teaching. In addition, ideas on the associations between inquiry processes and societal structures in the classroom were tested. Thus, among us, we had an ongoing, exciting set of phenomena in which to explore two basic themes. Each day a discussion was held on what was observed and two questions were asked: What happened today? How can we account for it? This, then, was a typical "exploratory" operation of the sort usually dismissed as nonresearch but without which decent research is impossible.

We gradually became aware of the fact that our reflections on classroom phenomena, interesting and stimulating as they were to us, were yielding no clear-cut results. We did not expect to be able to come up with a concise set of rules for future teachers to follow; but we did expect to be able to define relationships between self-direction and inquiry; between group stimulation and motivation; between planning of work and nature of subsequent performance. Actually what we discovered is that these and other relationships depend very much on *what sort of person the student is*. What made sense for one student did not for another; moreover, the significant differences between students did not seem to be as quantitative as they were qualitative. It was as if they represented different "types," with different approaches to learning, dif-

63

ferent ways of using social relationships, different kinds of rewards and punishments, different degrees to which any learning experience had importance for their own needs.

The following are three kinds of events that helped illustrate our discoveries:

1. Given the job of working algebra problems, twelve students seemed to work best alone, seeking help from the teacher on their own time after school; ten seemed to work best in groups of two or three, discussing all aspects of the work together; twelve seemed to work best in a rather formal "classroom" setting, with the teacher in direct charge and always available for help; and the remaining fourteen seemed to work equally well or badly under any of these three methods.

2. Six students who were outstanding in achievement were excused from further work in the three subjects during the last month of the school year. They were allowed to investigate on their own any topic which they and the teachers, sitting as a seminar, thought would be worthwhile. Three of these students turned out creative, perceptive work; the experience was challenging, exciting, and highly productive. The other three—equally bright and equally good achievers—probably did not do as well as they would have done within the "regular" class!

3. The three teachers taught by quite different methods. One was an excellent lecturer; another made use of committee-planned projects; the third guided intellectual discussion to analyze problems and to explain steps in problem solving. We discovered that these methods of teaching seemed to be appropriate for some students but not for others. It is true that a few students—possibly 12 out of the 50—worked well under all these methods. But for the most part they had decidedly different preferences, motivations, standards, and abilities under these different methods. Granted that teacher personality and subject "difficulty" account for some of the differences in response, we nonetheless felt that plenty of variance was left unaccounted for by these factors.

These and many other observations of "individual differences" were hardly unexpected. What was unexpected was that the differences were so vital—that they seemed to be the most influential. It became clear to us that the reason so much discussion of teaching in education courses seems vague and opinionated is that the validity of any statement depends on what the students—both individually and in a group—are "like;" and that until we can find some way to describe particular classes with precision, we shall be unable to make any statements except about very general policies or idealized images whose relationship to reality is unknown.

The net result of these reflections was the development of two propositions:

a. That students differ in their approaches to learning experiences; and that learners may be of several different "types."

b. That each type of learner will learn most effectively when taught by methods aimed at his "type."

The original aim of this project was to investigate the meanings and validity of these propositions. It launched us on a study of the various possible ways in which "types" of students might be identified.

TYPES OF STUDENTS AS PERCEIVED BY TEACHERS

Ever since we were soberly assured by a very fine elementary school teacher that pupils are either "wrigglers" or "squirmers," we had wanted to talk with more teachers about types. In the summer of 1958, at a workshop in Oklahoma City, we asked 70 teachers, supervisors, and principals to write out descriptions of the various types of students they found in their high school classrooms. We discovered that the 300 descriptions thus obtained could be classified under four major types of students: the good, the bad, the indifferent, and the lost.

The "good types" are those with whom teachers can work. Their behavior is responsive to task, group, and teacher, and on the whole they are "there to learn." They include the following:

1. *Natural leaders.* They not only go along with the task but identify with the teacher and guide others too. Thus they volunteer for responsibility; for example, in a project group they organize the work and the other students.

2. *Autonomous and self-directive.* These get excited about the subject, are challenged by it, and are capable of working on their own. They do not make trouble for others and they ask for help when they need it. They can be counted on for novel and stimulating interpretations.

3. *Interdependent, high achievers* are oriented to work, getting good grades, and getting along with the class and the teacher. They are bright and successful; they also stay within boundaries and expectations in the situation and do not often come up with creative ideas. They do what they are told to do well and with enjoyment.

4. *Interdependent, low achievers* are similar to the students mentioned, only not bright enough to be very successful. However, they are well-adjusted and nobody holds lack of achievement against them.

5. *Nonconforming but work-oriented.* These students accept the achievement task, but have to find a "different" way to approach it. The need for the "different" way is aimed only at being different.

6. *Nonconforming, creative.* These students need to be different not only with respect to ways of working but also with respect to the goal. Very often they set a more difficult task than is required. Their behavior has much in common with type 2, but they enter into it for the "wrong" reasons—reassurance rather than autonomy.

7. *Conforming and dependent* youngsters accept the goals and want to achieve, but they seem helpless and need to have others guide them. They may end up with good grades.

8. *Submissive.* These students often do not know what the task goals are. They only deliver the behavior the teacher wants, without question or understanding.

The "indifferent" students are innocuous in class. They do not care about work and education. They do enough to get by, and they do not make trouble. Some of them are seen as pleasant and likable.

9. *Happy-go-lucky.* This student has a good sense of humor, likes people, and enlivens the classroom routine with occasional teasing and non-hostile "wise cracks." He stays well within the bounds of decency and he "ain't mad at nobody." Enjoyable to have in class, once you give up trying to educate him.

10. *Beauty queen.* This one "preens during class, getting ready to strut in the halls between classes." She has a pleasant smile for the teacher, gets C's, and remains preoccupied with mysteries beyond the reach of the petty affairs of the educational program.

11. *Gone on athletics.* This young man daydreams about the masculine world of physical prowess. He is a cultist, unaroused by the hair-splitting verbal nonsense surrounding him.

12. *Duck-tail haircut.* Another cultist, with his leather jacket, jeans, wide belt, and preoccupation with the gang. Just waiting for the bell to ring and for his school-leaving birthday. Knows better than to try to "start something."

13. *Prig.* This one's resistance to involvement is achieved through a petty but crippling moral literal-mindedness. She sits in judgment on everyone, and sooner or later finds something to criticize about all of them. Narrow-minded and insular, reasons, goals, and causes are foreign to her.

14. *"I-don't-need-an-education."* This type may be bright, friendly, and outwardly cooperative. Since his father is a self-made man in a business

he will share someday, he sees nothing that school work can add to his probable success.

The "bad" students are the ones who anger the teacher. They are hard to handle and add nothing to the class. Teachers seldom are able to emphathize with these students enough to understand them, or even to control their own anxieties at not being able to deal with them.

15. *Teacher impressers.* These are big talkers, always putting on an immense show of interest and of being lost in a flurry of activity. Their unawareness of their own hypocrisy is so great that, when taken to task, they retreat into injured innocence.

16. *Short-cutters.* These seek the quick way to meet demands without effort, that is, the easy courses, the "soft" teachers. They want rewards and recognition, but they scheme rather than work for them. They are often smart and for the most part cynical. "Any kind of cheating is OK," "no sense of right and wrong," "sneaky."

17. *Clowns and attention seekers.* With reference to this group, our reporters really let themselves go—"always acting a part—must be center of attention;" "wants to annoy teacher and disturb class—mother says it's the school's fault;" "they know they can get the teacher's attention by tantalizing her;" "feels responsibility to entertain class."

18. *Misdirected superior.* "Delights in needling the teacher with floundering questions;" "thinks he knows more than the teacher;" "acts bored with explanations and assignments;" "scoffs at other kids' efforts;" "use cleverness to avoid work but can always pass because of high intelligence;" "lazy;" "doesn't care to share his knowledge."

19. *Social climbers.* "Those who attempt to organize cliques to gain importance socially and become frustrated when they meet with opposition. This usually creates problems at home and at school."

20. *Monopolizers.* These students think (?) out loud all the time, and go their own way, with little responsiveness to what the class is trying to do. They can not take criticism, have no respect for authority, can be aggressive.

21. *Hero worshippers and blind followers.* These idolize another student or the teacher; or simply slavishly follow the crowd. They work hard at giving up all signs of their own personality, and they live vicariously in others.

22. *Antisocial and destructive.* These differ from other antisocial types in that their behavior does not stem from misguided need for reassurance, but from hatred turned outward; their problems are always said to be the fault of others. "Defies the teacher," "doesn't want to work

and doesn't want anyone else to work," "a gang spirit," "delinquent," "poor sense of values," "uses profanity in class," "deep inadequacy covered up by daring attacks."

The "lost souls" are quiet types, fearful, withdrawn, and unhappy. They all have very little self-esteem.

23. The *rejected* think nobody likes them; every effort to help them is seen as a slight or insult. They trust nobody, not even themselves.

24. The *dreamers* are wrapped in an inpenetrable shroud of dreams; they are simply "not there;" unreachable.

25. The *sufferers* would like to participate, but find it too painful; being called on in class is torture. For them, avoiding pain is their main goal, and everything is painful.

26. The *passive* are seemingly without affect; they never express like or dislike, enthusiasm or resistance. They drag through required work, but seem almost totally uninvolved and detached from it.

This, then, is what the teacher contends with; these are his perception of the ways in which students relate to the classroom—and his own feelings about these different sorts of relationships. We may ask: Do these types exist? Are they real? The answer is that one behaves in terms of what he *thinks* is real. As long as teachers believe these types of students exist, they will react to students as if they fit these categories; and if this continues, then the students will also adopt this same image.

TYPES OF STUDENTS RESULTING FROM ASSESSMENT OF PERSONALITY

It seemed clear to us that the types of students perceived by teachers may be very largely images projected from their own needs: the good, bad, indifferent, and lost. We felt we wanted our types to be based on something more objective than this, and so we devised a test to assess those aspects of students' personalities that, hopefully, would be more significant for learning in the classroom.

We recalled[2] the following differences among our sophomores that we had had to cope with:

First, students do approach subjects differently. One child can understand algebra presented symbolically and theoretically; a second child probably needs to have the symbols related to objects like blocks, moving wheels, and data-producing experiments; a third youngster needs to see algebra in relation to how it is used in everyday affairs; a fourth is mostly intrigued by its puzzle-solving aspects, which are attractive partly because they are so remote from "life"; a fifth child is struck by the beauty of the systematic organization and logical coherence of the subject. Clearly implied is a need for different methods of teaching, with different emphases upon symbolic and operational experience, different mixtures and sequences of induction and deduction, and different contexts (social, experimental, physical) for algebraic problems and principles.

Second, students do seem to work best in particular kinds of social organizations. Thus one student seems to work problems best by himself; a second works best with a friend; a third does better with a small clique; and a fourth is least distracted and most stimulated in a larger group.

Third, students differ very markedly in the kinds and amounts of instructions they need in order to work effectively. One student works effectively only when he knows exactly what he is "supposed" to do next; a second student makes the most out of activities whose purpose is defined in general terms but whose materials and resources are not given; a third student is more challenged when he can plan the activity as well as execute it; a fourth is stimulated by hearing the ideas of others and then creates something different for himself, and so on.

Students' ideas differ about who should make the decisions that guide learning. Thus when we ask students "who should decide" each of 24 matters about the class, one student answers that he, the student, should make 22 of the decisions for himself; another thinks the teacher should make all but one; and yet another student wants to leave most of the decisions to the class!

Fourth, students need different supports and conflicts to stimulate their interest to learn. A student who challenges another to creative self-expression may drive a third to tears or sullen apathy; two friends may form a clique which is impenetrable for group purposes, or they may be a strong combination which gives the group excellent natural leadership; a student may be tied up in anxiety which can be released by the spontaneous expression of hostility by a classmate, yet the same kind of expression may tie another student in knots. And, to some extent, these considerations may apply to the teachers, too.

Fifth, students differ in the amount of knowledge and experience they bring to an investigation. This is the problem of resources for the group, and it probably reflects interests in the subject as well as personal variations in experience. At any rate, it is likely that group investigation is helped by having students who can relate questions and concepts to a variety of observations.

Sixth, and finally, includes physical energy, creativity, frustration tolerance, ego ideals, sex attitudes, spontaneity, self-concepts—all entering into the picture.

During this period, we also surveyed the literature, thought about group composition researches that had been going on in the laboratory since 1951,[3] talked things over with all the teachers we could, and thus formulated, in an article for *School Review*,[4] the most promising basic dimensions of the various types. These dimensions are: (*a*) the values the student holds with respect to classroom-relevant goals and assumptions; (*b*) the student's pattern of emotional reaction to stresses in learning situations; (*c*) the kind of teacher the student can "identify" with, and the nature of this identification; (*d*) the student's structure of threats and defenses with regard to his interaction with peers; (*e*) the "ability" of the student, defined in terms of "maturity" and "sophistication" with regard to subjects rather than in terms of IQ and/or some general index of "achievement;" and (*f*) the student's own motivational pattern as reflected in his preferences for different kinds of learning activities.

By this time, funds had become available through the Cooperative Research Branch of the U. S. Office of Education.[5] We recruited five research assistants and proceeded to the next step: the construction of the assessment battery. The battery slowly evolved through the successive stages of construction, try-out, modification, and validation by comparing interpretations from each test with impressions of teachers. Each member of the research team assumed responsibility for the development of at least one instrument, and the entire group participated in viewing results and offering suggestions for improvement. The battery, completed in January 1959, contains the following tests:

1. *"Situations."* Forced-choice questionnaire assessing the fight, flight, work, pairing, and dependency tendencies in social stress situations. This test is an objective form of the Reaction to Group Situations (sentence-completion type) test developed and validated in previous research in the laboratory.

2. *Words! Words!* Semantic differential test, associating 14 word-pair continua to 13 goal and person concepts. The word-pairs were developed by Professor Benjamin Wright; the first form was tried out in the Sophomore Project.

3. *Teacher Descriptions.* Rating and ranking of six given "types" of teachers with respect to "typicality," "learn most from," and "feel most comfortable with."

4. *Participation A and B.* Rating and ranking forms, respectively, ascertaining relative preferences for working, under five social condi-

tions (alone, friends, class, etc.), with five kinds of interaction (common purpose, uninvolved, threatening, etc.) and in two roles ("telling" and "listening").

5. *Ways of Doing Things.* Rating of the extent to which each of four social conditions (alone, group, etc.) has each of 20 proposed advantages (rewards) and disadvantages (punishments).

6. *Who Should Decide?* Checking which of five agents (you, teacher, class, etc.) should make each of 24 decisions about progress, materials, standards, etc. This was piloted in the Sophomore Project.

7. *Reactions to Groups.* In two contrasting situations, checking behaviors one would or would not do, whether a boy or girl would do it, whether one would approve or disapprove the other person doing it.

8. *Values.* Rating of value items keyed to the categories developed by Charles Morris.

9. *Classroom Activities.* Frequency and value preferences for described activities of four kinds. Piloted in Sophomore Project.

This battery ran to 43 pages, took three hours to administer, and elicited 715 responses from each student. From the battery, 172 scores were calculated for each student. The tests were administered to 750 students in 11 high schools located within driving distance of Chicago. For factor analysis, we selected 216 students in grades 8 through 11. In the sample there were as many boys as girls; there was equal representation of three ranges of economic "class" (laborer to professionally trained executive); IQ was evenly and comparably distributed through the class, grade, and sex groups.

The largest factor, accounting for about 11% of the data, is one we call the "goody-goody" factor. It is contributed to by all the scores through which a child says how well he likes things—teachers, methods of working, goals, other students, and so on. It is also contributed to by scores which, taken together, give a picture of conformity: the student who is high on this factor likes everything expected of him, no matter what it is. It is accompanied by rather low-level work, and by lack of emotional involvement. There is rejection of fight and flight, and of all but rather muted expressions of feeling. We could not help but wonder if this factor does not portray a highly successful adjustment to the demands of the typical classroom; and, if so, it should probably be called the "survival" factor. It is more characteristic of upper- than of lower-class (economically) children.

The second factor, accounting for about 7% of the data on these high school students, is a social-sexual factor. The sexual part has to do with discriminating between boys and girls, having different expectations for the two sexes—as compared with thinking of them as inter-changeable. Together with this are included acceptance of emotion, preference for active rather than passive interpersonal relationships, and a distinct liking for decisions to be made by the "group" rather than by oneself, teacher, or large class. This factor tends to be more typical of the younger and brighter students in the seventh to ninth-grade range, and probably spots a particular developmental task characteristic of this age.

The third factor, accounting for about 7% of the data, is character-ized by hesitancy and confusion in participating with other people, by uncertainty about what values are important, and by unstable indica-tions of personal security. There is confusion about one's own sex role, retreat into passivity, concern over personal-social relationships, and avoidance of emotional expression.

The fourth factor, accounting for about 5% of the data, appears to be a combination of rational consistency with needs to exploit one's peers. There is great preference for "telling" and not listening; more-over, what one speaks about is himself, his own feelings, his own opinions. Working together for a common goal is rejected, as is acceptance of responsibility for one's own progress. There is preference for activities involving the class as a whole (that is, those in which one is anonymous, where personal progress can not be checked on easily, and in which one can avoid responsibility). The most attractive value is sensual enjoyment. This factor is negatively related in IQ, and tends to be found with lower-class boys.

The fifth factor, accounting for about 4% of the data, is strongly female and is associated with low IQ; there is a tendency for lower-class and older students to be associated with this factor also. The domi-nant note is identification with boys' activities and behaviors. There is strong preference for listening rather than telling, for submission rather than dominance, for comfort rather than work. There is a good deal of interpersonal "sensitivity."

The sixth factor, accounting for about 3% of the data, is for boys. The strongest component is the value of social restraint, but it has noth-ing to do with altruism, which is the lowest rated value. It has instead to do with submissiveness, which shows up in just about every score that could be thus interpreted. The preferred teacher is the authori-tarian, the most worthwhile activities are teacher-dominated; listening is strongly preferred to telling. Identification is with female behavior; judgments are made critically and evaluatively of other people; nothing is voluntarily revealed about oneself.

The seventh factor, again 3% of the data, is a classical textbook picture of counterdependency; that is, of denial of one's own dependency. There is strong rebelliousness against adult authority, against the discipline of working on tasks. Peer groups are used to assert oneself, not to listen to others. At the same time, there is a seeking of warmth from others, and a strong rejection of opportunities to "be on one's own." There is evidence of confusion about the male role, and of deeper insecurity and feelings of inadequacy. This factor is shown most by boys of high IQ.

The eighth factor, also about 3%, is most represented in the younger children, and somewhat stronger for boys than girls. It seems to represent an effort to submerge oneself in group activities, preferably with a few other students. Probably likes to "do things" with a group of students, but adds very little to the group. Tends toward passivity and avoidance of responsibility. It is the picture of a "fringer."

The ninth factor, also about 3%, is for young, high IQ students. It shows a strongly teacher-centered person who wants the teacher to set out a respectable thought-out course of study, to stimulate the student and make demands on him, and to work closely with him. The student likes information and listening to reports. The value picture suggests thoughtfulness rather than mere "academic" achievement. The student rejects practically everything that has to do with the class, and probably has trouble coping with peers.

The tenth factor, another 3%, is rather similar to this last factor in its teacher-centeredness. A different kind of teacher is preferred, however, that of the rule-giver or authoritarian. There is strong preference for working alone, within boundaries set by the teacher. There is rejection of the teacher who tries to plan with the student, and rejection of class activities.[6]

Most interesting to us is the clear revelation of the very wide array of nonlearning concerns of children. Conformity, confusion, sex identifications, reactions to authority, relating to (or avoiding) peers—these sorts of problems and needs probably "drive" the interaction in the classroom much more than interest in anything academic. One suspects that the prescribed "materials of instruction" and academic tasks set by the teacher may be useful primarily to provide a content vehicle for exploring and working on these higher priority social-emotional-sexual developments.

To confound and confuse the picture further, no actual student can be represented by a single factor. Any of these ten factors presented may be strong, middling, or weak within a particular student, and all combinations are possible. It is clear that the dynamic world of the group, out of which a social order is created, is a world of phenomena that lies below consciousness. It is the world of motivations, tensions, and energy systems; and it makes insistent high priority demands on the realms of thought, memory, and behavior. Events in this submerged world, manifested in the over-all problem of reconciling psyche and socio systems, greatly influence the quality, amount, and meaning of learning.

EMPIRICALLY DETERMINED (TEACHABLE) TYPES

The factor analysis, although immensely interesting, was discouraging. We had to discard the notion that there would be a few, neat, and all-inclusive categories of students. The first ten factors accounted for only about half of the variance in the test data. A large number of even smaller factors, as yet undescribed, would be equally influential in the classroom.

Following a great deal of thought on this situation, we finally realized that the one certain fact we could count on is that in each classroom some students have more meaningful experiences than others. Perhaps the best way to compose a class would be simply to select, for each teacher, students like those who, *in his opinion*, had been most successful with him in the past! This became our definition of the "teachable" student—and we suspected that it would be a different definition for each teacher.

The remainder of this report details how we tested this impression, and with what results.

Three questions were explored in the effort to decide whether to act on the impression. First, to what extent is "teachability" a general factor, defined the same way by all teachers? Second, to what extent is it a unique factor, defined very differently from one teacher to the next? Third, can we describe this factor at all and, if we can, does it make sense in the light of other knowledge?

The extent to which teachability is a general factor could be assessed by asking teachers to name the students who, in their opinion, had the most worthwhile experiences in their classes. If they all chose the same students, then we would conclude that "teachability" meant the same thing to all the teachers. But if they chose different students, it would mean that the property of "teachability" differed from teacher to teacher. We already had some data on this point. During the Sophomore Project, the three teachers had been asked to tell us which of the 50 students they thought were getting most out of class.

One teacher selected 7 and the other two 9. Of these, only three students (6% of the group) were selected by all three teachers, and five additional students were selected by two teachers. Of the eight students nominated by at least two teachers, seven had taken an extensive questionnaire of "what classroom activities the students considered most worthwhile." Here are the items selected by at least four of these students. (The number in parentheses tells how many.) We have grouped the items according to what appear to be their common themes.

Personal Trust in the Teacher, and Acceptance of the Teacher in the Role of Expert and Authority

Obtaining feedback—test scores and teacher's opinions about how well you are doing. (6)

Obtaining help during conference hour (from the teacher). (6)

Listening to a lecture by (the social studies) teacher. (7)

Being a member of (the math teacher's) class. (4)

Listening to a lecture on closed-circuit TV by the (social studies) teacher. (4)

Listening to explanations by the English teacher to a committee of which you are a member. (4)

The English teacher's insistence on "good working conditions" (discipline) for the group. (4)

Interest in Ideas and Information

Watching a movie. (5)

Listening to "outside speakers" from the University itself. (4)

"Achievement" and Grades

Getting ready for an exam by class review. (5)

Going over a test (after it is graded and handed back). (4)

Taking a social studies examination. (4)

Answering questions in class. (4)

Interaction with Other Students

Discussing current events in a group with other students. (4)

Seeing problems put on the board by another student. (4)

Individual Responsibility

Doing outside reading in preparation for a report to the class. (5)

Setting up equipment, running the recorders, operating the telephone switchboard (that connects the students by phone). (4)

Practicing your part for a production. (4)

Writing a paper on an assigned topic. (4)

Personal Involvement in the Work

Writing an original paper voluntarily. (5)
Deciding who you will work with. (4)
Planning your own work yourself. (4)
Thinking about and deciding which aspects of a unit (of work) you wish
to specialize in. (4)

The students chosen by these teachers apparently willingly accept the teacher's central role, they accept his guidance, they are motivated to "achieve," they enjoy taking responsibility, and they are personally involved in the class.

Considering the small degree of agreement of the teachers choice of "teachable" students, and also the small number of items on which the seven students agreed, it seemed reasonable to conclude that each teacher has his or her own idea as to what is meant by "teachability." There is, however, a common element running through the agreements: the items are all symptoms of superior maturity—a conclusion which very accurately anticipated the extensive analysis presented in Chapter 5.

In another preliminary study, we made up a Q-sort, consisting of 50 behavioral traits of students. Forty teachers were asked to sort out the list, indicating which traits best described the kind of student they considered superior and productive. There was very little agreement in their reports. They placed markedly different emphases upon critical thinking, social adequacy and cooperation, and personal maturity. The fact that the image of the preferred student—presumably the kind the teacher aims his instruction at—differed from teacher to teacher added weight to our impression that different students learn best under various teachers and teachers probably differ in the kinds of students they are able to "reach."

Finally, we asked one of the teachers, many of whose students had already been tested on the assessment battery, to give us the names of several who, in her opinion, "got a lot out of class," and several who "got very little out of class." Then we analyzed the tests to see what differences they revealed between these two groups of students. The results were: First, the successful and unsuccessful students did not differ very markedly on any single score, but they did differ a little bit on many scores. This was of considerable interest because it suggested that no one or even several factors like IQ, age, interest in working in groups, etc., could be used by themselves as selection factors. Second, the more successful students were in many ways quite unlike the teacher. Complementary factors rather than congruent ones may well have been more the rule. Thus the teacher appeared to prefer a rather remote relationship to others, was somewhat passive in interactive situations, and tended to see himself in the role of a rationally oriented and powerful expert. The students she picked as successful differed from the unsuccessful in that although they accepted her role for purposes of learning, they did not feel very comfortable with it; and themselves tended to be active with a preference for committee and friendship groups, and they accepted considerably more emotion than the teacher did. Thus there was homogeneity in the expectation of the teacher's role but complementation in the areas of functional adequacy—with the students, by and large, adapting to the teacher rather than vice versa. These findings, derived from one teacher, seemed eminently reasonable, and we had no reason to suppose that the situation would be very different with other teachers.

The notion of selecting students to fit an empirically determined model seemed to us attractive. It would not depend for its success on premature theories or prejudices. If being bright, for example, were an important factor, it would appear among the differences between successful and unsuccessful students for a particular teacher. If it were not a significant characteristic for that teacher, then it would not appear. Then, too, the approach could be applied routinely, and would thus be more practical for schools.

On the other hand, the approach would have its limitations. We might very well miss types of students the teacher had not encountered in the past but who might still profit from his instruction in the future. And we would be very much at the mercy of the teacher's selection of past successful students—with no very clear assurance of what the teacher meant by "success," or of whether the teacher's idea of success in any way coincided with those of the students.

In the progress report of the research at that time (June 2, 1959), we summarized our expectations as follows:

"The purpose of next year's experiments, of course, is to find out if our hunch is valid. The hypothesis is not that "teachable" classes will be more comfortable or congenial than the usual randomly selected classes (although this might turn out to be true) but rather that the students in the teachable classes will have less energy tied up in nonlearning concerns and anxieties about interpersonal relationships, authority, sex identification and so on. Presumably if this is the case, then the students ought to be more able to put that energy into learning tasks and they ought to be able to learn more. This we shall attempt to find out, using pre and post achievement tests.

There are, however, certain reservations that ought to be made, and which, if made properly, will tend to bolster the findings. The first reservation is that the differences between "teachable" and regular classes should be greatest for teachers whose method of teaching calls for interaction among pupils; it should be least, let us say, for a teacher who lectures all the time or whose class "discussions" are mostly perfunctory recitation periods. The second reservation is that differences will be greatest with teachers who challenge the class most; that is, the less the teacher expects of his classes, the less likelihood that one will perform any more or better than another.

The third reservation takes us into very large educational issues which go way beyond the scope of this experiment, but whose existence we somehow have to take account of. Two kinds of observations may suffice to limn the issue: first, that experiments with teaching methods tend to show little difference with respect to learning outcomes as generally defined and tested; and second, it is not uncommon for teachers to have the impression that some students who get low grades nevertheless get a great deal from their classes whereas others, including some high achievers, may get little. It appears that achievement, as generally measured and testified to on report cards, does not tell the whole educational story. The part it doesn't tell has to do with the "meaning" of the information and principles to the individual student. It is probably this part of the learning outcome that is most influenced by the social milieu of the classroom; and it is this part which probably contributes to the child's character. In any case, we shall attempt to get data systematically for the purpose of forming an opinion about the likelihood the student is "getting something out of the class"—apart from what achievement tests show."

THE COURSE OF THE INVESTIGATION

In the spring of 1960, 15 teachers agreed to participate in the experiment. These teachers were located in eight high schools and junior high schools (Arlington Heights, Niles Township, Lincolnway, Nicolet, Forest Road, Rich Township, Mishawaka, and Bloom Townships) in Illinois, Wisconsin and Indiana. The grades taught ranged from 8 through 11, and the subjects were English, American literature, social studies, geometry, advanced algebra, biology, world history, and American history. (The data were incomplete for two of these teachers, so our report is based on the results with 13 teachers.)

During the spring, the teachers designated 15 to 24 currently "successful" students and 0 to 20 "unsuccessful" students who were getting, respectively, "much" or "little" out of class as judged by the teacher.

These students were tested with the large assessment battery, which, on the basis of the earlier tryouts, had been reduced from 715 to 405 responses. In addition, all 1640 students available for the teachers' next year's classes were tested. This number of students to select from ranged from 62 (Teacher No. 10) to 224 (Teacher No. 14).

During the summer, the responses of the successful and unsuccessful students were counted, and compared. Significantly different responses ($p \leqq 0.1$, chi-squared test) were incorporated into a scoring key for each teacher. The tests of the other students in the available population were scored with this key, and the highest scoring students were selected to become the experimental class for that teacher. The control class for each teacher was selected from the remaining available students by the school officers, using their regular selection procedures.

During the academic year 1960–1961, the 30 classes were studied in detail. Each class was observed from three to five times by a team of at least two observers. From one to three sessions in each class were tape-recorded, and the tape record analyzed and coded, statement-by-statement. Diagnostic conferences pooled the impressions of all the observers of each class. Ten of the Post Meeting Reaction sheets filled in by the students at the end of class sessions were selected randomly with respect to time from the larger number administered during the year. The students also took the Student Opinion Survey, Sociometrics, and Guess Who test during the spring of 1961. The teachers took the Sociometrics, and provided us with grades, achievement records, and lesson plans. They also were interviewed from two to five hours by the observers on different occasions.

During the spring, summer, and fall of 1960, the tremendous mass of data was coded, tabulated, significance-tested, and otherwise processed by the observer-researchers. This report was written during 1961.

THE REPORT OF THE EXPERIMENT

We felt that if our previous impression were substantiated we could hold the reader's attention. Accordingly, the first matter to be discussed is the educational results, Chapter four.

The independent variable is the greater teachability of the students in the experimental classes, and this variable is responsible for most of the differences between the classes. Chapter five considers to what extent there is a common "teachability" factor, what it is composed of, and how greatly it varies among the teachers.

Since "teachability" is meaningful only in terms of a defined style or method of teaching, Chapter Six describes the "general" style of the teachers, the differences in this general style caused by the general teachability factor, and the extent to which this general picture actually fits the 13 individual teachers.

The relationships among style of teaching, "teachability" of students, and results, differ from teacher to teacher and probably involves somewhat different dynamics. In Chapter Seven we study all the data on one teacher, and attempt to show what happened and to explain why. Chapter Seven is a long didactic case study of "teachability" at work.

Chapter Eight presents briefly the results of similar analyses of how teachability factors worked to produce differences within the pairs of classes of four other teachers: a "high-level" academic teacher, a "person-oriented" teacher, a "technical-routine" teacher, and a "literary-appreciation" teacher.

Chapter Nine analyzes the changes, from the beginning to the end of the school year, in the attitudes, interests, values, etc., of teacher No. 14 and his experimental and control students.

Chapter Ten presents the conclusions about teachability grouping: for whom and under what conditions it works best; our reservations, or the dangers we see in it; and some practical alternative ways of getting teachable groups.

The Appendix contains our instruments: the assessment battery, the observation schedules, the questionnaires; and detailed data on the teacher discussed in Chapter Seven.

NOTES

1. Thelen, H. A., *Education and the Human Quest,* New York: Harper and Brothers, 1960, pp. 224.
2. Thelen, H. A., *op. cit.,* pp. 134–135.
3. These researches are reported in: Stock, D., and H. A., Thelen, *Emotional Dynamics and Group Culture,* New York: New York.
4. Thelen, H. A., "Classroom Grouping of Students, *School Review,* **67,** (Spring 1959) pp. 60–78.
5. Proposal for Research to the Commissioner of Education: "Development of Educational Methods for Different Types of Students," *Appendix A. Project 428* (April, 1958).
6. This description of factors is quoted from Thelen, *op. cit.,* Reference 1, pp. 122–125.

Chapter Four

OUTCOMES: Educational Achievement and Personal Satisfactions

Teachers Marks and Gains on Achievement Tests · Pupils Satisfaction with Activities · Interpersonal Relationships · Summary of Differences Related to Teachability

"Grouping," or the selection of students to be in a particular class with a particular teacher, was based on a simple universal observation: that each teacher finds some students more "teachable" than others. With these students he feels he does a better educational job; he is likely to be more at ease with them, to believe that they respond better, to feel that in many ways his teaching is primarily "beamed" to them. These students have what it takes to make the teacher perceive them as "successful" in his class. The definition of this "something" varies from one teacher to the next, for each teacher makes somewhat different demands on the students, may have different feelings about what goals are really important, and certainly identifies differently with different students.

With these considerations in mind, we decided to try to give each teacher a class composed of "teachable" students, and to compare it with an "ordinary" class. We used 13 teachers so that there would be an adequate base for drawing generalizations. The independent variable, and difference "built-in" between the teachable ("experimental") class and the regular ("control") class, was created by our selection of students for the experimental classes; the control classes were selected by the "regular" procedures in each school. All other factors, such as time, method of teaching, teacher personality, etc., were either identical or subject only to "random variation."

Our general hypothesis was that giving each teacher a class of students he could teach should result in better teaching. We also believed that it would make more difference to some teachers than to others, and we had some ideas about who would be most helped by our method of selecting his class. After all, the "teachability factor," the qualities that make the student successful in the classroom, differs for each teacher and enters differently into their interactions with the class. But the first point to establish is that a "teachability factor" exists, can be used to group students, and results in better teaching. Once this point is established we can then relax and talk about what this factor is in general, how it differs among teachers, and how it operates.

We think the first thing the reader would wish to know is whether our method of grouping accomplished anything, and if so, what. Four kinds of evidence were used to estimate the extent to which learning differed between the experimental and control classes of 13 teachers.

The comparisons are of two sorts, and it may be helpful to explain these briefly now. First, the classes had been composed in such a way that the average "teachability score" of the students in each experimental class is significantly higher statistically ($p \leq .01$) than in the corresponding control class of the same teacher. Second, it is also possible to make comparisons within a single class. Since there is a range of teachability scores within each class, it may be divided into halves, with one-half containing the students having higher scores and the other half lower scores on the teachability factor.

Thus we can compare the experimental *class,* having generally higher teachability scores with the control *class;* and we can *also* compare the higher and lower teachability students within each class. The trends should be the same in the comparisons.

TEACHERS' MARKS AND GAINS ON ACHIEVEMENT TESTS

Each teacher gave each student a mark or grade, and this can be taken to represent the teacher's best over-all judgment of "what the student learned" during the year. In addition, each teacher administered the same course examination to both classes at the beginning and end of the year, so that it was possible to say how large the gain was in whatever learning the examination measured. We will call this gain *achievement.* In some cases, the teacher's mark was probably based solely on achievement, but in most cases the teacher's mark took other factors into account as well. In the profession at large, most teachers believe that the educational values of classroom experience are by no means all measured by achievement tests. In one school system, for example, the teacher's mark is based on achievement test results (50%), judgments of "ability" (25%), and judgments of "motivation" (25%). Thus in this system achievement represents only half of what the teacher's grade is supposed to take into account.

Table 2 compares marks given to six pairs of control and experimental classes at the end of the first semester and all 13 pairs at the end of the school year.

The findings are that in the six classes where teachers gave grades for the first semester, all six of the experimental classes received higher marks, even though four of the control classes gained more on achievement tests. At the end of the year, all 13 teachers gave marks, and 11 experimental classes and one control class received the better marks— even though seven control classes and only five experimental classes gained more on the achievement tests. It is rather startling to find that a class may gain more on achievement tests and yet be given lower marks than those received by a class that gained less! Apparently the presumably "objective" justice of achievement tests may be tempered by other more subjective (or self-concerned) observations which will be discussed later.

The differences, however, are not large. In only two cases is the difference in average marks between classes as large as one grade point. And the class that gained more than its counterpart on achievement tests still gained an average of only 16 to 20% more. These are not impressive differences. What is impressive is not the difference but its direction. However small the difference (which is affected by how good the test, by whether the teacher "covered" it, by previous background of the students, etc.), there is a marked tendency for the class receiving the higher marks to be the "teachable" one. (The tendency is further bolstered when we consider what happened to the one exception to the rule.)

In every case, the students were selected in such a way that the average teachability score of students in the experimental class is significantly

Table 2. Comparison of Teachers' Grades and Achievement Gains for Experimental and Control Classes

Class Gaining Most on Achievement Tests	Teachers' Marks					
	First Semester Class with Higher Marks			Final Class with Higher Marks		
	Experimental	Control	Neither	Experimental	Control	Neither
Experimental	2	0	0	5	0	0
Control	4	0	0	6	1	1
Totals	6	0	0	11	1	1

Table 3. Comparison of Teachers' Grades and Achievement Gains for High and Low Teachable Students

Group Gaining Most in Achievement	Within Experimental Classes Groups Having Higher Grades			Within Control Classes Groups Having Higher Grades		
	High Teachable	Low Teachable	Neither	High Teachable	Low Teachable	Neither
High Teachable	6	1	0	3	0	1
Low Teachable	3	2	0	4	1	0
Neither	1	0	0	4	0	0
Totals	10	3	0	11	1	0

higher than in the control class (mean score in the experimental class is 83.4 and in the control class 41.4% of possible). Hence the high and low teachable students in the two classes are distributed around different mean "levels." In Table 3, we compare the relationships between achievement gains and teachers' marks for high and low teachable students in the experimental classes and in the control classes.

The findings revealed that in 10 of the 13 experimental classes, and 11 of the 13 control classes, the higher teachables received better marks than the lower teachable students. The high teachable students within the experimental classes tended also to have higher achievement scores while in the control classes, the high teachables had approximately the same achievement.

The findings are most dramatic when we examine all the marks given by teachers and all the tests from which gains can be calculated. Table 4 displays how the marks were assigned.

Of the 13 teachers, 9 gave two grades, one for English and another for Social Studies. Thus, in the 26 classes, there were 44 distributions of grades. In each class, comparisons were made of the grades received

Table 4. Teacher Grade versus High and Low Teachability Students

Teachability	Number of Cases	Number of Cases Getting Higher Marks*	Average Difference in Marks
Upper half	44	35	0.35
Lower half	44	6	0.38

* In three cases, upper and lower halves got equal marks.

Table 5. Achievement Test Gains versus High and Low
Teachability Students

Teachability	Number of Tests	Group with Higher Gain	Amount of Difference in Gain (%)
Upper half	34	17	2.2
Lower half	34	17	3.8

by the students having the top half of the teachability scores with those
having the lower half of the scores. The difference between marks of A
and B, B and C, etc., is numerically equal to 1.0.

The finding is that the half of the class with higher teachability scores
is $35/6 = 5.8$ times as likely on the average to get better grades from
the teacher. The amount of the difference averages to about a third of
a grade point.

Finally, pre- and post-achievement test measurements were conducted once in 18 classes and twice in the remaining 8 classes, yielding
a total of 34 measurements of gains. Table 5 shows who gained most.

The finding is that the half of the class with the higher teachability
scores is *neither more nor less likely* to make higher gains on achievement
tests. In other words, whatever it is that is meant by "teachability" is
not correlated with achievement as measured by gains on achievement
tests, even though, as just observed, a student's teachability *is* quite closely
related to his ability to get better grades.

We should consider the possibility that any teacher might well be
pleasantly disposed toward an experimental class of his prescription and
for his benefit, and the higher marks in 11 of the experimental classes
could lend substance to such a conviction. But the possibility fades when
one notes that *within* the classes, *regardless* of whether they are experimental or control, the more teachable students get the higher marks
and the teacher simply had no way of knowing within a class what teachability score belonged to each student.

Thus, no matter how we examine the data, we get a quite consistent
picture: the students with the higher "teachability" scores obtain higher
grades, whether the comparison is between classes or within classes; and
they are just as likely to get higher *or* lower gains on achievement tests.

PUPIL SATISFACTION WITH ACTIVITIES

It may be argued with some reason that if a student is challenged, interested, and hard-working during each class activity he is

becoming educated. In other words, the quality of classroom experiences ought to bear some relationship to what the student profits from the experience. Questionnaires called Post-Meeting Reaction Sheets, administered immediately after a class session, can be interpreted to give us a rough idea of whether the day's experiences were involving, challenging, and apparently worthwhile to the student.

Unlike the achievement tests which were different for each pair of classes, the questions on the Post-Meeting Reactions Sheet were the same for all classes.

In most classes* these sheets were distributed ten times between September and December, 1959, and three times during May and June, 1960. In each pair of classes, the questionnaires were administered on the same day following comparable activities.

The questionnaire comprises eight items. The average response of each class was calculated for each item and each administration. The number of days on which each experimental class indicated greater satisfaction than its corresponding control class, and vice versa, was calculated. Every item showed greater satisfaction in the experimental classes than in the control classes, although two (inadvertently) ambiguous items do not show significant superiority. Arranged in order of favorability of the experimental classes, beginning with the most favorable, the items are the following.

How did you feel this class meeting was today? (1) This item introduces the check list with an opportunity for the student to indicate his overall reaction to the session. It is scaled from total dissatisfaction ("no good") to complete satisfaction ("excellent").

Higher satisfaction: 9 experimental classes, 2 control classes, 1 tie.

How often were the questions and comments of the students really understood and replied to fairly and helpfully? (4) The student is asked for his perception of the teacher's facility in interaction. Is he sensitive? Trustworthy? The item is scaled from total failure, or possibly *absence* of teacher's effort ("never") to highly successful efforts to be helpful ("very frequently").

More helpful response to: 9 experimental classes and 3 control classes.

How clearly did you understand exactly what the class was supposed to do today? (5) Was the definition of the task such that the student knew what was expected of him? Satisfaction ("perfectly") would indicate sufficient clarity for the student to work freely; ambiguity ("not at all") implies frustration and consequent dissatisfaction.

---

* One teacher administered the questionnaires only three times and this is too scanty a basis for generalization. Consequently, the discussion in this section is based on findings from 12 of the 13 teachers.

Greater clarity of understanding: 9 experimental classes and 3 control classes.

What part of the class was really working on the lesson today? (7) The student is asked for his perception of the group's involvement in the task. Scored for an entire class, it indicates commitment to and satisfaction with the task ("everybody") ranging down to flight, play, or other nonwork activities ("almost nobody").

Nearly everybody: 9 experimental classes, 3 control classes.

How often did you find yourself wanting to say things to the class, but for one reason or another you did not actually say them? (2) This item delineates the student's perception of the limits on expression. The scale implies supportive opportunities for communication at one extreme ("never") to a maximum perception of restriction and threat at the other ("very frequently").

Higher freedom: 8 experimental classes, 4 control classes.

How worthwhile to you was what you learned in class today? (3) Requires that the student assess his personal involvement with the task or goal of the session. This item is scaled from lack of meaning or commitment ("worthless; waste of time") to pointed personal significance ("highly meaningful; most worthwhile").

More worthwhile: 7 experimental classes, 4 control classes, 1 tie.

How difficult was the lesson today? (6) This item requires the student to compare his expectations for himself with the teacher's demands. Ideally, the teacher's timing and pacing should provide an *optimal* challenge, neither minimal ("too simple; baby stuff") nor maximally demanding ("very difficult; over my head"). There is some ambiguity in this item, for the student may conceivably feel most comfortable in a situation perceived as "easy." In scoring this item, the midpoint score on the scale (rather than top score) was considered best.

Middling difficult: 6 experimental classes, 5 control classes, 1 tie.

Item number 6 is odd in that there is no confident basis for deciding what rating along the scale corresponds to highest satisfaction. The decision to count the midpoint as most satisfactory is convenient, but has no empirical justification.

How satisfied were you with the part you played in class today? (8) This item tests the student's ability and opportunity to meet his own role expectations in the classroom. Did he find a rewarding place for himself ("rather delighted and pleased") or did the situation provoke a sense of failure ("really disappointed or discouraged").

More satisfied: 5 experimental classes, 4 control classes, 3 ties.

Item number 8 indexes satisfaction but it is difficult to evaluate it. Is satisfaction with one's own role a sign that the activity was unchallenging or that it was really worthwhile? How legitimate is satisfaction with oneself as an index to productivity of experience? In other words, what degree of satisfaction would reflect an educationally sound activity? The answer probably would differ among students.

INTERPERSONAL RELATIONSHIPS

The teacher's influence is extraordinarily great and has much to do with whether classroom experience will be oriented to learning, to self-protection, to approval-seeking, or to other goals, many of which are not very educative. Given one kind of teacher-pupil relationship we would predict that a great deal of educative learning may occur; given another sort of relationship, we would expect very little educative learning. We do not regard teacher-pupil relationship as an educational outcome, but we suggest that it is a condition which may help confirm and explain findings about educational outcomes.

Interpersonal relationships were assessed by means of sociometric ratings made during the last two months of the school year. Each student rated each other student and the teacher in his class; in addition, the teacher rated each of his students. The ratings were on a five-point scale of liking for two different kinds of association with the person: "work with" and "chat with." Presumably, the "chat with" relationship is voluntary and friendly, whereas the "work with" relationship is oriented to effectiveness in work.

In view of the higher grades, coupled with no greater achievement in the experimental classes, one's first guess would be that the teacher probably likes the students in his experimental classes more than in his control classes. The findings, based on average ratings each teacher accorded the students in his two classes, are that six experimental classes were preferred by their teachers for both "work with" and "chat with," and one control class was preferred. In addition, three teachers preferred the experimental class for work and the control for chat, and the remaining three teachers had the opposite preferences.

The data show that the teacher tends to prefer his experimental class and that he gives it higher grades. If these two facts are directly related, then it would be reasonable to suppose that the more the teacher likes the class the higher the grades he will assign to it.

In fact, however, the *amount* of grade superiority has no relationship to the *amount* of the teacher's preference for working with and chatting with the students. Half of the six classes most preferred to work with are among the six showing *greater* grade superiority, whereas the other half have *lower* grade superiority. Similarly, no tendency is found that the classes most preferred for chatting with have the more superior grades.

It is reasonable that the teachers would tend to prefer their experimental classes: the teachers, after all, participated in selecting students known from past experience to be "successful" in their classes and thus presumably to facilitate the classroom interaction and activities of the teacher.

But what of the students' preferences for the teacher? How do these students selected by the teacher feel about him? Do they reciprocate his preference for them? Experimental and control classes were compared in two ways: (1) the mean or average rating given by all the students in each class; and (2) the number of students in each class rating the teacher first choice to work with and to chat with.

The findings are that the "average" student (mean ratings) in nine *control* classes tends to prefer the teacher more both to work with and to chat with! At the same time, the same number, five, of both control and experimental classes contain a greater number of students who rate the teacher first choice to work with and to chat with.

These findings call for explanation, but we will have to know more about the classes to have much confidence in any explanation. But at this point, let us be aware of some possibilities.

1. There may be a bit of personal exploitation involved. That is, the teacher has selected students that he can successfully teach; these are students who can meet the teacher's needs. To the extent that the teacher's needs are met through his participation in activities that also meet needs of the students, there is no exploitation involved. But if the teacher has needs that cannot be so channeled, and especially if these needs are somewhat threatening to the students, then one might expect the students to feel some resentment toward the teacher even though they go ahead and help meet the teacher's needs (after all, that's partly the reason they were selected).

There is some observational information that supports this kind of explanation, and we shall consider it in connection with our case studies. In anticipation, however, one teacher tended to prefer and establish a joking relationship with the students. Most of the jokes were at the expense of students who would laugh but would also cringe. And the students tended to perceive that they had a good time and they liked each other very much; yet they also did not care for the teacher. At the same time, the teacher considered the class to be one of the best he ever had, and he strongly preferred it over his control class.

2. A second explanation, suggested by Professor Dan Katz, assumes that the experimental classes were more productive and work oriented —as indeed they tended to be. In this case, one would expect standards

of evaluation to be more explicit, higher, and more in control of activities. The existence of these standards would provide criteria for judging, and would make it easier for the students to distinguish between the teacher's role as a teacher and his personal role as an individual. Hence they could be generally more positive about the class and yet less "positive" about the teacher. Professor Katz suggested that the development of such standards often tends to create heterogeneity in the group: for the standards to develop and to be enforced, a good number of students must "go along" with them and presumably these would be students who could identify with and cooperate with the teacher. At the same time, there would be other students who simply construed the higher standards as being more demanding, and, although socially cooperative, these students may very well remain psychically uninvolved in the developments, and they would not feel especially positive toward the teacher.

It seems that these two explanations are consistent with each other, and that they come close to portraying the actual situation. Some indication of how generally this situation occurred may be obtained by considering the reciprocity of liking between teacher and class.

The findings are that three of the nine experimental classes and three of the four control classes preferred by the teacher to work with also preferred him. Thus with respect to work with, there is reciprocity in six of the thirteen cases. Of the nine experimental and four control classes preferred by the teacher to chat with, four reciprocated the feeling. The fact that there appears to be less reciprocity with respect to the more personal activity (chat with) is consistent with the reasoning above.

What about the interpersonal feelings among the students? Several lines of reasoning would lead one to expect more cohesion (more positive interpersonal choices) in the experimental groups. First, if there is some sense of being exploited, then, unless it is too dangerous, we would expect the students to be drawn together through mutual identification in their common plight. Second, there should be a greater communality of interest among the "teachable" students because they were selected from the same image. Third, if the experimental groups are more productive (as already implied by higher grades), then their members may be more actively cooperative. On the other hand, less cohesion might be expected if the teacher has enforced psychic demands that split the group, or if the teachable students are all alike and in need of some other "type" to complement their capabilities, or if the group is frustrated by having nothing to do (no common purposes which would provide a rationale for interdependence).

The findings are that of the thirteen comparisons, eight experimental classes and two control classes choose their members more strongly both for work with and chat with. Eleven experimental groups are higher for chat with, and eight for work with. The tendency, then, is for the experimental classes to be the more cohesive, and for this cohesiveness to be due more to interpersonal "psychic" elements than to social cooperative elements. In short, the experimental class tends to be one with greater solidarity—a conclusion which is further substantiated by the evidence presented in Chapter Five.

SUMMARY OF DIFFERENCES RELATED TO TEACHABILITY

.1. The basis of the teachability factor was a comparison of students each teacher thought were "getting a great deal out of class" with their opposites. The traits that distinguish the two lists of students offered by each teacher were grouped under the name Teachability Factor. To the extent that we managed to load the experimental class with students higher on this factor, the teacher found the experimental class more teachable, which resulted in its members receiving higher marks.

2. The teachability factor is found to bear no relationship to whatever it is that accounts for gains on achievement tests. A positive or negative relationship might exist for any one particular teacher, but over thirteen teachers it averages out. Thus teachability is not necessarily connected to cognitive factors, such as IQ and past achievement scores. The implication is that a teachable class is not necessarily a "high ability" class and, on the other hand, a homogeneous high ability class is not necessarily "teachable." Both depend on the teacher, as other researchers have surmised (see Chapter 1).

3. The discovery of greater satisfaction of the teachable students with classroom activities clearly agrees with the notion that they are having more "meaningful" experience. It also shows that the teachers were fairly accurate in their earlier selection of these students as "getting a lot out of class;" and that the selection procedure we used did succeed in identifying students fitting this model. It also suggests that the "more meaningful experience" communicates to the teacher as "learning more," and hence the higher grades.

4. The friendlier feelings of the teachable students for each other and of their teacher for them agrees with other research and training studies which associate good interpersonal relations with personally meaningful experience. The experimental classes are more cohesive, and they may also be more oriented to work.

5. The finding that control classes prefer their teacher more than the corresponding experimental classes do suggests that in the less anxious climate of the experimental classes the teacher encountered fewer barriers against exploiting the student for his own needs; or that the more work-oriented cohesive experimental classes set higher standards for themselves, creating at the same time, hidden resentments which focused on the teacher.

On the whole, then, we interpret the results to show that the teachable classes *were* more teachable, with the students having better feelings toward each other; with the feeling that activities were more satisfying and interest-provoking; and with the teacher testifying that the experience of the students was more educational. At the same time, the students did no better on achievement tests and did not have more of a personal liking for their teacher.

We conclude that, judging by the results, the word teachability is precisely correct for the name of the characteristics that biased the selection of students for the experimental classes.

Chapter Five

TEACHABILITY: The General Factor and Its Variability among Teachers

Assessment of Teachability · Summary · Variations of Teachability among the Thirteen Teachers

As we have seen, thirteen teachers each selected students who served as the models for selecting students for the "teachable" (experimental) classes. By comparing the two kinds of students, more and less "teachable," we can find a pattern of differences which we have named the "teachability" factor.

The teachability factor is not necessarily composed of the same pattern of traits, attitudes, etc., for the students of each teacher although there are, of course, some common elements for many of the teachers. The number of these elements would be insufficient for a complete definition of teachable children for two different teachers because the *common* elements could not take into account the *differences* in personalities and methods of the two teachers. What the common elements can define, however, is general *tendencies* that mark the "successful" or teachable child in the range of teaching situations we studied. Just as our thirteen teachers have common elements in their teaching and achieved many results in common in our experiment, so the teachable classes have some characteristics in common that are different from those of the control classes.

ASSESSMENT OF TEACHABILITY

The data for describing the commonality among the teachability factors of the 13 teachers are responses on our 405-item Assessment Battery (see Appendix C). The several kinds of evidence from the assessment battery contribute to the picture of how "teachable" students tend to view the world of the classroom, themselves, the teacher, and their classmates.

1. We asked the students to rate the frequency of occurrence of 48 suggested possible *disadvantages* when they work alone, with the teacher, with a few other students (for example, subgroup or committee), and with the class (see Appendix, "Ways of Doing Things"). For the purpose of counting responses, the five-point frequency scale was divided into halves, with the top half representing nearly complete denial that a certain disadvantage (item) ever occurs.

2. We listed 40 specific activities that might occur in the classroom, and we asked the students to rate on a 5-point scale how much they preferred each activity (see Appendix, "Classroom Activities"). Their responses are divided into two categories: high preference (top ratings) and low preference (bottom ratings).

3. We listed 50 kinds of roles or acts in which a student might "participate," and asked them to rate their preferences for these on a five-point scale (see Appendix, "Participation"). Their responses were further categorized as indicating high or low preference.

4. We proposed seven topic words or concepts (for example, *boy, myself, having power*), and then offered for each concept ten identical scales anchored at the two ends by a pair of words (for example, *wet-dry, pretty-ugly*). The students were asked to rate each concept along these ten "dimensions" (see Appendix, "Semantic Differential"). We counted the number of responses in each half of each scale (for example, more "wet" than "dry"). This is a more or less standard type of word association test.

5. We described, in a sentence or phrase, 50 situations that occur in classrooms, and asked the students to check which of two responses best approximated their ideas, feelings, or actions in such a situation (see Appendix, "Situations"). We counted how many students checked each alternative.

6. We described, in a paragraph, each of six "types" of teachers, and asked the students to rank these types with respect to (*a*) how typical they are of teachers in general, (*b*) how comfortable the student feels in a class with each type, and (*c*) how well the student learns from each type (see Appendix, "Teacher Description"). We classified responses as top or bottom, depending on whether the rating of a paragraph was among the top or bottom three ratings, respectively.

7. We listed 60 statements of "values" or generalized ways of behaving to which persons might aspire. Each student was asked to rate, on a nine-point scale, how "important" each such aspiration was to him (see Appendix, pp. 220–222). The scale was divided in half, and we counted the number of students rating each item "positively" (top half of the "importance" scale) and negatively.

8. We listed 24 decisions that must be made in the classroom, and asked the students to check who should make each one. Choices were: the teacher, you (the student), the class-as-a-whole, a small group or committee, and you plus the teacher. Each response was counted.

9. Another section containing 45 items contributed no items to the general factor. This section is therefore not discussed in this chapter.

Our task with the data was to devise a procedure for selecting from the 360 item battery the items that discriminate between high and low teachable students. The procedure involved first identifying the items that discriminated for the students of each teacher, and then counting the number of teachers for whom each item discriminated.

The selection of discriminating items for each teacher's class was done empirically by counting how many high and low teachable students selected each of the responses. Then we applied a statistical screen (chi-squared test, cut-off at the 0.1 level) to select the responses for which the differences between high and low teachable groups were large enough to give us confidence that they existed—that they were not the result of "accident" or chance.

The index of discrimination, telling us how importantly each item discriminates for all the teachers, is the algebraic sum of four figures based on means: (a) the number of high teachable groups that made the response; (b) the number of high teachable groups that rejected the response (by making an opposite response); (c) the number of low teachable groups that made the response; and (d) the number of low teachable groups that rejected the response (by making an opposite response). The best discrimination would occur when all the high teachable groups made the response and all the low teachable groups rejected the response. In this case, a and d would each be 13, and b and c would each be zero. The index, then, is $a - b - c + d$.

In Table 6, we display the 66 most discriminating items arranged in order of their discrimination indices. With respect to a particular item, 4 out of the 13 teachable groups would by "chance" be significantly higher than their corresponding control groups only once out of 33 times. Five would be higher once out of 160 times; and 6 would be higher once out of 825 times. The likelihood that 7 or more groups would be higher by "chance" is practically zero. (Incidentally, these estimates are generous to "chance," for they are based on the least discriminating items (0.1 level) in the table).

The items appearing at the top of the table are most common to the differences between all pairs of high and low teachable groups. As we go down the table, the items are less discriminating for the whole popu-

Table 6. The Sixty-Six Items Best Discriminating between High and Low "Teachable" Students

Item No.	Discrimi- nation Index	Teachable High +	High −	Low +	Low −	Item	Teachability Response
1	14	10	0	0	4	When doing things by myself I find it hard to consider ideas	Denial
2	11	8	0	0	3	Have teacher lead a discussion in which basic principles are explained	Prefer
3	11	7	0	0	4	Be grateful and undemanding in my acceptance of life experience	Important (Accept)
4	10	9	0	0	1	Get individual help and instruction from teacher during class work	Prefer
5	10	8	0	0	2	When I do something with a teacher I get confused in my work	Denial
6	10	7	0	0	3	When doing things with a teacher I feel very little enjoyment	Denial
7	10	7	0	0	3	Being one of the more active persons during a lively class discussion	Prefer
8	10	7	0	0	3	While doing things with a few other students I forget ideas that have been explained	Denial
9	9	7	0	0	2	When doing things with a few other students I find it hard to consider ideas	Denial
10	9	7	0	0	2	Have a conference with the teacher concerning your progress in class	Prefer
11	9	7	0	0	2	When doing something with a teacher I waste time	Denial
12	9	7	0	0	2	I feel very little enjoyment when doing things by myself	Denial
13	9	7	1	0	3	Pointing out good ideas and attacking bad ideas offered during class discussion	Prefer
14	9	5	0	0	4	Prepare on your own to make a report to the class	Prefer
15	8	7	0	0	1	When doing things as a member of the class I get into trouble with others	Denial
16	8	7	0	0	1	When I have work to do with a teacher I don't feel like getting started	Denial
17	8	7	0	0	1	When talking with a teacher I lose the thread of conversation	Denial
18	8	7	1	0	2	Plunge courageously into the challenges of life	Important (Accept)
19	8	6	0	0	2	"Myself" is more "good" than "bad"	Association
20	8	6	0	0	2	When doing things with a few other students I get confused in my work	Denial

Table 6 *(Continued)*

Item No.	Discrimi- nation Index	Teachable High + −	Teachable Low + −	Item	Teachability Response
21	8	6 0	1 3	When doing something with a teacher I feel difficulty asking for help	Denial
22	8	5 0	0 3	Study basic course content as a member of a small group of students	Prefer
23	8	5 0	0 3	When doing things as a member of a class I have difficulty expressing my feelings	Denial
24	8	5 0	0 3	Be willing to make sacrifices for the welfare of others	Important (Accept)
25	7	7 1	1 2	Thinking about an argument you might use to persuade others	Prefer
26	7	6 0	0 1	When doing things with a teacher I become upset easily	Denial
27	7	6 0	0 1	When discussing with the teacher I lose interest in ideas	Denial
28	7	6 0	0 1	When doing something with the teacher I get confused in my thinking	Denial
29	7	6 1	0 2	When doing things by myself I lose interest in ideas	Denial
30	6	7 1	1 1	Be aware of and understand my innermost thoughts	Important (Accept)
31	6	6 0	0 0	Perform a demonstration or experiment for the class	Prefer
32	6	6 0	0 0	Work hard to attain the good things of life honestly	Important (Accept)
33	6	6 1	0 1	When doing things as a member of a class I learn very little for my work efforts	Denial
34	6	5 0	0 1	"Myself" is more "safe" than "dangerous"	Association
35	6	5 0	0 1	When doing things with a few other students, I get confused in my thinking	Denial
36	6	5 0	0 1	"Being popular" is more "good" than "bad"	Association
37	6	4 0	0 2	When the group agreed it needed more information, I: (A) described my feelings; (B) wasn't sure I wanted to discuss my feelings	A
38	6	4 0	0 2	Use the wisdom of the past in order to make a better future	Important (Accept)
39	5	6 1	1 1	"Being popular" is more "tight" than "loose"	Association

Table 6 *(Continued)*

Item No.	Discrimination Index	Teachable High +	Teachable High −	Teachable Low +	Teachable Low −	Item	Teachability Response
40	5	6	2	0	1	Reading a story in which the author describes the innermost private feelings of his characters	Prefer
41	5	6	0	1	0	"Having power" is more "big" than "little"	Association
42	5	6	0	1	0	"Boy" is more "strong" than "weak"	Association
43	5	5	0	0	0	"Girl" is more "pretty" than "ugly"	Association
44	5	5	0	0	0	Live a moral life of high ideals	Important (Accept)
45	5	5	0	0	0	Do things actively and with enthusiasm	Important (Accept)
46	5	5	0	0	0	Who should decide: Whether you are making satisfactory progress?	You plus teacher
47	5	5	0	1	1	"Boy" is more "new" than "old"	Association
48	5	5	1	0	1	Have confidence in my personal strength and ability to do things on my own	Important (Accept)
49	5	4	0	0	1	Most comfortable with "planning type" teacher	Prefer
50	5	4	0	1	2	Try always to act in a socially acceptable manner	Important (Accept)
51	5	4	1	0	2	Live a life of service to others	Important (Accept)
52	4	5	0	0	1	Live a refined and well-mannered life	Important (Reject)
53	4	5	1	0	0	"Having power" is more "tight" than "loose"	Association
54	4	5	0	1	0	Learn most from "expert type" teacher	Prefer
55	4	5	0	1	0	Who should decide: whether your project group should meet after school?	Committee
56	4	4	0	1	1	Develop understanding of others through self-awareness	Important (Accept)
57	4	4	0	0	0	When Henry was annoyed, Ray: (A) thought of a way to explain; (B) realized how he felt	A
58	4	4	0	0	0	Most comfortable with "traditional-professional type" teacher	Prefer
59	4	4	0	0	0	Learn most from "traditional-professional type" teacher	Prefer
60	4	4	0	0	0	Who should decide: when you will come in for a conference with the teacher	You plus teacher

Table 6 *(Continued)*

Item No.	Discrimi- nation Index	Teachable High + −	Low + −	Item	Teachability Response
61	4	4 0	0 0	Who should decide: how good a job the teacher did today?	Class
62	4	4 0	0 0	Who should decide: whether it is all right to ask questions to end someone's boring report?	Teacher
63	4	4 0	0 0	Who should decide: to what extent the behavior of another student is out of line?	Teacher
64	4	3 0	0 1	When Hal felt hostile to the group, he: (A) wished he would not have to come to the meeting; (B) was glad that Bob felt the same way.	A
65	4	3 1	0 2	Learn most from "authoritarian type" teacher	Prefer
66	4	1 3	2 0	When Glenn bawled me out, I: (A) lost interest in what we were supposed to be doing; (B) thought that some of his ideas would be useful	B

lation of groups, and the figures show the number of groups for which they do discriminate. It is not impossible that the same class could contain both a lesser tendency and its opposite; or that an item could be answered one way by one teachable class and the opposite way by another. Such occurrences are indicated by the four figures that come before each item in the table.

The task of interpreting the data may be approached in several different ways, and the reader may use his own method. What we wish to find out is whether there are any central "themes" that are characteristic of "teachability." We want to know what these themes are, how consistently they are supported by all the items, what kinds of situations elicit these themes, and what subthemes are there.

Our procedure will be (1) to see what the general tendencies are; (2) to select the most discriminating items as "keynote" items; and (3) to then see how the rest of the items affect the keynote themes.

Tendencies in the Table of Discriminating Items

To us, the most striking shifts as we go down the table are in the *kinds* of items. Thus, in the discrimination range from 14 through 7, 59% of the items all come from the same test. In this test the student is asked to check

71466

how often (on a scale from "frequently" to "never") various "disadvantages" occur. The top half of the discrimination range, then, portrays the most discriminating behavior as denial that one ever is uncomfortable, confused, forgetful, etc. The more "teachable" students either are in fact more "adequate" in a wide range of situations involving the teacher, class, a few others or no others—or they simply want us to think so. Their greatest commonality is the image of adequacy that they project in these statements about themselves.

Also, within the top range of discrimination (14 through 7) 24% of the items are judgments of "worthwhileness" of classroom activities. Such judgments, of activities set up by someone else and external to one's self, do call for little defense of one's self-concept, and we would expect these judgments to be closer to actual observed behavior. If these items are consistent with the "denial" items we will feel more confident that the denials express what the students feel rather than what they think they ought to feel. In other words, the activity items may enable us to decide whether the more teachable students are alike in their conception of stereotypes about a "good" student or whether they are alike in having similar feelings about working alone and with others. Either finding would say something about "teachable" students, but the two findings would suggest quite different degrees of "conformity."

Moving down to the discrimination range of 6 and 5, the character of the discriminating items changes. In this range, 36% of the items are judgments of the importance of certain values or aspirations, and, again, we must judge whether the responses are stereotypic or whether they truly represent the child's actual preferences. Interestingly, 32% of the items in this same range are word associations; and these are believed to be about as "tamper-proof" as items can be. Thus the two sorts of items, representing the opposites of abstract-verbal and subconscious-associative behaviors, may serve to check each other.

Finally, moving to the lowest range, with discrimination index of 4, the items again shift in character, with 80% of them quite possibly representing the results of specific experiences in classrooms (as distinguished from ethical and sex-cultural norms and values). Thus the most frequent items tell who in the classroom "should" make certain decisions, what sort of teacher the student finds most comfortable and effective, and how the student would respond to certain interpersonal stresses. The closeness of these items to experience probably also explains their lesser commonality, for it is with respect to these items that different teachers' ideas of teachability would be expected to make the most difference. The "behavioral level" here represented should be consistent with the more general levels in the upper part of the table, but would be expected to represent less of the picture: other behaviors, equally consistent, could exist too.

Keynote Items and Themes

Let us now consider the possibility of major "themes" within the set of discriminating items. We would reason that of the 360 items in the battery it is not unlikely that one or two would very directly represent something quite central in teachability; they would, in effect, be "anchor" or keynote items which would give us the best cues for organizing the other items into a coherent picture.

The top item, number 1, is strong denial of "When doing things by myself I find it hard to consider ideas." The student is denying that he must depend on the thinking of others; he is asserting confidence in his ability to think by himself. To the extent that thinking by oneself is a central requirement in the classroom, the self-confidence expressed here may be a dominant attitude. It remains to be seen whether the student's performance is likely to be consistent with this theme.

The second highest discriminating item, number 2, judges the activity "Have teacher lead a discussion in which basic principles are explained." Teachable students judge this activity as very worthwhile. We note that it is intellectually oriented, accepts the teacher as an expert, and provides for interaction among the students and teacher.

The third item, number 3, is an expression of "value" or aspiration: "Be grateful and undemanding in my acceptance of life experience." An item at this level of abstraction is susceptible to somewhat conflicting interpretations—which is one reason why we have many additional items on the test. Generally speaking, one can see in this item a "goody-goody" quality of submissiveness or he can see an optimistic acceptance of reality, or both. The self-confidence theme of the first item disposes us to the "reality" interpretation of this item. We shall propose, subject to the evidence of the other items, that the student is here saying "let life come to me; I shan't resist it, and it is so good that it will reward me." Or, in terms of the first theme, "I expect to be able to cope with whatever comes."

Do the other items clarify and substantiate these themes of self-confidence, adequacy, and reality-orientedness, or do they support an impression of weakness, defensiveness, submissiveness, and possibly hypocrisy?

Elaboration of the Themes

It is interesting that five of the eleven next most common items (discrimination index 10 and 9) refer to the teacher. Two of them, numbers 4 and 10, tell us that of 40 classroom activities, the students judged as the most worthwhile only two that involved the teacher. The other "teacher" items, 5, 6, and 11, deny discomforts; the teachable children, more than the others, deny the occurrence of confusion, disenjoyment, and time-wasting, respectively, in their contacts with the teacher. It appears that the students are confident they can deal with the teacher, and they also perceive him as someone tangible to whom they can relate.

Item 7 suggests that the teachable child likes interaction; items 8 and 9 add that he is not distracted by other children, and item 13 reinforces a strong sense of personal adequacy in being free to attack and commend others. Item 12 denies psychic dependence on others and item 14 blends the feeling of personal strength and ability to think alone with the notion of getting response from others. Item 14, along with the two keynote items, is most rejected by the low-teachable students.

This brings us to items 15 through 24 (discrimination index 8). Item 15 suggests that the child thinks he can attack and commend others without getting into trouble—that is, that his interaction is neither hostile nor disorderly. Items 16 and 17 add little that is new about relationships to the teacher. Item 18, the second value statement in the table, is consistent with the "reality" theme of item 3, and most certainly contradicts the "submissiveness" hypothesis. Item 19 adds a clear impression of higher self-esteem among "teachable" students, and strengthens the "adequacy" theme. Items 20, 21, and 23 further clarify the impression of adequacy in interpersonal activity, and item 22 selects the most interactive situation (studying with a small group of students) as also highly worthwhile or productive.

Item 24 brings in a new note of altruism, and it stands alone. As a statement of aspiration it suggests that the students want to see their interpersonal interactions as helpful to others, rather than as merely self-gratifying or self-aggrandizing. It further reinforces the student's perception that his behavior is nonhostile (item 15). One may theorize, too, that this altruistic perception gives the student the "right" to expect more from other people, since he is open to give as well as to receive.

Items 25 through 29, discrimination index 7, add to the picture of self-adequacy (number 29), and interest in interaction (number 25); and they further spell out the impression of "ease" with the teacher (numbers 26–28).

Items 30 through 51, discrimination index 6 and 5, present an interesting counterpoint between the 8 "value-abstract" items and the 7 "association-subconscious" items; with the remaining seven items providing confirming evidence from perceptions of behavior. Our interpretation will move back and forth among these three sorts of items.

Number 30 places a high value on awareness of innermost thoughts, and this is supported by number 40, high preference for reading about innermost thoughts of characters in a book. Two elements suggest themselves: first, concern with one's own feelings, and second, willingness to face up to them. Concern may suggest a component of anxiety; willingness to face up suggests strength to live with or overcome the anxiety. Number 34, associating safety rather than danger to one's self, supports the hypothesis of strength and adequacy. Number 48, a value item, makes this an explicit aspiration, and it adds support to the extent that aspirations are projections of existing qualities. Numbers 33 and 35, implying personal autonomy in the classroom, provide further support at the level of perception of one's own performance. The aspiration to "do things actively and with enthusiasm," number 45, adds to the image of adequacy.

More theoretically, items 42, 47, and 43, reflecting psychically "good" sexual orientation, are necessary conditions for the hypothesis of personal adequacy to be acceptable.

Continuing into more social aspects, item 41 suggests that power— either over others or of others over oneself—is "big," that is, potent, a reality that makes a difference. Items 45 and 48, already discussed, imply a "power" dimension in personal adequacy; and number 31 represents an activity in which one is dominant. This dominance, however, is contingent upon, and subsidiary to work; it is legitimized by group purpose. This qualification is rationalized in the value of "service to others," item 51, and in the value of acting "in a socially acceptable manner," item 50. Thus the picture emerges of self-confidence and adequacy which, however, is to be expressed in power over others only when the expression does not clash with the rights and needs of the others. Further evidence is seen in relation to items 36 and 39, "Being popular." Popularity is a kind of social power which reflects charisma; it is good, but it is also "tight," that is, constrained and stressful. Power through contribution to work is not anxious; but power through charisma is, and one must have a code through which he can direct his power-capabilities (stemming from personal adequacy) into legitimate channels. Items 32, 38, and 44, stressing honesty and hard work, wisdom, and morality, provide such a code.

The behavioral policy which resolves these dilemmas is *cooperation*, both as a means to legitimize one's power and to control the power of others. Thus the student is most comfortable with a teacher who plans activities with the class, item 49. And he would prefer that assessments be made of him, not by himself or the teacher alone, but by the two of them together, item 46. An item which well summarizes the various elements is number 37. The sort of cooperation here represented, namely telling how one feels when such data are required, calls for personal adequacy, acceptance of one's own feelings, acceptance of a social framework, and possibly (along with item 31) a touch of narcissism.

In the last group of items, numbers 52 through 66, discrimination index 4, several items appear to further substantiate statements already made, whereas other items add new components to the picture of the "teachable" student.

Item 53 suggests some anxiety about power; item 56 strengthens the picture of psychic adequacy; item 57 brings the elements of power, cooperation, and service together in a work context; item 60 emphasizes cooperation as a means to protect autonomy, and item 55 extends the principle to a group of which one is a member. Items 64 and 66 both deal with hostility, 66 portrays a person who is adequate in the face of hostility of others, and 64 suggests some anxiety about acting in a socially acceptable manner when one is himself hostile. Avoidance of the hostility-provoking situation is selected as the better course.

The novel elements clarify the kinds of external controls (or external supports for internal controls) which the student desires. Our students are adequate and independent enough to want to evaluate the teacher for themselves, but they also want to protect themselves from the consequences of making such evaluations and they seek this protection in impersonal, more objective standards set up by the entire class (item 61). This also, incidentally, recognizes and accepts interdependence with other students as an aid to oneself in the face of danger.

The teachable student also wants a firm, strong teacher whose authority is impersonal—items 54, 58, 59, and 65. Such a teacher presents an attractive solution to the student's own control problems, and we may infer that the student can "identify" with this sort of person. And finally, the student looks to the teacher to protect the social order by taking action in those interpersonal hostility situations in which the student does not fully trust himself, items 62 and 63. Finally, the desire for a robust, active, and adventurous life is implied in the rejection involved in item 52.

SUMMARY

The General Factor of Teachability

In capsule form, our summary of the tendencies of a teachable student is the following.

1. He has a high degree of personal, psychological adequacy.

2. He seeks to realize his strengths.

3. He has not yet developed easy control over the expressions of his strengths.

4. He seeks to develop the necessary controls (a) through acceptance of social values, (b) cooperative modes of working, and (c) being "work-oriented."

5. He seeks external controls from a "firm" teacher with whom he can identify.

As a footnote, we may consider why such a student would tend to be selected as "getting a lot out of class." First, his personal adequacy would be attractive and admired by many teachers. Second, he would be seen as aspiring and "motivated." Third, he would be seen as desiring to work "with" the group and teacher. Fourth, his need for a "firm" teacher would be supportive of the expert, authoritarian, and traditional-professional types that are predominant in our experiment.

VARIATIONS OF "TEACHABILITY" AMONG THE THIRTEEN TEACHERS

Having arrived at an overall description of the teachability factor, it is now appropriate to consider what this definition includes and what it leaves out, how "universal" or general a factor it is, and to what extent this description would provide a model of the "teachable child" for all teachers.

First, let us remember that the sections of the assessment battery from which these items were selected contained 360 items. The 66 teachability items thus represent only an 18% sample of the behaviors measured by the test. In other words, 82% of the things the test measured have little or no relationship to "teachability" as an attribute of the entire population of students in this experiment.

Next, let us remember that the assessment test itself by no means attempts to assess all aspects of "personality" and of a world view or orientation. The test is stringently limited by two boundaries. First, the items are only intended to get at "group-relevant" aspects of personality, that is, those personal attributes that would, in theory, bear some relationship to how one would participate in a face-to-face group. And second, the situational context of every item is the classroom. Thus the test is delimited to group-relevant aspects of personality as it functions in the classroom. These are very severe delimitations, and do not entitle us to make broad generalizations as to "personality" or to probable performance in other social settings.

We may conclude that a classroom full of teachable students is by no means "homogeneous" or "all alike." They do, however, tend to have some limited factor in common, and this factor does make a difference within the situation and typical purposes of the classroom. An analogy might help us to evaluate this factor. Suppose a lecture is given by a foreigner with a heavy accent. Those in the audience who are accustomed to this accent will understand the lecture much better than those who are not. The ability to deal with the accent is certainly a trivial factor from the standpoint of total personality; yet in this particular situation of the lecture, this trivial factor makes an almost crucial difference. If you consider 13 lecturers, each with a somewhat different "accent," and group the generalized abilities required to be successful with most of them, you would end up with a composite picture of a student with great linguistic understanding, ability to cope with frustration, and, possibly, great interest or positivity toward foreigners. But to comprehend any one of these lecturers, only particular skills, attitudes, and compatibilities are required.

We think that "teachability" is similiar to this. The picture of a student who could deal best with all 13 teachers is the one we have presented. This student is a generally "healthy" person able to cope with all personalities. However, a student who could on an average best deal with all 13 teachers may not necessarily be able to deal best with certain ones of them; that is, he might do superbly with one of the teachers and miserably with another. In general this student's average performance in dealing with 13 teachers would be good.

To deal with one teacher in a particular situation requires less generalized abilities than to deal with 13 each in a somewhat different situation. The practical deduction from this is that the full teachability factor, as we have defined it for a population of 13 teachers, may not be at all required to cope with any of them. We will present evidence on this point shortly. But before we do that, let us complete the picture. There may be special skills or attributes that are important in dealing with a particular teacher. In other words, the teachability factor as defined for 13 teachers may not only be unnecessarily inclusive for a particular teacher—but it may leave out some other characteristics that are vital to that particular teacher. Thus one might have the linguistic ability and interest that gives one an edge in dealing with foreigners in general; yet from time to time one would encounter a strongly aggressive, academic, or indoctrinated foreigner with whom one could still not cope. The aggressiveness, intellectuality, or value-attitude involved would in these cases be at least as important as the linguistic-cultural abilities.

These possibilities, which we have felt represented strong probabilities, explain why we defined teachability separately for each teacher. Thus we have the data we need to test the ideas. Let us consider the evidence relevant to this discussion and ask the following questions.

1. How "big" a factor is teachability? That is, how many differences exist between low and high teachable students? Operationally speaking, of the 360 items in the total battery, how many significantly differentiate between high and low teachable students selected by each teacher?

Column A, Table 7, shows that "teachability" for the various teachers comprehends from 18% to 50% of the 360 items, with the average being 33% or 119 items.

2. To what extent is the general teachability factor which is most typical of the whole population, represented in the discrimination pattern of each teacher? How nearly alike are teachability in general and teachability with reference to a particular teacher?

Column B, Table 7, shows that the core items (general factor) are somewhat more heavily represented than the other items. In the various teachability patterns, from 33% to 65% of the core items are selected with the mean at 47%. These figures represent the extent to which the teacher's pattern overlaps the general factor.

Table 7. Relationships between General and Specific Teachability Factors

Teacher Number	Column A Percent of 360 Test Items Discriminating for Each Teacher	Column B Percent of *core* Items Discriminating For Each Teacher	Column C Core Items	Column D Noncore
			Percent of Each Teacher's Pattern Represented by:	
1	32	56	32	68
2	29	52	33	67
3	27	42	29	71
4	34	45	25	75
5	50	65	24	76
6	18	38	38	62
7	40	53	24	76
8	34	35	19	81
9	36	45	23	77
10	32	33	19	81
12	34	53	29	71
13	34	47	26	74
14	34	50	27	73
Means	33	47	27	73

3. What part of the teacher's pattern is composed of the general core items and what part is unique to the teacher?

Column C, Table 7, shows that the general teachability factor accounts for from 19 to 38% of the individual patterns, with the mean at 27%. Column D subtracts the figures of Column C from 100, emphasizing that from 62 to 81% of what each teacher means by "teachable" is *not* included in the general teachability factor.

The picture of quantitative differences among the various teachers' definitions of "teachability" shows that there is great variation from teacher to teacher both in the number of test items and in the number of the general teachability factor items that discriminate between high and low teachable students for each teacher. These differences are further elucidated and extended when we consider how the various sections of the test enter into teachability.

4. Do the various sections of the test discriminate differently from teacher to teacher?

The A columns in Table 8 show what percentage of all the items in each of the eight sections of the test are discriminating for each teacher. Thus, for example, of the 48 items in the section "Ways of Doing Things," 19% discriminate between high and low teachable students for teacher 8, where as 77% discriminate high and low teachable students for teacher 5. The smallest range of discrimination across all the teachers is yielded by the 50 items of the section "Situations": 2 to 28%.

Looking down the columns, we see that the range of discrimination across the eight sections of the test is lowest for teacher 6 (low 6, high 28, range 22) and for teacher 13 (low 22, high 48, range 26). The greatest range or variation of discrimination among the eight sections is highest for teacher 12 (low 14, high 67, range 53), for teacher 10 (low 2, high 53, range 51), and for teacher 5 (low 26, high 77, range 51). Teachers 4 and 12 are interesting because they have exactly the same total number of items in their discrimination pattern (34%, Table 10) and at the same time almost the greatest differences within their patterns.

5. Do the various aspects of the general teachability factor discriminate differently from teacher to teacher?

The B columns in Table 8 are calculated like the A columns except that the percentage is of the number of items from each section that are drawn, not from the whole test but from the general teachability factor. Thus the B columns show how the internal composition of teachability, defined by each teacher, compares with teachability as defined by commonalities among all 13 teachers.

Thus we see that 83% of the "Who Should Decide Items" from the general teachability factor are included in the discrimination patterns

Table 8. Percentage of All Items (A), and Core Items (B) Included from Each Section of the Test within the Discrimination Pattern of Each Teacher

Test Section	Teacher																										
	1		2		3		4		5		6		7		8		9		10		12		13		14	
	A	B	A	B	A	B	A	B	A	B	A	B	A	B	A	B	A	B	A	B	A	B	A	B	A	B
Who should decide?	58	83	29	50	17	00	37	67	50	50	13	33	25	33	42	33	17	17	33	17	33	83	33	33	50	33
Classroom activities	30	50	25	17	23	50	35	50	58	83	20	33	45	67	45	33	45	67	53	67	67	67	48	83	53	50
Participation	32	75	40	75	20	50	28	25	68	100	16	75	46	75	38	75	46	25	38	25	38	75	38	75	44	75
Situations	22	25	26	50	26	50	16	00	26	25	6	50	18	50	20	25	28	75	2	00	14	00	22	25	16	50
Teacher description	28	40	6	20	28	80	44	20	33	20	28	20	39	60	17	00	22	20	17	00	33	40	22	20	44	60
Ways of doing things	44	63	31	53	46	63	46	58	77	95	27	32	52	68	19	32	58	74	35	53	37	63	27	16	33	42
Values	18	46	32	69	20	15	30	31	45	54	28	62	40	38	33	38	28	23	22	23	32	38	43	92	32	62
Words, words	34	56	13	56	15	33	40	67	37	44	11	11	4	33	46	44	31	33	49	33	40	44	30	44	24	44

of teachers 1 and 12, whereas none of these items appears in the pattern for teacher 3. "Ways of Doing Things" and "Values" are the sections that contribute most heavily to the general teachability factor; yet the range across the teachers for the "Ways of Doing Things" items is from 16% (teacher 13) to 95% (teacher 5), and for "Values," the range is 15% (teacher 3) to 92% (teacher 13).

The general teachability factor represents the total population of discrimination patterns of the 13 teachers; but it describes no one such pattern very well. The differences between each teacher's pattern and the general factor are so great that we can believe that students will have to be selected according to the separate patterns of each teacher.

Chapter Six

FACILITATION: The General Tendencies and Their Variability

The Observational Data · Description of the Control Classes · The Differences Teachability Made · Summary · Variations among the Thirteen Teachers

The selection of "teachable" students for each teacher thus introduces prejudice into the classroom. Compared to the usual class, the teachable class should, theoretically, be easier to teach. The events in the classroom should have a different quality about them, and this quality should be conducive to greater effectiveness, whatever that may mean for each teacher. If the teacher is concerned with "achievement" of the sort that achievement tests measure, his more "teachable" class should gain more. If the teacher is not concerned with "achievement," and in fact provides no more or better activities or relationships designed to further achievement, then the achievement gain should not be greater. It was this reasoning that led us to think of the selection factor as a "teachability" factor rather than as an "achievement" factor.

THE OBSERVATIONAL DATA

The question of what exactly the teacher is trying to teach, and of the ways and the extent he is in fact facilitated, can only be answered by interpreting observations of what goes on in his classroom. The data to be discussed in this section are reports of observations of events within the 26 classes of the 13 teachers. The data are the following:

1. Classification of teacher comments within a set of categories. This analysis was made from tape-recorded samples of classroom conversation. Three research assistants, each of whom was thoroughly familiar with the class, categorized the statements of the teacher. They then analyzed their differences of judgment together. The categories of

data obtained in this way comprise "Observation Schedule 1." (Appendix D and E)

2. Number of occurrences of various kinds of behavior engaged in by students. This was observed in the classroom and tallied. It is reported as a frequency count (Observation Schedule 2, Appendix F)

3. Generalized ratings, made at the end of the year by the students, of how often (on a five-point scale) different behaviors were engaged in by the teacher and by the students (Guess Who—Frequencies, Appendix I)

4. Ratings (on a five-point scale) by the students of the extent to which the teacher approved or disapproved of each of these behaviors (Guess Who—Approval, Appendix I)

5. The students' rank ordering of their class as compared to other classes (Student Opinion Survey) in not strictly observational data, but we included the data at this point because the one item that was significant is very helpful to interpretation of the rest of the data. (Appendix H)

Our first task was to discover which of these items or categories discriminate between teachable and control groups. The medians were found for each class, and we counted the number of comparisons in which the experimental class was higher than the control class, and vice versa. The discrimination index is the difference between the number of comparisons in which the experimental class is higher than the control class. An index of three or more is considered as suggesting a difference in tendency.

The first question we ask of the data is how many differences are found to discriminate between experimental and control groups. Table 9 shows the number and percent of items or categories that discriminate.

Table 9 shows that 34% of the behaviors observed by the researchers or students discriminate within the 13 comparisons of experimental and control classes.

The second question is how large the differences are, that is, how different the classes are from each other. For the most part the data show (Table 11) that the differences are quite small. It is the number of comparisons rather than the size of the differences that can be called significant. Our confidence is based on the fact that a large number of small differences form a consistent pattern which is in accord with the theory.

Given this information about the data, our next question is what our strategy of interpretation shall be. First, we attempt to describe the control classes, making a composite or "median" picture from the 13 observed control classes. This discussion will be based on Table 10 and

**Table 9. Distribution of Discriminating Items
or Categories of Observation**

Source of Item or Category	Number of Items or Categories Possible	Number of Discriminating Items or Categories	Percent of Discriminating Items or Categories
1. Observation Schedule No. 1			
(a) Teacher comments	13	6*	46
(b) Teacher affect (Emotionality)	12	3	25
2. Observation Schedule No. 2 (Student behaviors)	16	7	44
3. Guess Who—Frequencies			
(a) Students	18	4	22
(b) Teacher	18	6	33
4. Guess Who—Approval	18	8	44
Total	95	34	36

* In addition, the teacher talked more, a statistic which "adds up" these categories.

will be limited to the 34 items or categories which differentiate between experimental and control groups. Second, we shall note in which direction each of these 34 aspects was biased in the experimental groups (Table 11). Third we shall attempt to diagnose and generalize the pattern of differences.

DESCRIPTION OF THE CONTROL CLASSES

The salient items are presented in Table 10. We shall now discuss them briefly, adding additional information to clarify the picture.

The first ten items are from Observation Schedule No. 1. Of these, the first seven are percentages of the total observed behavior, and the last three are average number of times certain behaviors occurred during a class period.

In the control classes, the teacher talked about 76% of the time. Ninety-one percent of his comments are "technical," which means in our category system that they simply carry out predetermined plans and activities or "cover-the-ground" by giving information, either via discussion or lecture. In 12.5% of the comments, the teacher is talking about concepts and relationships, rather than simply giving information or description. Eight percent of the comments are "professional," which means that they are primarily influenced by learning-oriented responses

Table 10. Items Characterizing the Control Classes

Items	Control Groups
Observation Schedule No. 1	
Proportion of time during which teacher talks	C: md $= 76\%$
Teacher behavior determined by rules and prior considerations such as defined procedures, ground to be covered, or academic lesson	C: md $= 91\%$
Teacher instruction that focuses on the meaning and significance of ideas with particular concern for pointing out the relationship between one concept or variable and another	C: mean $= 12.5\%$
Teacher behavior determined by situational demands and student interest, with effort to lead students into self-initiated decision-making processes	C: md $= 8.0\%$
Teacher statements that are concerned explicitly with group standards, morale, organization, and/or role expectations	C: md $= 4\%$
Attempts by teacher to condition the student to acceptance of a value orientation similar to the teacher's	C: md $= 3\%$
Teacher expression about own experience, fantasy, hunch, or opinion	C: md $= 1\%$
Teacher behavior that is irrelevant to the cognitive task demands—thus a freer expression and association of ideas	C: mean $= 0.5$/class hour (mdn $= 0$)
Affect of pairing expressed by the teacher to the class during discussion or course of lesson	C: md $= 0$/class hour
Greater quantity of unidentified affect in E classes	C: md $= 0$/class hour
Generalized Ratings by Students (Guess Who—Teacher)	
Frequency that teacher presents ideas which influence the class	C: usually
Frequency that teacher offers compromises when there are several sides being taken on a topic	C: usually
Frequency that teacher thinks his or her idea is best	C: usually
Frequency that teacher talks out of turn	C: rarely
Frequency that teacher brings in his own outside work relating to this class	C: rarely
Frequency that teacher seems to get upset when unable to answer questions	C: never
Student Ratings of Approval and Disapproval (Guess Who—Approval)	
Extent of teacher approval when a student brings in a lot of extra work that he or she has done on subjects relating to class	C: shows approval
Extent of teacher approval when a student offers compromises when there are several sides being taken on a topic	C: shows approval

Table 10 *(Continued)*

Items	Control Groups
Extent of teacher approval when a student suggests new ideas when the group seems to be at a standstill	C: shows approval
Extent of teacher approval when a student continually asks questions in class	C: neither approves nor disapproves
Extent of teacher approval when a student sympathizes with others when it is needed most	C: neither approves nor disapproves
Extent of teacher approval when a student thinks his or her idea is best	C: neither approves nor disapproves
Extent of teacher approval when student talks out of turn	C: tolerates
Extent of teacher approval when student disrupts the work of the class by clowning	C: tries to prevent

Observations of Students, Schedule No. 2

Student raising hand for recognition by teacher following question asked by the class	C: md = 32/class hour
Voluntary, task-oriented student verbal behavior when called on after raising hand	C: md = 10.5/class hour
Frequency of teacher's calling on students by name —hand not raised	C: md = 23/class hour
Impulsive answers to teacher questions by students who simply blurt out their answer without waiting for teacher recognition	C: md = 5.0/class hour
Quantity of instances when students initiate a new topic or request additional information	C: md = 23/class hour
Student behavior that evidences preoccupation with activity other than class lesson—for example, doodling, daydreaming, etc.	C: md = 15.5/class hour
Student behavior that interferes with the work effort of others	C: md = 1/class hour

Guess Who, Students

Frequency that students sympathize with others when this is needed most	C: occasionally
Frequency that students get things done when most of the class is confused	C: occasionally
Frequency that students talk out of turn	C: occasionally
Frequency that students disrupt the work of the class by clowning and fooling around	C: rarely

Student Comparison of His Class with Other Classes

Extent that a student would like to work with the same group of students again next year	C: $x = 6.5$*

* Mean derived from ten-point scale with 1 equaling "not at all" and 10 equaling "completely."

and concerns of students. This is the part of educative interaction which is "emergent" rather than predetermined or impervious to needs of students as expressed in their behavior.

Four percent of the teacher's comments are moralistic or motivating. That is, they try to make the activities, homework, or conclusions more palatable by appeals to duty, requirements of an "education," and so forth. In 3% of the statements, the observers detect the effort to persuade the students to believe or think similarly with the teacher and to accept a value orientation similar to the teacher's. The teacher's value orientation is, however, for the most part normative and impersonal, for only 1% of his statements expresses subjective or personal opinions.

The teacher's impersonality with regard to ideas and subject content is further seen in the statistic that less than half the teachers ever come up with a personal idea that appears to the observers to be irrelevant to the subject under study.

Finally, the observers noted no instances of warm interpersonal affects of the sorts known as "pairing," and "diffuse affect" on the part of more than half the teachers.

The next six items represent observations by the students of how often, in their opinion, the teacher engages in certain behaviors. According to the students, the teacher's ideas are usually influential, he usually settles arguments by seeking acceptable compromises, and he usually thinks his own idea is the best one. On the other hand, he rarely "talks out of turn," and rarely does "extra work" on behalf of the class. Further, he never gets upset when he cannot answer questions raised by the students.

To us these six observations by the students reinforce the researcher's observations. The teacher appears to be unflustered, powerful, authoritative, and impersonal. He knows what has to be done and does it. He is secure enough to allow the students to get into conflict, and usually finds some compromise among their positions.

The next eight items portray the student's perceptions of what will be approved or disapproved of by the teacher. The teacher is not "really glad" about any of the 18 behaviors, but he is seen as "showing approval" of three: extra work done by the student, compromise suggestions offered by students, and new ideas offered by students to get the group from a standstill. The teacher is seen as neutral or indifferent to continual questioning by a student, expressions of sympathy from one student for another, and self-congratulatory or aggrandizing remarks by a student. Finally the teacher is seen as tolerating (more negative than being indifferent to) a student when he "talks out of turn" and as trying to prevent "goofing off" by the student. These items suggest that the teacher approves behaviors that help him, is either indifferent to or uninvolved in needs expressed in interpersonal behaviors of students, and attempts to secure order by persuasion (for example, moralizing).

So far we have been describing the teacher. The next seven items present the researcher's observations of the students. The most frequent behaviors that distinguish between experimental and control groups during the 24% time that the students have the floor are the asking and answering of questions. Where the teacher asks the question, hands are raised 32 times during the hour; of these, the teacher calls on about one-third. The teacher is more likely to call on someone who did not raise his hand (23 times during the hour), and in five instances a student blurts out the answer without being recognized. Thus the teacher asks about 38 questions during the hour. In addition, the students raise 23 questions. During the hour, also, the observers noted about 16 instances of doodling, daydreaming, or other, presumably inattentive behavior, and about one instance where such behavior interfered with the work of others.

The students perceive that they rarely disrupt the class, that occasionally they sympathize with each other, are able to operate in the face of confusion, and "talk out of turn." Finally, on the Opinion Survey, they indicate mild liking for the idea of working with the same group of students next year.

Our picture of the control classes, built only from the 36% of the items and categories that distinguish it from the experimental class, portrays those aspects of the pattern that are influenced by teachability. In summary, these aspects add to a teacher-dominated, routine, recitation-type lesson, with considerable give and take during the lesson-oriented discussion, and with half the recitaton "conscripted" by the teacher calling on students who do not offer to answer his questions.

THE DIFFERENCES TEACHABILITY MADE

The picture of the control classes is also substantially the same as the experimental classes. There are no marked differences in method of teaching, ways of dealing with students, types of activity, etc. It is very clearly the same person teaching both classes. The differences are primarily caused by the teacher responding somewhat differently to the two classes, and in many cases there is little evidence that the teacher even knows he is behaving any differently. Most of our teachers were aware of differences in liking one class or the other, but most of the other differences they told us about were attributed to particular strong or weak individual students, not to the classes as groups. Nevertheless, the discrimination index shows us that there were many differences, mostly small, that "went in the same direction" a significant number of times, and the examination we are about to undertake will show that these differences do add up to a consistent picture.

The most discriminating item in Table 11 is supported by the largest number of comparisons as well as by markedly different behavior: the item is observed-student inattentiveness or private play. The most obvious thing about the students teachers judged as "getting most out of class" would appear to have been that they were "work-oriented" and presented less of a "management problem."

Item 2 suggests that some of the control or curbing of tendencies to play comes from within, for in nine of the comparisons the median liking of each other as people to work with is higher in the experimental groups. The greater regard for each other as companions in work may well imply a higher regard for work.

Item 3 shows a higher reward for doing extra work; the teacher is perceived as being "really glad" rather than merely "shows approval."

In item 4, the observers report some loosening of the constricted technical, routine, and predetermined teacher behavior, from a median of 91% to a median of 83% of all teacher behavior.

In item 5 we learn that the students see the teacher as more permissive in the face of clowning. There is only one-eighth as much clowning, and the teacher is less concerned with trying to prevent it, probably because there is much less to prevent.

These five items are, in our opinion, the keynote items. The plurality of comparisons "favoring" the experimental groups is in each case 6 to 8, which is certainly way beyond "chance." Already in these five items we have the basic themes which we will expect the other items to illustrate in more detail:

1. A more work-oriented, less inattentive and distracted class.
2. More work-solidarity among the students.
3. More enthusiasm in the teacher's approval of work.
4. Less rigidity, more flexibility in the teaching.
5. Greater permissiveness with respect to disruptive behavior which occurs much less frequently.

The greater flexibility, permissiveness, and enthusiasm of the teacher could, one might suppose, also imply a greater personal involvement of the teacher. In item 6, the students portray the teacher as rarely (rather than never) getting upset when he cannot answer questions. Item 7

Table 11. Differences Between Experimental and Control Classes

Item No.	Discrimination Index	$E = C$	Item	Finding	Source of Item
1	8	2-1-10	Student behavior that evidences preoccupation with activity other than class lesson—for example, doodling, daydreaming, etc.	E: md = 2 observed instances/class hour C: md = 15.5/class hour	Observation 2 (private play)
2	7	2-2-9	Extent that a student would like to work with the same group of students again next year	E: x = 7.2 C: x = 6.5*	Student Opinion Survey (Item 4)
3	7	1-4-8	Extent of teacher approval when a student brings in a lot of extra work that he or she has done on things relating to class	E: really glad C: shows approval	Guess Who? (Item 6)
4	6	3-1-9	Teacher behavior determined by rules and prior considerations such as defined procedures, ground to be covered, or academic lesson	E: md = 83% of teacher statements/class hour C: md = 91%	Observation 1 Teacher Role (technical)
5	6	3-1-9	Extent of teacher approval when student disrupts the work of the class by clowning	E: tolerates C: tries to prevent	Guess Who? (Item 12)
6	5	4-0-9	Frequency that teacher seems to get upset when unable to answer questions	E: rarely C: never	Guess Who? (Item 17)
7	5	3-2-8	Teacher expression about own experience, fantasy, hunch or opinion	E: md = 5% of teacher statements/class hour C: md = 1%/class hour	Observation 1 Level of Concern (subjective)
8	5	3-2-8	Extent of teacher approval when a student continually asks questions in class	E: shows approval C: neither approves nor disapproves	Guess Who? (Item 2)
9	5	2-4-7	Greater quantity of such affect in E classes	E: md = 2 observed instances/class hour C: 0/class hour	Observation 1 Emotionality (unidentified affect)
10	5	1-6-6	Student behavior that interferes with the work effort of others	E: md = 0 observed instances/class hour C: md = 1/class hour	Observation 2 (disturbs others)

Table 11 (*Continued*)

Item No.	Discrimination Index	E = C	Item	Finding	Source of Item
11	5	0-8-5	Affect of pairing expressed by the teacher to the class during discussion or course of lesson	E: md = 2 observed instances/class hour C: md = 0/class hour	Observation 1 Emotionality (Pairing with group)
12	4	4-1-8	Teacher behavior determined by situational demands and student interest, with effort to lead students into self-initiated decision-making processes	E: md = 8.5% of teacher statements/class hour C: md = 8.0%	Observation 1 Teacher Role (Professional)
13	4	4-1-8	Frequency of teacher's calling on students by name—hand not raised	E: md = 32.5 observed instances/class hour C: md = 23/class hour	Observation 2 (conscripted answers)
14	4	4-1-8	Extent of teacher approval when a student sympathizes with others when it is needed most	E: shows approval C: neither approves nor disapproves	Guess Who? (Item 15)
15	4	3-3-7	Teacher instruction that focuses on the meaning and significance of ideas with particular concern for pointing out the relationship of one concept or variable to another	E: mean = 14.7% of teacher statements/class hour C: mean = 12.5%/class	Observation 1 Level of Concern (Relationships among concepts)
16	4	3-3-7	Voluntary, task-oriented student verbal behavior; called on after student raises hand	E: md = 9.5 observed instances/class hour C: md = 10.5/class hour	Observation 2 (student comments)
17	4	3-3-7	Extent of teacher approval when a student suggests new ideas when the group seems to be at a standstill	E: really glad C: shows approval	Guess Who? (Item 1)
18	4	3-3-7	Extent of teacher approval when a student thinks his or her idea is best	E: tolerates C: neither approves nor disapproves	Guess Who? (Item 7)

Table 11 (*Continued*)

Item No.	Discrimination Index	$E = C$	Item	Finding	Source of Item
19	4	3-3-7	Frequency that teacher thinks his or her idea is best	*E:* occasionally *C:* usually	Guess Who? (Item 7)
20	4	3-3-7	Frequency that students get things done when most of the class is confused	*E:* usually *C:* occasionally	Guess Who? (Item 8)
21	4	3-3-7	Frequency that students sympathize with others when this is needed most	*E:* usually *C:* occasionally	Guess Who? (Item 15)
22	4	3-3-7	Frequency that students talk out of turn	*E:* rarely *C:* occasionally	Guess Who? (Item 16)
23	4	2-5-6	Teacher behavior that is irrelevant to the cognitive task demands—thus a freer expression and association of ideas	*E:* mean = 1 time/class hour when observed *C:* mean = .5/class hour	Observation 1 Emotionality (flight-escape)
24	4	1-7-5	Greater quantity of attempts by teacher to condition the student to acceptance	*E:* md = 9% of teacher statements/class hour *C:* md = 3%/class hour	Observation 1 Teacher Role (generalized adult)
25	3	5-0-8	Proportion of time during which teacher talks	*E:* md = 78% of class time *C:* md = 76%	Observation 1 Teacher statements
26	3	5-0-8	Extent of teacher approval when a student offers compromises when there are several sides being taken on a topic	*E:* really glad *C:* shows approval	Guess Who? (Item 10)
27	3	4-2-7	Teacher statements that are concerned explicitly with group standards, morale, organization, and/or role expectations	*E:* md = 2% of teacher statements/class hours *C:* md = 4%	Observation 1 Topic of Discussion (Group centered)
28	3	4-2-7	Impulsive answers to teacher questions by students who simply blurt out their answer without waiting for teacher recognition	*E:* md = 4.5 observed instances/class hour *C:* md = 5.0/class hour	Observation 2 (spoken out)

121

Table 11 *(Continued)*

Item No.	Discrimination Index	E = C	Item	Finding	Source of Item
29	3	4-2-7	Student raising hand for recognition by teacher following question asked of class	E: md = 23 observed instances/class hour C: md = 32/class hour	Observation 2 (volunteer answers)
30	3	4-2-7	Quantity of instances when students initiate a new topic or request additional information—ask questions	E: mean = 26.2 instances/class hour C: mean = 23.4/class hour	Observation 2 (student questions)
31	3	4-2-7	Frequency that teacher brings in a lot of extra work that he has done on things relating to this class	E: usually C: rarely	Guess Who? (Item 6)
32	3	4-2-7	Frequency that teacher offers compromises when there are several sides being taken on a topic	E: always C: usually	Guess Who? (Item 10)
33	3	4-2-7	Frequency that teacher talks out of turn	E: occasionally C: rarely	Guess Who? (Item 16)
34	3	4-2-7	Frequency that teacher presents ideas which influence the class	E: always C: usually	Guess Who? (Item 18)
35	3	3-4-6	Frequency that students disrupt the work of the class by clowning and fooling around	E: occasionally C: rarely	Guess Who? (Item 12)
36	3	3-4-6	Extent of teacher approval when student talks out of turn	E: tries to prevent C: tolerates	Guess Who? (Item 16)

* Mean derived from ten-point scale with 1 equaling "not at all" and 10 equaling "completely."

shows a fivefold increase in the number of subjective and personal comments of the teacher—which is also consistent with his lessened rigidity.

In item 8, the teacher is able to be a little more approving "when a student continually asks questions in class." Item 11 shows us that the permissiveness goes along with slightly more positive and warm expressions of the teacher toward the students, and item 9 says that affect in general is at a slightly higher level.

In item 10 the observers note no instances of student behavior that disturbs others, which suggest that the tolerant attitude, ascribed to the teacher in item 5, is not very difficult to maintain.

Item 12 is especially interesting when coupled with item 4. It suggests that the "loosening up" of the rigid technical pattern, while distinctively in the direction of a more responsive co-determination of work, is mostly to be accounted for in other behaviors, and we shall see that these other behaviors are mostly the offering of more personal, subjective, and "involved" comments by the teacher. Item 15, at the same level of discrimination, suggests that the teacher is digging deeper, conceptually speaking, and this suggests that the greater amount of subjectivity may signify involvement rather than irresponsibility.

Item 13, showing 50% more frequency of calling on students by name, is open to two interpretations. The fact that these are students who did not raise their hands could be interpreted to mean that the teacher is more frequently checking up on the quiet ones. This could be viewed either as an attempt to catch them off guard, or it could be viewed as an expression of concern for them. The other items gives considerably more support for this second hypothesis.

Item 14 gives slightly more substance to the allegation of more warmth from teacher to class (item 11), and item 17 suggests that the teacher's greater involvement includes process as well as task work; he gives more reward to those who help the class.

Among the remaining items at this same level of discrimination, number 24 enables us to organize the information from several others. We see here that the teacher makes more effort to persuade students to adopt his own beliefs. He is more involved, more concerned to get across his ideas, and he maintains more strong control of participation (he calls on more people who do not have their hands up—item 14, and on fewer who do, item 16). He is a little freer to exploit the class with personal, irrelevant remarks (item 23). And he is less tolerant of possessive students (item 18). At the same time, he is also less dogmatic (item 19), and he has a stronger, rather than a weaker class (items 20, 21, and 22) as perceived by the students.

The remaining items, discrimination index 3, add further details.

The slightly greater percent of time during which the teacher talks (item 25) is consistent with his greater involvement, and item 26 reaffirms the teacher's concern with the class making progress. Item 27 shows the teacher as less dogmatic, authoritarian, and self-concerned. Item 28 shows the students as slightly more self-disciplined and item 30 suggests once again that the source of the discipline is their interest in work. Item 29 which shows fewer hands raised when the teacher asks questions, suggests, when taken with item 13, that he probably asks his questions of particular individuals rather than of the class as a whole—which reinforces the notion of greater concern and involvement with the students.

The last six items give us further perceptions of the students, and these add a little more to the picture. The students see the teacher as usually, rather than rarely, doing extra work for the class (item 31), a sign of greater involvement and enthusiasm. The teacher always, rather than usually, moderates arguments (item 32), a sign of greater involvement in the class's problems as a group. He occasionally, as compared to rarely, talks out of turn (item 33), a sign of greater emotional freedom. Interestingly, his ideas always, rather than usually, influence the class (item 34), which suggests a greater readiness of the class to accept them. The students see each other as more often clowning and fooling around (item 35) which in the face of contradictory evidence from the observers, can be taken as an expression of the feeling of greater permissiveness. Finally the teacher clamps down harder, according to the students, on "talking out of turn" (item 36); and this could be an expression of greater guilt feelings on such occasions or of a perception of greater work-orientedness on the part of the teacher.

SUMMARY

Considering the five themes of the first five items and the additional nuances added by the other items, we see that one central theme comprehends all the details: the differences are subsumed under the concept of *greater solidarity*. The composite picture of the differences in operation of the experimental classes as compared to the control classes is the picture of a better or more fully developed group. It is both more work-oriented and more permissive. The leader is more of a person, more psychically free, more influential, more enthusiastic—and at the same time less rigid and dogmatic. The students have more self-control and more regard for each other and they see the teacher as more rewarding and more ready to exert himself on their behalf.

The sociometrics and teacher marks displayed in Chapter 4 further reflect these differences. The finding that "teachability" represents more personal adequacy, energy, and psychic freedom (Chapter 5) provides the "explanation."

The style of teaching in the experimental groups can be briefly summarized: it is the old style adapted, for the most part involuntarily, to a higher solidarity group.

VARIATIONS AMONG THE 13 TEACHERS

Our description of the changes in classroom operation yielded by the teachability factor is, of course, a composite description constructed from 13 comparisons among pairs of classes. The changes describe a large population which exists simply by virtue of our ability to add numbers. There is no assurance that any actual teacher or comparison between two of his classes would "fit" the picture.

Therefore it is appropriate at this point to consider the range of individual possibilities covered up by the statistics on population. Perhaps the simplest strategy is to ask ourselves: How nearly alike are the patterns of differences produced among the teachers? If these patterns are very similar, then the population statistics must also fairly represent all the situations; but if they are markedly different, then the population statistic is indeed merely a convenient fiction—useful, to be sure, at the level of propositions, but an unsafe basis for prediction in any individual case.

Let us consider the evidence. We shall ask the following:

1. How extensive is the pattern of differences between experimental and control groups from teacher to teacher? Operationally speaking, of the 95 observation categories, how many significantly differentiate between experimental and control groups for each teacher?

Column A, Table 12, shows that of the 95 possible differences our instruments could register, the range is from 21% in the case of teacher No. 10 to 46% in the case of teacher No. 5. The mean is 35%, or 33 categories.

2. To what extent is the general pattern of differences, representing the whole population, discriminating for each comparison of an experimental group with its corresponding control group?

Column B, Table 12, shows that the items that discriminate for the whole population also discriminate somewhat more heavily than other items for most of the teachers. The range is from 26% for teacher No. 10 to 59% for teacher No. 5. The mean is 40%, or 43 categories.

3. What part of the pattern of differences between the experimental

Table 12. The Representation of Observational Categories in the Differences between Experimental and Control Classes

Teacher Number	Column A Percent of 95 Categories Discriminating for Teacher	Column B Percent of 34 Core Categories Discriminating for Each Teacher	Column C Percent of Each Teacher's Pattern Represented by Core Categories	Column D Noncore Categories
1	39	47	43	57
2	36	35	35	65
3	34	32	34	66
4	38	44	42	58
5	46	59	47	53
6	43	38	33	67
7	30	29	36	64
8	40	41	38	62
9	29	35	44	56
10	21	26	45	55
12	37	44	43	57
13	38	47	44	56
14	35	47	49	51
Means	35	40	41	59

and control group of each teacher is composed of categories discriminating for the population as a whole?

Column C, Table 12, shows that from 33% (teacher 6) to 49% (teacher 14) of the individual patterns is composed of categories which discriminate for the whole population. The mean is 41%. By the same token, the part of the pattern for each teacher that is *not* included in the general pattern ranges from 67 to 51%.

4. Do the various kinds of observation categories discriminate differently from teacher to teacher?

The A columns in Table 13 show what percentage of each set of categories discriminates between control and experimental groups for each teacher. Observation schedule No. 1, representing the coding of 13 aspects of the teacher's comments, varies most markedly in its ability to discriminate. For teacher No. 9, only 8% of the categories discriminate, whereas for teacher No. 5, 77% of the categories discriminate. The smallest range of discrimination is provided by Observation Schedule No. 2, which provides the categories within which student behaviors were classified. The range is from 47%, teacher No. 14, to 80%, teacher No. 1.

Table 13. Percentages of All and of Core Categories in Each Set That Discriminate between Experimental and Control Classes

																		Teacher									
	1		2		3		4		5		6		7		8		9		10		12		13		14	
Categories	A	B	A	B	A	B	A	B	A	B	A	B	A	B	A	B	A	B	A	B	A	B	A	B	A	B
Guess Who																										
Teacher-Frequency Core	39	33	56	17	67	67	50	83	33	50	56	67	28	17	33	33	44	33	33	33	72	100	39	67	33	17
Student-Frequency Core	22	25	11	25	22	25	39	50	50	75	44	25	33	25	50	25	28	50	28	25	28	50	50	50	22	50
Teacher Approval Core	33	13	33	25	28	25	33	13	50	50	39	00	11	13	17	13	28	25	28	38	28	13	22	25	28	25
Observation Schedule No. 1																										
Comments Core	46	83	39	50	15	33	23	50	77	100	39	67	31	33	39	83	8	17	31	50	31	17	39	50	69	83
Emotionality Core	17	33	25	00	8	00	17	00	8	00	8	00	8	00	42	00	00	00	00	00	00	00	8	00	17	67
Observation Schedule No. 2																										
Student Behavior Core	80	86	53	71	53	29	60	57	53	57	60	57	67	71	67	71	53	71			53	71	67	71	47	57

Looking down the A columns, we see that the various kinds of categories contribute very differently to the discrimination patterns. The emotionality counts, Observation Schedule No. 1, contribute nothing to the patterns of teachers No. 10 and 12 (among others). Yet the teacher behaviors rated by the students (guess who—teacher) contribute 33% of their categories to teacher No. 10, and 72% to teacher No. 12.

5. Do the categories that discriminate for the whole population discriminate differently from teacher to teacher?

The B columns of Table 13 show what percentage of the generally discriminating categories ("core" categories) in each set are included within the discrimination pattern of each teacher. Two sets of core categories (teacher behaviors as rated by students and teacher behaviors as rated by observers) show the greatest variation in their contributions to the patterns for each teacher: the range is from 17 to 100%. The smallest range of discrimination is shown by the categories of student behavior and teacher approval as rated by the students: 25 to 75% and 0 to 50%, respectively.

Looking down the B columns, we see that the various core categories contribute very differently to different teachers. Thus all the core items having to do with teacher behaviors in Observation Schedule No. 1 discriminate experimental and control classes for teacher No. 5, but none of the core items having to do with emotionality discriminate.

As with the teachability factor, it is amply clear that the general pattern of differences between the populations of 13 comparisons of experimental and control classes does not at all well describe the differences between experimental and control groups of any single teacher.

Each teacher has *his* own way of teaching and is facilitated by a class of students who conform to *his* definition of teachability. The resulting classroom processes are different from teacher to teacher. The general proposition that a teacher is more effective when he works with teachable students seems to us to be correct, but the terms of this proposition are quite different from one teacher to the next.

Chapter Seven

CONGRUENCE: The Fit between One Teacher's Style and His Teachable Students

Overview of the General Trends in the Data · Detailed Examination of the Effects of the Teachable Class · Characteristics of Teachability · Resumé · The Fit between Teachability and Teaching

By putting together the observations of 13 control or unselected classes, we formulated a composite, fictitious, "median" description of the usual teaching style of our 13 teachers. Then, through the contrivance of a "discrimination index" we showed that the median teaching style is changed when the teacher is given a "teachable" class. This new style is quickly summarized: it is the old style adapted to a higher solidarity group.

A complete summary of the results obtained from the composite picture of the 26 classes is: a predominantly "technical-routine" style of teaching will shift toward a more personally involved, psychologically interactive style when applied to a higher solidarity group. The outcomes will also shift, with the greatest shifts (teacher marks, satisfaction, and interpersonal liking) reflecting the changed psychological interaction, and the least shifts being in the areas most remote from psychological interaction (achievement tests, stereotypic perceptions of the course).

But does this generalization apply to all our individual teachers? Did they all have a "technical-routine" style of teaching? Was the change introduced by grouping always toward greater solidarity in the classroom? We have already noted that each teacher defines teachability somewhat differently, and that the differences in classroom operation between control and experimental groups form different patterns. Is it not likely, then, that there may well be 13 quite different equations all having the following form?

$$\begin{array}{ccccccc}
\text{Regular (control)} & & \text{More teachable} & & \text{Changed classroom} & & \text{Better educational} \\
\textit{style} \text{ of teaching} & + & \text{students selected} & = & \text{operation, more in} & + & \text{outcomes, as judged} \\
\text{of each teacher} & & \text{for each teacher} & & \text{line with each} & & \text{by each teacher} \\
& & & & \text{teacher's purposes} & &
\end{array}$$

This equation assumes that each teacher has an "established" or habitual style of teaching. We attempted to justify this assumption by selecting experienced teachers who were judged by the administrators to have a stable, "well worked-out" course. Teacher style, then, is a set of "givens" in the experiment.

The "more teachable students" represent the independent variable. The students whose performance we studied were not selected by the teacher; they were selected by us on the basis of their similarity to the "model" students selected by the teacher from his earlier classes. In composing the teachable classes, exactly the same procedure was followed in every case, and the judgments are all completely empirical. The only assumptions involved in the independent variable are that: (1) each teacher does a better job of teaching some students than others; (2) the teacher, after seven months of working with a class, can point out the students "getting most and least out of class"; (3) a long and heterogeneous assessment battery will show a sufficient number of items significantly differentiating between more and less teachable students; and (4) students selected from a large population on the basis of these significant items will be "similar" to the model teachable children with respect to the most salient aspects of teachability.

There should be a close relationship between the first two terms of the equation. In his dealing with the class, each teacher expects certain things from the students, and he makes certain demands upon them. These expectations and demands are inherent in his "style" of teaching. From observation of his style of teaching, it should be possible to describe the teacher's demands and expectations. And a "teachable" student would then be defined as a student who could meet the demands and live up to the expectations. In this and Chapter 8 we shall discuss the extent to which knowledge of the way the teacher normally teaches (that is, in his control class) enables us to forecast characteristics of his teachable students.

The third term of the equation carries the argument a step further. It reasons that the teacher is successful to the extent that his students can meet the demands imposed on them by the teacher's style of teaching. In short, a teachable class should facilitate the achievement of the teacher's purposes. The operation of the teachable class should represent a higher development of the teacher's style. In practical terms, we would expect two things: (1) fewer management problems in the teachable class (except in the unlikely instance of a teacher whose purpose is to create management problems); and (2) more accentuated "pure" or self-consistent role performance by the teacher. He should not only be able to improve the sort of things he is already trying to do (in the control class), but he should be able to do these things with fewer distractions and fewer wasted motions. Thus, in this and Chapter 8, our interest will be in the extent to which the modifications of teaching, resulting from a class of teachable students, are directed toward a higher quality, more consistent style of teaching.

Finally, the fourth term of the equation simply says that if the above reasoning is correct, the teacher will perceive that the class is learning more of whatever the teacher is trying to teach. We have already noted the discrepancy between marks and achievement test gains and feel justified in rejecting the common assumption that achievement tests necessarily measure what the teacher is "really" trying to teach. The teacher's mark expresses his final, incontrovertible, and professional judgment of the extent to which he thinks the student learned what he was trying to teach. And in nearly all cases this judgment was found to be more affirmative in the "teachable" classes. We shall not, in this chapter or the next, raise further questions about the fourth term of our equation.

OVERVIEW OF GENERAL TRENDS IN THE DATA: TEACHER NO. 5

Our portrayal of the style of teacher No. 5 will be based on detailed examination of the 95 categories of data discussed in the preceding chapter, plus the 19 items of the Post-Meeting Reaction Sheet and Student Opinion Survey. Thus we shall consider 114 discrete sorts of information about the teacher. These data are presented in Tables 14 through 20.

The data are represented in two ways. First, the actual mean or median value of each category is given. Second, this figure is compared with the corresponding figures for the other 12 teachers, and is given a quintile ranking. That is, we show whether the figure is about at the average (Quintile C) of the 13 teachers, whether it is somewhat higher (Quintile B) or lower (Quintile D) than average; or whether it is quite deviate, with 10 or 11 of the other teachers being higher (Quintile E) or lower (Quintile A). The reason for these quintile ranks is to give us a "base line." The composite picture of the control groups already presented represents the "average" (Quintile C) teaching, and we shall find it easier to understand teacher No. 5 by seeing how he differs from

Table 14. Overview of Teacher No. 5's Style in his Experimental and Control Classes

			Shifts of Quintiles from Control to Experimental-Percent of Categories				
Categories	Number of Categories	Percent C Control	No Shift	Toward C	Away from C	More Extreme	Reversal
Observation Schedule No. 1	28	64	36	11	42	7	4
Observation Schedule No. 2	13	8	45	16	8	8	23
Post Meeting Reactions	8	12	63		12	25	0
Student Opinion Survey	11	36	0	18	36	0	46
Sociometrics	6	17	17	50	33	0	0
Guess Who:							
Teacher behavior	16	69	63	12	19	0	6
Student behavior	16	88	63	0	31	0	0
Teacher approval	16	81	50	6	38	0	6
Total	114						
Quintile Shifts (represented in columns)			A → A B → B C → C D → D E → E	A,B,D,E → C	C → A,B,D,E	B → A D → E	A,B → D,E; D,E → A,B

the "average" style rather than by trying to describe his style in absolute terms.

The same tables also include the corresponding data for the experimental class of teacher No. 5. The quintile ranks are again based on the distribution of *control* classes, so that we can estimate the significance of the modifications of teaching produced in the experimental class. Thus we see that teacher No. 5's control class asks fewer questions (two per period) than does any other control class (Table 16). Then we note that his experimental class asks many more questions (23 per period); and finally we note that the rank of the satisfaction is in the top quintile of the control classes. In other words, teacher No. 5 moves from the least to the most questions raised by students simply by having a teachable class.

In considering teacher No. 5's style let us start by noting some of the trends in the data. Table 14 shows the various sources of data and how many categories are contributed by each source. It also shows what percent of the categories are ranked in Quintile C for teacher No. 5's control group.

We note that the operation of the control class is reasonably typical of the average control class (64 to 88% C ratings) with respect to observed teacher behavior and the 16 behaviors rated on the "Guess Who" test. Teacher No. 5 is most atypical with respect to observed student behavior, having only one of the 13 categories (or 8%) in the middle range. The other three kinds of data, all reflecting student feeling about the course, range from 12 to 36% average.

The next column, labeled "no shift" shows the percentage of categories that are the same in both experimental and control groups. From 0 to 63% of the categories are the same; or, conversely, from 100 to 37% of the categories are modified by the teachable students.

Next we note the categories (0 to 50%) in which the experimental group is more like the average of the control groups; the percent (12 to 42%) of the ratings that shift from average (C quintile) in the control group to some other value in the experimental; the percent (0 to 25) of nonaverage categories, quintiles B and D, that become more extreme (A and E); and finally, the percentage of the categories in which the control and experimental groups both deviate, but in opposite directions, from the "average."

Certain impressions emerge when we look at the shifts. The teacher's behavior, Observation Schedule No. 1, shifts in general to more personal freedom of the teacher to voice his opinions and feelings. The greatest change in student behavior is the reversal, from quiet and somewhat apathetic to intrigued and active. The post-meeting reactions shift from above average to even more liking for the classroom activities. The student's ratings of the course as compared to their other courses shift from average or negative judgments to highly positive judgments. The sociometrics reveal a confused picture which we will want to consider carefully in our more detailed analysis. The major shift of the Guess Who ratings is from average to more positive.

DETAILED EXAMINATION OF THE EFFECTS
OF THE TEACHABLE CLASS

In Table 15, the quintile ranks of the categories of observations of the teacher's behavior in the control class reveal that the teacher talks very little and the class a great deal as compared to other classes (1, E and 2, A). There are also fewest comments generally addressed to the classes (4, E) and a correspondingly larger number addressed to persons, either the teacher (3, B) or particular students (5, B). Yet, for all this impression of person-to-person interaction, this teacher is unusually low in the percent of comments about persons in the class (9, D). But he is more likely than other teachers to offer his own opinion about topics (11, B) and he appears somewhat less interested in conceptual meanings (12, D). He tends to be somewhat lower than average on "professional" behavior (15, D), which, in our category system, comprises reality-oriented creative participation. He is average in the expression of emotion except "facilitative humor," on which he is higher than average (27, B).

Summarizing, we see that teacher No. 5 has a high degree of person-directed interaction, expresses his own opinions a little more than average, and is less concept- and work-oriented than average. But he is for the most part "average" (64%, Table 14).

Giving teacher No. 5 a teachable class produced striking and dramatic changes. The largest shift (9, D to A) is in personal remarks about students. About one-sixth of his comments now refer to their peculiarities, interests, family, hopes, etc. He speaks much more impulsively—"acting out" his feelings (13, C to A). He offers a great deal of advice, admonishment, and ideas about right and wrong (16, C to A). More of his comments seem motivated by self-concern (17, C to A), and the number of subjective opinions rises drastically (11, B to A). He responds somewhat more to his students' interests (12 and 15, D to C+). His "cover-the-ground" or routine-technical operation is lessened (6, C to D; 10, C to E; 14, C to E). He has become more spontaneous in his expression of emotion (increase in five categories), he has become more dominant and central in the classroom (3, B to A, and 5, B to C), and he even talks somewhat more (1, 51 to 55% of the time).

Table 15. Observation Schedule No. 1, Teacher No. 5

	Percent of Total Number of Statements—Means		Ranking Among 13 Control Classes—Quintiles	
Observed Category	Control	Experimental	Control	Experimental
1. Statements by teacher	51	55	E	E
2. Statements by students addressed to	49	45	A	A
3. Teacher	40	48	B	A
4. Class	40	34	E	E
5. Particular student topic, "content"	20	18	B	C
6. Ideational	89	77	C	D
7. Group operation	5	2	C	C
8. Activity	5	4	C	C
9. Personal form	0	17	D	A
10. Descriptive	80	32	C	E
11. Subjective	11	44	B	A
12. Relationship	9	15	D	C+
13. Impulsive frame of reference	0	9	C	A
14. Technical	91	48	C	E
15. Professional	5	13	D	C+
16. Generalized adult	4	26	C	A
17. Self-concern	0	13	C	A
	Number of Incidents per Class Period			
Emotionality				
18. Fight: teacher	2	7	C	A
19. threatening	1	2	C	C
20. Dependency: rules	0	1	C	C
21. Flight: breakdown	0	1	C	C
22. escape	0	1	C	C
23. irrelevancy	0	2	C	B
24. Pairing: person	6	8	C	B
25. group	0	2	C	B
26. Unidentified affect	1	3	C	B
27. Humor: facilitative	2	4	B	B
28. disruptive	0	1	C	C

The increased personal involvement and spontaneity of the teacher is responded to by the experimental class (Table 16). There is a striking increase in the number of questions asked by students (7, from 2 to 23 per period, E to A). And hands are up wherever the teacher looks (3, D to A). There are more comments offered gratis by students (6, D to B) and answers are occasionally given by students without waiting for

Table 16. Observation Schedule No. 2, Teacher No. 5

	Number of Observed Instances per Class Period		Ranking among 13 Control Classes—Quintiles	
Observed Category	Control	Experimental	Control	Experimental
1. Teacher questions	36	32	B	C
2. Conscripted answers	13	16	C	B
3. Raise hands	33	115	D	A
4. Volunteer answers	19	17	B	B
5. Speak out answer	0	4	E	C+
6. Student comments	2	12	D	B
7. Student questions	2	23	E	A
8. Lesson participation	8	25	B	A
9. Study for other class	0	0	D	D
10. Whisper	1	5	E	E
11. Private play	1	0	E	E
12. Disturb others	0	0	D	D
13. Blow off (violent, impertinent)	0	0	D	D

recognition (5, E to C+). The teacher has more students demonstrating, reading aloud, or presenting material (8, B to A), and he gives less guidance by asking questions (1, B to C). Interestingly enough, the experimental class, although far more active, remains, like the control group, a very orderly class (9-13). In general, the shift in student behavior is toward increased initiative taken by students. And, in spite of the teacher's somewhat more central, privileged, and self-centered posture, the students actually carry a greater load of determining and influencing events in the classroom. The teacher, in "coming to life" as a person, has brought the students to life, too.

The Post Meeting Reaction Sheets are summarized in Table 17. The control and experimental classes are for the most part very well satisfied with the meetings—the control class mean is between A and B, and the experimental class mean is A. There are three shifts. Satisfaction with the teacher's responses to questions shifts from C to A (4); satisfaction with one's own role shifts from B to A (8); and overall satisfaction with the meeting shifts from B to A (1). The percent of days on which the experimental class gives higher ratings than the control class gives a more emphatic picture of the same differences. The experimental class is consistently the more satisfied class, even though the numerical measures for the two classes are closely similar.

When the students are asked to compare their class with other classes through the medium of the Student Opinion Survey, Table 18,

Table 17. Post Meeting Reactions, Teacher No. 5

	Percent of Days Satisfaction is Higher in		Mean Satisfaction Quintiles	
	Control	Experimental	Control	Experimental
1. How did you feel this class meeting was today?	15	85	B	A
2. How often did you find yourself wanting to say things to the class, but did not?	39	61	A	A
3. How worthwhile to you was what you learned in class?	50	50	A	A
4. How often were questions and comments of students really understood and replied to fairly and helpfully?	8	92	C	A
5. How clearly did you understand exactly what the class was supposed to do today?	15	85	A	A
6. How difficult was the lesson?	54	46	B	B
7. What part of the class was really working on the lesson?	15	85	A	A
8. How satisfied were you with the part you played in class?	25	75	B	A

the results are more striking. The average rating goes from D in the control class to B in the experimental. The highest ratings, C, in the control group form a clear pattern: they delineate a psyche group but not a socio group. All the C ratings are with respect to items which describe a voluntary discussion group: it discusses interesting topics (3), the students like each other (4), they are willing to do the work (5), and they like the teacher (9). It is true that these are not highly positive ratings as compared to other classes, but they do establish something about the class: it is primarily oriented to interpersonal relations. Compared to other classes, it is less meaningful (1, D), makes less use of materials of a sort the student would like to go on with (2, E), provides less basis for planning for the future (6, D), points less toward other

Table 18. Student Opinion Survey, Teacher No. 5

Criteria	Mean Ratings 10—Extreme Satisfaction 1—Extreme Dissatisfaction		Ranking Among Thirteen Control Classes—Quintiles	
	Control	Experimental	Control	Experimental
1. Is each class meaningful and rewarding?	6.1	7.3	D	B
2. Does each class make use of subject materials of the sort you would like to study and work with next year?	5.2	6.4	E	C
3. Does each class deal with topics that are interesting to talk about outside of class?	6.0	7.8	C	B
4. Is each of your classes a group of students you would like to work with again next year?	6.8	8.6	C	A
5. Are you willing to do the work required in each of your classes?	7.5	7.9	C	B
6. Does each class further your plans for things you want to do after leaving high school?	5.7	7.3	D	B
7. Has each class opened new interests or things for you to do?	5.5	7.6	E	B
8. Is the time of each class spent on activities which you enjoy?	5.3	7.0	D	B
9. Does each class have a teacher with whom you would like to work again next year?	7.6	8.7	C	B
10. Do you look forward to going to each of these classes?	6.0	7.4	D	B
11. Has each of the classes given you opportunity to practice or try out some special skill or talent which you have?	5.6	6.3	D	C

interesting activities (7, E), provides less opportunity for practice of skill or talent (11, D). It is looked forward to less (10, D) and its activities (for example, lessons) are less enjoyable (8, D). Thus the control class sees itself as an average discussion group but one whose meetings have little value apart from the interpersonal interactions.

The experimental class rates itself tops as "a group of students you would like to work with again next year," (4, A). It finds only average appeal in the materials (2, C) and only average opportunity to practice skill or exercise talent (11, C). There is much greater interest in the topics discussed (3, B), greater motivation (5, B), enjoyment (8, B), anticipation (10, B). The experience of the class is more meaningful and rewarding (1, B); it furthers plans for "after high school" (6, B) and it opens new interests (7, B). And the students express more interest in working with the same teacher next year (9, B). It appears that, whatever the reason, the students in the experimental group feel more adequate and self-confident. They not only see the class as a pleasurable discussion group; they also see it as contributing to broader educational goals.

Before going on to the remainder of the data, it may be useful to review the themes that have so far emerged, and to add some comments based on the observers' anecdotal reports as follows:

1. Teacher No. 5 in the control group is a somewhat impersonal, technical-routine teacher who makes much use of student-teacher discussion. He has good "order," and the students tend to be subdued, presumably docile, and rather positive in their evaluation of the course. In the experimental group, the teacher is much more personally involved, acts more impulsively, expresses more affect, and is freer with moralizing advice or wisdom. The students are far more active, take much more initiative, and are somewhat more positive in their evaluations of the course.

2. The experimental class is psychologically a far "stronger" class, able to argue with the teacher and to cope with his stepped-up psychic (emotional) demands; and they find the interaction enjoyable.

3. In neither class is their much intellectual work or structured purposive activity. The teacher's emphasis in the control class is on "covering-the-ground." In the experimental class, the emphasis is on affective give-and-take at a rather high level of emotionality. There is much more stimulation, but it is primarily interpersonal provocation rather than the challenge of conceptual work and problems.

4. The subject is social studies, and the discussion is primarily centered around how to behave in a variety of situations. The method of

learning is primarily conditioning, and the teacher's tactics include shock, sarcasm, "personal" remarks, moralizing, experience-swapping, etc. The subject matter and objectives of the teacher thus tend to legitimize his method of teaching; and it is a method which appeals to the experimental students in its own right.

5. The teacher is unable to implement this method in the control group. He is skillful in judging just how far he can go with his stress tactics, and he does not push the psychologically weaker control class. He sticks to the text, restrains his impulses, and maintains an equable level of politeness. Judging by his performance in the experimental class, he is "under wraps" in the control class, and the result is a pleasant but routine situation.

The question which all this raises in our minds is to what extent the teacher is exploiting the experimental class primarily to meet his own personal (rather than professional) needs? Two remaining sorts of evidence may throw light on this issue: the reward system of the group, and the sociometrics.

The reward system is partly revealed in the "Guess Who" instrument. We would expect that a different pattern of behaviors in the two classes might well suggest a different set of standards; and differences between the students' perceptions of the extent of the teacher's approval of the various behaviors might confirm this idea. Table 19 presents the data on 16 behaviors from the Guess Who test.

The first set of columns shows the frequency with which the teacher is perceived as engaging in the various behaviors. Compared to the control class, in the experimental class the teacher is seen as less of a questioner (2, B to C), more attentive (5, B to C−), slightly more likely to exert himself for the class (6, D to C−), less likely to "talk out of turn" (16, C to D−), and less likely to get upset when unable to answer questions (17, C to D−). He is also seen as slightly more likely to blame and criticize the students (11, C to B−). Thus we get a curious picture of the teacher as a "better" group member who, at the same time, may be somewhat more punitive—possibly because he expects and demands more from the students and thus can be disappointed more readily.

The experimental students see themselves as paying better attention (5, C to D−), engaging in less disruptive behavior (12, C to E−), less likely to "talk out of turn" (16, C to D−), and more likely to keep going in the face of confusion (8, C to B−). They also suggest a slightly higher level of personal stress: they worry a little more about how well they are doing (14, C to B−), and they are a little more likely to be-

Table 19. Guess Who, Teacher No. 5

Behavior	Teacher Frequency (1—always, 5—never)				Student Frequency (1—always, 5—never)				Teacher Approval (1—really glad, 5—wish to prevent)			
	Means C	Ex.	Quintiles C	Ex.	Means C	Ex.	Quintiles C	Ex.	Means C	Ex.	Quintiles C	Ex.
1. Suggests new ideas when the group seems to be stuck	1.7	1.6	C	C	3.5	3.6	C	C	1.2	1.3	C	C
2. Continually asks questions in class	1.8	2.3	B	C	3.4	3.1	C	C	1.8	2.2	A	C−
3. Talks the most	1.6	1.6	B	B	3.5	3.6	E	E	3.7	3.2	C	B−
4. Usually comes up with answers	1.8	1.9	C	C	3.0	3.1	C	C	1.5	1.5	C	C
5. Does not pay attention in class	4.1	4.4	B	C−	3.4	3.8	C	D−	4.6	4.6	D	D
6. Bring in a lot of extra work on things relating to this class	3.2	2.9	D	C−	3.6	3.7	C	C	1.5	1.3	C	B−
7. Usually thinks his or her idea is best	2.7	2.9	D	D	3.8	3.9	C	C	3.0	3.4	C	B−
8. Gets things done when most of the class is confused	1.4	1.4	C	C	3.0	2.6	C	B−	1.8	1.3	C	B−
10. Offers compromises when there are several sides being taken on topic	1.8	1.6	C	C	3.4	3.3	C	C	2.1	1.6	C	B−
11. Usually criticizes and blames other peoples' actions or ideas	3.5	3.1	C	B−	4.0	4.3	C	C	3.8	4.0	C	C
12. Disrupts the work of the class by clowning and fooling around	4.0	4.2	C	C	3.5	4.4	C	E−	4.5	4.4	C	C
14. Worries about how well he is doing	2.9	3.0	C	C	2.0	1.7	C	B−	2.7	2.3	C	C
15. Sympathizes with others when this is needed most	2.3	2.5	C	C	3.0	2.9	C	C	2.5	2.2	C	B−
16. Usually talks out of turn	3.9	4.4	C	D−	3.7	4.0	C	D−	4.1	4.3	C	C
17. Seems to get upset when unable to answer questions	4.1	4.8	C	D−	3.9	3.3	D	C−	3.2	3.3	C	C
18. Presents ideas which influence the class	1.4	1.4	C	C	3.6	3.5	C	C	3.9	1.6	E	C−

141

come flustered by questions (17, D to C—). From the first four of these items we get further confirmation of the "strength," including both involvement and self-discipline, of the class; and the last two suggest that this strength is not necessarily a sign of greater security—that is, it may have other roots.

The students' perceptions of the behaviors that will be approved (rewarded) by the teacher are much the same in both classes, although the many slight differences do form a consistent pattern. The largest differences are both open to somewhat conflicting interpretations. The teacher gives far less approval to the student who "continually asks questions in class" (2, A to C—). We may suspect that in the dull control class such behavior would be a help, but in the active experimental class it would be an obstacle to discussion. It would also, perhaps, be a threat or challenge to the more self-centered teacher's dominance. Thus the teacher could disapprove because he is trying to protect either the class or himself.

With respect to students who "present ideas which influence the class," the teacher is far more approving in the experimental class (18, E to C—) although his approval is only average as compared to all the control classes. The teacher appears to allow (or yield) the students' "stronger" roles in the experimental class; and this view is supported by practically all the other shifts. He is slightly more approving of students who talk a lot (3, C to B—), of extra work done by students (6, C to B—), of students who are self-assured or possessive (7, C to B—), of students who offer compromises during occasions of conflict (10, C to B—) and of students who give sympathy to others "when it is needed most" (15, C to B—). In short, the teacher is seen as giving more approval to group-building and ego-assertive roles. We take this as further confirmation that it is to the teacher's interest to have a "strong" group, for in such a group he can "let himself go."

The sociometric data, Table 20, are at first glance rather curious; but we shall attempt to show that they fit the picture and give it more focus. The curious thing is that the students have been found to like the class very much; in addition, we have the teacher's own testimony that the experimental class is the best class he ever had during his six years of teaching. We may, therefore, be somewhat startled to discover that the teacher prefers the persons in his control class more than in his experimental class; and, although the experimental students prefer the teacher slightly more than the control students, the preference is still no more than the average of the 13 control classes. It is obvious that the teacher and the students are able to distinguish between interpersonal liking on the one hand and self-gratification or satisfaction on the other.

The sociometric picture of the control class presents no problem. The

Table 20. Sociometric Ratings, Teacher No. 5

Choice	Mean Ratings (1—Strong liking, 5—Strong rejection)		Ranking Among Thirteen Control Classes—Quintiles	
	Control	Experimental	Control	Experimental
1. Teacher: work with students	2.00	2.35	B	C
2. Teacher: chat with students	2.00	2.21	B	C
3. Students: work with students	2.63	2.44	B	A
4. Students: chat with students	2.63	2.38	B	A
5. Students: work with teacher	1.87	1.58	D	C
6. Students: chat with teacher	1.91	1.72	C	C

teacher gives the students more of a chance to participate and interact than they encounter in their other classes; hence all concerned have a better chance than usual to "become acquainted." The teacher, "under wraps" is no threat to the students, nor are they to him. Conversation is polite, demands are few, and there are no management problems to speak of. The class tends to be smaller than most (23 students, as compared to 29 in the experimental group). Since the class size is small, it seems reasonable that the teacher, who has strong interpersonal curiosity and interest, could get to know the children as persons and under nonthreatening conditions. Hence his B ratings of the students. At the same time, the smaller group with greater opportunity for interaction results in development of more relationships among the students; and the teacher tends to encourage rather than discourage these relationships. Hence the students' B ratings of each other, and their marked satisfaction with the class's interactive activities. Finally, the teacher's lack of involvement, the superficiality of the subject matter, the routineness of the teaching, all conspire to give the teacher an average rating by the students: he is indistinguishable from all the other technical-routine teachers they have. The fact that they rate him a little higher to chat with than to work with is consistent with their perception that the interpersonal and discussion components of their experience are somewhat more rewarding than the work components.

In the experimental group, the picture is very different. In a word, the teacher and students both find gratification in the provocative, interactive, emotionally charged discussion. But the teacher, with his lack of restraint, his sarcasm, his self-concern, his "personal" remarks is, as a person, threatening, and the students do not especially like him. In the same way, the students, with their active initiative, questioning, and greater emotional maturity provide the teacher with the foil he needs for meeting his own needs; but they also challenge and provoke him, as his defensive ratings (blaming and criticizing) suggest. Thus, although the teacher receives a large amount of gratification from the situation, he does not especially like the students as persons.

Both these interpretations are bolstered by the finding of very high interpersonal liking among the students. This liking is contributed to by all the participation-related factors present in the control class, but these factors are accentuated. There is more emotion shared, a condition which usually results in greater liking. But, in addition, there is a new factor: the emotional demand and threat of the teacher. Unlike a work threat which can be dealt with rationally, the emotional threat is capricious, unpredictable, and, coming from a person with the power of the teacher, practically impossible to deal with. Hence there is a "banding together" against the teacher, with the cohesion based on greater identification of the students with each other's plight. The students mean more to each other, are more necessary to each other, and rate each other higher. At the same time, they see the teacher somewhat as an enemy, and they tend to shut him out—and this in turn would increase his perception of their threat to him.

Thus we conclude that the teacher and class are necessary to each other in the sense that they increase each other's gratification, but they do not feel especial warmth or identification with each other. We think that such a situation is entitled to be labeled somewhat exploitative.

Our final conclusion is that the teachable class did make things easier for the teacher. He was primarily interested in obtaining a certain gratifying quality of interpersonal interaction. He was quite well able to recognize it when he had it—as shown in part by his ability to give us good models of the sort of student he wanted in class. His teaching changed the most of any of the 13 teachers because the particular nature of his students exerted the strongest influence on his teaching. Both students and teacher had a more gratifying experience together, and the educational results, while somewhat better (as shown by grades) were less important all around than the greater rewards of the interpersonal interaction.

Returning briefly to our questions about the general "equation" at the beginning of this chapter, we find ourselves in doubt about the answer to the first question, and quite confident about the answer to the second. The first question was "to what extent does knowledge of the way the teacher normally teaches (that is, in his control group) enable us to forecast the characteristics of his teachable students?"

In the case of teacher No. 5, the observer would note the large amount of student interaction, the subdued manner of the class, the impersonal manner of the teacher, the dominance of the assigned text assignments, and the lack of conceptual inquiry. In order to answer the question we have posed, the observer would have to be able to diagnose two things: (1) with respect to what part of his functioning might a change in class personnel help the teacher, and (2) if such help were available, would he be able to utilize it. These questions are both important. Thus teacher No. 5 might be helped to have students who can participate more adequately and also students who have strong conceptual interests. But it is likely that he could use the help of the former—as we have seen— but not of the latter. Thus we conclude that our first question cannot be safely answered merely by observing the teacher's style in the control class. We must also take into account his own purposes and needs, his "readinesses" and potentials. And this is exactly what we do when we ask him simply to point out the students who in his opinion "get a lot out of class." For this selection is realistic and operational: the teacher's goal is to have more interaction of the sort he has already had with certain students. The model is concrete, and the "readiness" has already developed (provided, of course, the teacher really does select students according to the criterion of "gets a lot out of class").

The second question asks about "the extent to which the modifications of teaching, resulting from giving the teacher a class of teachable students, are directed toward a higher quality, more-consistent style of teaching." In the case of teacher No. 5, we think our discussion thus far has given an affirmative and complete answer.

CHARACTERISTICS OF "TEACHABILITY" FOR TEACHER NO. 5

Having discovered that teacher No. 5 was facilitated by having teachable students, it is now appropriate to define more specifically what "teachability" means for teacher No. 5. We have already seen enough of the behavior of these students to make some inferences about them. They are clearly "strong" personalities, able to enter into give-and-take interactions with an adult, capable of dealing with a rather emotional person who also has power over them, and capable of being aroused to a high degree of enthusiasm in at least some situations involving their active participation. They are also students who can identify with and be attracted to other students. These, then, are characteristics they "must" have if our observations are to be believed. And if we find, on the basis of clinical assessment, that they do indeed have such characteristics, then our confidence in the preceding analysis will be considerably greater.

Teachability is defined by the differences between "successful" and "unsuccessful" students selected for us by the teacher. The differences are ascertained by analyzing responses on a 405-item assessment test. For the "model" children selected by the teacher, 145 responses were found to be characteristic of the "successful" or teachable group, and 139 other responses were characteristic of the unsuccessful group. If a student had all the earmarks of teachability, his score would be 145. By subtracting the number of "unsuccessful" responses from the number of "successful" responses, we arrive at a score for "net" teachability.

Teacher No. 5's classes were selected from the population of 158 students available to take the course. All of these students were tested, and their "teachability" scores computed. The experimental class was then composed of students having the highest scores, ranging from the 71st to 100th percentile for the population, with a mean score of 45.8. The control class was selected at random from the 129 students left after the experimental class had been taken out of the population. Its scores range from the 2nd to the 89th percentile, with a mean score of 18.1. The overlap between the distributions is accounted for by scheduling problems; three students who should have been in the teachable group had to be scheduled into the control group. This amount of overlap probably does not significantly vitiate the results. We assume, therefore, that the observed differences between experimental and control classes reflect differences in their "teachability." But teachability is contributed to by a very large number of items, and the teachability score of each student is made up of a different sampling from these items. A score of 35 for one student might be composed of altogether different items from those producing a score of 35 for another student.

In the analysis to follow, we shall work with the full range of items which discriminated between the students selected by teacher No. 5 as successful and as unsuccessful. The most interesting responses are "doubly discriminating;" that is, a response strongly accepted by the successful students would be strongly rejected by the unsuccessful students. Such items were contributed by five sections of the assessment battery, and will be designated as $S+$ and $U-$ items. In addition, some responses show significant agreement among the S (or U) students themselves but no agreement among the U and S students. These responses could be said to be characteristic of S or U but nondiscriminating between S and U. They are represented as $S+$ or $U-$ responses. Table 21 shows the number and percent of these three kinds of items contributed by the five most discriminating sections of the battery. Tables 22–25, in the appendix, list the items.

We shall take up the items, section by section, in the order of their

Table 21. Doubly Discriminating and Characteristic Items

Section of Test	Number of Items in Section	Number of Items			Percent		
		$S+U-$	$S+$	$U-$	$S+U-$	$S+$	$U-$
Words, Words, Words (Semantic differential)	70	8	9	9	11	13	13
Ways of Doing Things	48	23	9	6	48	19	13
Participation	50	13	14	7	26	28	14
Classroom Activities	40	12	11	6	30	28	15
Who Should Decide	24	6	3	3	25	13	13

listing in Table 21. Then we shall turn to the characteristic items in three sections of the test that contributed no double discriminating items.

1. Words, Words, Words. This is a word-association type test, and the responses of the student are fairly "deep." We shall consider this test first because it provides the evidence most susceptible to "dynamic" interpretation; that is, the items of this test are most likely to be "keynote" or thematic items.

The most striking difference between S and U students is the evaluation of "Myself." To the S students, *myself* is *safe* and *good*. To the U students, *myself* is *dangerous* and *bad*. In addition, the S students see *myself* as more *wet* than *dry*—that is, more flexible and adaptable; and the U students see *myself* as *strong* and *big*—that is, something to be concerned about or something that matters and is involved in many situations. Thus the first keynote theme is the positive feeling toward the self of worth, security, and adaptability of the S students as compared to the negative feelings of badness, danger (fearfulness), and concern of the U students.

Both groups associate activity with *being comfortable,* with the U group seeing it as more active and, in addition, as bad.

Being popular, for the U group, is highly potent—that is, they are deeply concerned about it; it is also flexible, it has no specific description. To the S group, *being popular* is hardly a matter of concern; it is conventional and inactive. In short, the U people worry about popularity whereas the S group takes it for granted.

Having power is a matter of some concern to both groups, with the S group being the more concerned. At the same time, the S group also sees this concept as fairly rigid and conventional, which suggests that although it is important it is not particularly threatening.

The reactions to *girl* and *boy* also distinguish between the groups.

The *S* students see *boy* as *loud*, that is, quite literally, noisy, and more figuratively, aggressive. *Girl* is *little, tight,* and *wet*—that is, not a matter of concern, conventional, but somewhat flexible. To the *U* students, *boy* is *soft, loose,* and *fat*—namely, secure, flexible, and passive; whereas *girl* is *new,* that is, very active. The *S* students appear to feel they have control over girls and identify aggressiveness with boys, whereas the *U* students see boys as passive and girls as endowed with activity and life.

When it comes to work, the *U* students tend to be impressed with its "goodness" whereas the *S* students note its active or vital character.

It appears from these responses that the *S* students, more than the *U* students, feel more personally worthy, adequate, and accept themselves. They consider striving for power to be important, although they are not anxious about it. They take popularity for granted, and their feelings about girls and boys represent healthy adjustments in our culture. And work is active and vital. The *U* students, more than *S* students, are anxious about popularity, have somewhat reversed feelings about the sexes, and admire work. Further, the *U* students see comfort as vital yet at the same time as somewhat bad; comfort is mixed with guilt.

2. Ways of Doing Things. The students rated the frequency of occurrence of the 48 "disadvantages" listed in this test. The significant discrimination is between "never" and "occasionally." On 23 items, the *S* students significantly chose "never" and the *U* students chose "occasionally." In the parlance of everyday life, the assertion that some interpersonal event or condition "never" occurs is a bit rash, and it bespeaks a good deal of self-confidence. On this assumption, the characteristic most significantly distinguishing *S* from *U* students is their self-confidence.

The ways the *U* students differ from *S* students provide a study in negative self-appraisal and interpersonal anxiety. The student sees himself as *less adequate* to interact with others, and he has *less energy available* at his command. Thus he more often encounters difficulty in talking to others, expressing feelings, learning from others, asking for help, and becoming interested (items 96, 99, 116, 125, 126, 130, 132 and 134). He displays lack of psychic vigor in more frequently becoming confused, distracted, forgetful, and inattentive (items 92, 93, 98, 103, 104, 105, 107, 110, 111, 114, 117, 121, 123, 127, 128). These difficulties occur in many situations but they tend to be manifested most frequently in the situations which most demand interaction, namely, with a small group of peers.

Of the nine items for which the *S* students significantly choose "never" and for which the *U* students have no agreement, four items depict greater ease and productivity with the teacher, two further develop the theme of personal adequacy, and three extend the picture of security in interpersonal activity.

Of the six items for which "never" is significantly rejected by U students and for which the S students show no significant agreement, three portray unproductive relationships with students and teacher, and three further the image of distractability.

3. Participation. The 50 items of this test are keyed to five kinds of situations and five qualities of interaction in these situations. Each of the 25 combinations of situation and interaction occur twice: once as a "telling" (initiating, dominating) behavior, and once as a "listening" (passive) behavior. Thirteen items are doubly discriminating; that is, the S students are significantly high and the U students significantly low.

Of these 13 items, 9 represent telling or initiating behavior calling for vigor and/or risk-taking. The four "listening" items all involve either threat to the self or anxiety about interpersonal relationships. More than the U students, the S students enjoy:

(a) Sitting by themselves: thinking and remembering (items 77 and 91).

(b) Awareness of feeling: reading about, talking about one's own feelings (items 57 and 53).

(c) Expressing affect: criticizing TV program, being active during lively discussion (items 81 and 80).

(d) Communication of ideas: hearing those of others, reporting on own readings, giving information (items 46, 78, and 67).

(e) Problem-solving, cooperative: telling and listening to ideas about problems common to their age group (items 86 and 73).

(f) Persuading, dominating: trying to interest another in one's hobby, (items 84 and 86).

There are 14 additional items on which the S students are significantly high whereas the U groups are either divided or indifferent. Five of these items portray dominance in interactive discussions; three involve mutuality or cooperation, three represent giving or receiving relatively "neutral" information; and the other three are concerned with expression of feeling.

Finally, there are seven items significantly rejected by the U students but showing indifference or divided reaction by the S students. Of these, five refer to expressing or hearing feelings (for example, criticizing or being criticized, intimacy).

4. Classroom Activities. The 40 items of this test describe more or less typical activities that go on in classrooms, and the students are asked to rate their *worthwhileness*. Presumably a worthwhile activity is one in which the student either finds personal self-realization or else accomplishes some task whose demands he considers legitimate. Twelve items doubly discriminate, with significant acceptance by the S students and rejection by the U students. More than U students, the S students consider worthwhile activities having the following qualities:

(a) Autonomous, self-directing work: research for term paper, preparing a report "on your own," studying for a test, beginning a homework assignment (items 15, 27, 33, and 37).

(b) Man-to-man relationship with teacher: discussing plans and progress (items 18 and 23).

(c) "Structuring" by teacher: explanation and demonstration of ideas, making expectations clear and explicit (items 28 and 39).

(d) Work-oriented interaction with other students: class "drill" on fundamentals, subgroup discussion, evaluation, and preparation of report (items 29, 25, 40 and 8).

Eleven further items are significantly accepted as worthwhile by the S students, whereas the U students are divided or indifferent to them. Of these, eight represent work-oriented interaction (discussion, demonstration, explanation, cooperative preparation) with other students. Two represent "independent" work, and one involves getting help from the teacher.

Of the six items significantly rejected by the U students but matters of indifference or division among the S students, four call for active work-oriented cooperation with other students (planning, organizing, studying, working); one requires listening to explanations made by other students; and one involves grading or evaluating one's own performance.

5. Who Should Decide? The 24 items of this test designate decisions that "somebody" has to make. The student tells who he thinks should make each.

Six of these items are doubly discriminating, in that the S students agree significantly on one response whereas the U students agree significantly on a different response.

The responses of the S students show that they expect:

(a) the *teacher* to lay down rules as to whether you are to work alone, whom you sit next to, control of discussion (items 2, 20 and 24).

(b) the *student* to judge and evaluate how much help to accept

from others, how "good" was the teaching, and when your skit is
ready to present to the class (items 3, 10, and 23).

The responses of the U students to the same six items show that they
expect:

(a) the "*crowd*" to decide behavioral standards such as whether
you should work alone (class), how much help you should accept
from others (committee), and control of discussion (class) (items 2,
3 and 24).

(b) the *student* to avoid risk-taking: the teacher evaluates teaching, not the student; and the student decides whom he will sit next
to (items 10 and 20).

(c) the *teacher* to "protect" the student by helping the student decide when his skit is ready to present to the class (item 23).

In three further items, the S students significantly agree and the
U students are divided: "evaluation of your contribution to the class
discussion" is to be by the teacher; "evaluation of your committee's
work" is to be by you plus the teacher, and the committee decides for
itself "how to discipline its members." By contrast to these active
judgmental activities, the items selected significantly by U students,
with the S students divided, continue with the theme of following the
crowd and evading responsibility for oneself; these items state that the
committee is to decide what conclusions should be reached, the class is
to judge student conduct, and the teacher is to help the student decide
when he should see a counselor.

6. Other Differences. Three sections of the test yielded no doubly
discriminating items. They do, however, display items on which there
is significant agreement by either the S or U students. And these agreements, while less useful for the clear-cut discrimination of S and U
students, do help present a complete picture.

The *Situations* test contains 50 items. Each item presents a stress
situation and two alternate ways to react. These alternatives are keyed
to work, fight, flight, dependency, and pairing (intimacy seeking). The
S students have the same response of work on only two items. "When
no one was sticking to the point," they "call for clarification of the
topic" rather than getting "bored with the whole thing." "When the
group agreed that it needed more information about how members
felt," they "described my feelings to the group" rather than "wasn't
sure I wanted to discuss my feelings."

By contrast, the U group shows agreement on 13 items. Of these agreements, five are on fight alternatives, six are on flight alternatives, and two are on pairing alternatives. Of the pairing items, one has a slightly hostile feeling, in that it identifies with a person who criticizes another, and the second offers warm encouragement to someone who is seen as needing "a lot of help."

Thus the *Situations* items further the picture of evasion and weakness, but add to it a quality of fight which can be called irritation, suspicion, resistance, and resentment. The fight is covert and inward; it might better be labeled rage.

The *Teacher Description* test presents paragraph descriptions of six teachers and asks the students to rank them in three ways: the teacher who seems most typical of all teachers, the teacher the student would be most comfortable with, and the teacher from whom the most could be learned.

For typicality, the *S* students give high ratings to the "subject matter expert," the "challenger" and the "traditional professional" types. The composite picture is that of a teacher who sets the structure of activities, provides a variety of materials and activities which he has perfected over the years, and stimulates the students to inquire for themselves. This appears to add up to a rather high opinion of the competence and experience of teachers in general. And the *S* students pick the traditional-professional as the one they would feel most comfortable with.

The *U* students have no agreement on the image of the typical teacher. They do agree on the matter of comfort: the most comfortable teacher is the "buddy-buddy" type who makes few demands and tries to be "one of the boys." The most uncomfortable is the "pupil-teacher planning" type, who demands that the students take on a great deal of responsibility for planning, organizing, and evaluating their work. The *U* students also agree in rejecting the "rules" type (authoritarian) as someone they can learn from.

In short, the *S* students are there to learn, see teachers as teachers, and are most comfortable with a skillful, decisive, and experienced teacher. The *U* students are not interested in achievement, select a teacher who makes few demands for work, and rejects the teacher who most clearly symbolizes the authority of adults.

The *values* test asks the students to rate 60 items as to their importance. The items are all rather abstract statements of values. The items are keyed to six general values or ways of life: social restraint and self control, adventure and initiation of change, withdrawal and self-sufficiency, altruism and receptivity, traditional middle-class norms, and sensual enjoyment.

The *S* groups agree, with extreme positivity, on 21 items taken from five of the six categories. The sixth category, sensual enjoyment, is marked positively, but not extremely so. The following comments pretty well sum up the 21 statements: The *S* students (1) appear more actively desirous of making a better world for themselves and others; (2) appear more concerned with the needs and welfare of others, and are willing to go out of their way to help them; (3) appear to value intimacy with others; and (4) appear to value self-sufficiency and independence, self-awareness, and mastery of their affectual desires.

The *U* students agree on low ratings of five items. They strongly reject two: "be at ease both physically and mentally without being too ambitious" and "enjoy good food and drink with a group of friends." Since they strongly reject what the rest of the analysis would lead us to think they would want, it seems reasonable to conclude that they feel guilty about these desires, and that the desires are strong and need to be put down decisively. The other three items are agreed upon with mild positivity (obviously negative compared to the *S* group), and look like a very lukewarm acceptance of aspirations they "should" value but have little hope of achieving: a well-organized and productive life, hard work and pioneering in some endeavor, and a life in harmony with nature and other men.

RESUMÉ

The Teachability Factor for Teacher No. 5

We collected and organized the above differences under the headings of Self, Emotion, Interpersonal Relations, Expectations of Teacher, and Work. The outstanding themes that emerged were:

1. *Self:*

> Sense of personal adequacy (confidence, risk-taking, autonomy, self-evaluation)
> > versus
> Sense of fear and threat (risk-avoidance, rejection of sensuousness, submissiveness to stereotypic goals)

2. *Emotion:*

> Emotional security and range (awareness, expressiveness)
> > versus
> Defensiveness (flight, rage, covertness, fear expression, fear of intimacy, fear of criticism)

3. *Interpersonal Relations:*

> Vigorous, interactive, mutuality (power, persuasion, dominance, communication, concern for others, cooperation)
> > versus
>
> Anxious, nonvigorous, other-directed (distraction, confusion, fear of listening, intimacy, fear to demand, follow crowd, anonymity, evade responsibility)

4. *Expectations of Teacher:*

> Strong, professional, useful (boundary-setter, helper, man-to-man, stimulator, self-confident)
> > versus
>
> Protective, undemanding (buddy-buddy, nonauthoritarian)

5. *Work:*

> Active, cooperative, self-directed (problem-solving, vital, purposive)
> > versus
>
> Avoidance (admiration, avoid responsibility for self, others, jobs)

THE FIT BETWEEN TEACHABILITY AND TEACHING

It seems unnecessary to labor the point further that the teacher obtained the results he wanted. We have seen the differences in his teaching of the experimental and control classes. We have imagined what sort of persons the teachable students must have been as judged by their behavior. After studying the data from the assessment test data, we found these impressions very strongly confirmed. In the instance of teacher No. 5, then, the demonstration that the teacher can be facilitated by giving him students of the sort he thinks he teaches best seems to be complete, thorough, and solid.

But what about the students? How well did this teacher fit their needs, interests, and capabilities? Does selecting students to facilitate the teacher automatically result in students having teachers who are good for them? Obviously the only way to test this theory is to repeat the experiment, letting the students (counselors, or others) choose the type of teacher to give to each student. Without repeating the experiment in this way, we can only reach a tentative and hesitant conclusion.

The first three basic themes seem to suggest that the students probably received as much as they gave. The teacher provided unusual opportunity for emotionalized, adventurous, interpersonal interaction, and all the data, both from the class and the assessment battery, suggest that the students should and could make good use of the opportunity.

The fourth and fifth themes, however, incite us to speculation. In the teachable class, teacher No. 5 does not seem quite to fill the bill for these students. He is far more personally oriented, and far less "professional" than the teachable students seem to be calling for. His activities have a rather low component of work, and afford very little opportunity for self-directed problem-solving. The teacher tends to give his own opinion or some quasi-moral precept as the answer to questions raised by students; there is very seldom any translation of a question into a problem to be solved by the student's own effort. It seems likely that this teacher probably failed to challenge and stimulate the students' capabilities and possible needs for self-directed work and inquiry.

Chapter Eight

PATTERNS: Four Additional Styles and Compatibilities

Teacher No. 13 · Teacher No. 8 · Teacher No. 7 · Teacher No. 14

The most distinctive feature of "teachability" grouping is its assumption, consistently applied, that every teacher is a special case. Students who are facilitative of one teacher may not be so for another; and facilitation may itself mean different things from one teacher to the next. Certainly the detailed case study of teacher No. 5 portrays a unique individual, and the effects of his teachable class were uniquely determined by the nature of his interaction with the students.

Since each case is unique, there is little that any one of them can establish beyond whether or not "teachability grouping" is beneficial (or not) in that case. There is no reason to expect that the plan would work equally well for all teachers. If they are unique individuals, then individuality could even extend to whether or not a change in the composition of the class would make a difference.

The case for or against "teachability grouping" can perhaps be best explored by observing what happened in the widest range of situations. Accordingly, we have selected the four teachers who differ most among themselves—their styles of teaching, the sort of classroom climate they typically produce, and our impressions of their purposes in teaching. We shall consider the same range of data that we utilized in our analysis of teacher No. 5, but we will demonstrate much less of the analytical procedure. The data are in the appendix of the technical research report; we will present the shortest account that clarifies what the teachers meant by teachability and the consequences resulting from their having teachable students.

TEACHER No. 13:

Classroom Operation

Of the thirteen teachers, number 13 is the most "academic-professional." The development of an understanding of algebra is the teacher's goal. His classes are strongly work-oriented and "intellectually" demanding. We get a clear picture of teacher No. 13 from this telegraphic summary of the perceptions of the observers.

Observers' Summary: The Style of Teacher No. 13

Re: Teaching Methods

The teacher uses modified lecture-discussion approach. Technique includes use of a problem (previously assigned or presently introduced) as a demonstration vehicle. Approaches problem through various means, pointing out advantages and disadvantages of each. Calls for questions from students with respect to his demonstration. Provides for student practice with problem either at board or at their seats. Board work normally involves having the student explain the steps that he took leading to problem solution.

Asks questions of students as a check to be sure that they understand and can explain principles and methods used in handling assigned problems. Seeks volunteers but will call on students who do not raise their hands. Allows time for students to think about the questions that he asks—works along with the student who is responding in effort to help the student in his thinking. Patient with "insightful mistakes." Doesn't rush through material. Makes his presentation in terms of what he thinks the student needs to know. Takes time to get feedback from students on points which are not clear to them. Normally does not go on to next point or problem until there are no further questions from students. Supplies answers only when there seems to be no student who can.

Sometimes teacher uses blackboard for a class "think-aloud session." Puts formula on board and raises questions with respect to it (why is this true, how do I arrive at this formula, etc.). Poses problem and acts as blackboard secretary as students suggest ways of dealing with it. Goes through equation with the class and points out need to see the significant steps and procedures. Places stress on understanding vocabulary of Algebra as well as the orderly steps of problem solution.

Teacher's statements normally fluctuate from technical, factual "givens" to professional relationship type. Sometimes gets above the heads of the students as he moves to abstract theoretical level. Tries to stimulate thinking and will phrase his questions so as to have students deliberate. Emotionality not a major part of teacher's approach. He is supportive and commends correct responses, work done well, etc. Shows displeasure with playful, non-work oriented behavior. Sometimes tends to be moralistic about the importance of the subject and the need to work hard at it.

Re: Expectations for Students

Essentially, the students are to be young apprentices in the field of mathematics. They are to follow the teacher who has been over the road many times before. The student is to let the teacher know when he has difficulty in following him over "the road."

Come to class prepared to work. Enter into discussion of problems set before the class. Try out and reason through the different approaches to handling various problems. Be somewhat curious. Raise questions when clarification or further explanation is needed. See the relationships among concepts and beyond specific problems to broader theoretical concerns. Understand and use the proper math vocabulary. Feel free to enter into controversy over points related to issue, topic, or problem, *but* have logical explanation for opinions expressed. Try to follow through in doing problems. Volunteer for problems for by doing them or attempting to do them you help others and help yourself.

The observation schedules demonstrate that most of the talking (88%) is done by the teacher, and most of it is addressed to the class as a whole. 96% of the content is ideational—straight algebra subject matter, and in 19% of his comments the teacher is dealing with relationships and principles. He is rated among the more "professional" teachers (quintile B), with 19% of his comments being directly responsive to the students' performances. The teacher is about average for subjective, personal statements, and none of his motivation seems to be based in self-concern. He is average in the expression of emotion, with, perhaps a tendency toward less interpersonal warmth and more facilitative humor. He sometimes acts impulsively and with "fight."

Participation of students, in spite of their limited opportunity to talk, is above average in most instances. More than average, they volunteer and ask questions, speak out answers, and participate in presenting the lesson. They also whisper among themselves more, and engage in more episodes of emotional "blow-off."

With the experimental class, the picture is the same in most respects. The teacher makes more statements about the activities of the class and about its problems of operation. He utilizes feedback from the students more extensively ("professional" statements, are up 50%). His "relationship" statements remain at the same level; it is the "technical-routine" category that decreases. The teacher's emotional expressions now include no "fight," and his other affects are unchanged.

There is a marked shift in teacher dominance. He now asks 50% more questions, and the students only ask one-third as many. The class is far more orderly, with only one-quarter as much whispering and other disturbances.

In short, the teacher appears to be driving harder with a more work-oriented class. It moves with a faster tempo, with more direction from the teacher, and with less nonwork and emotional behavior.

The impression of a higher level of work is strengthened by the post-meeting reaction data. In the experimental class, the "part of the class really working on the lesson" is up (C to B); the student's satisfaction with his own performance is similarly up; more lessons are felt to be more difficult, and yet understanding of what the class "was supposed to do" is greater (from E to C). The learning has more value (B to A), and personal frustration is drastically reduced (D to A).

The student opinion survey also adds to the picture of a work-oriented class: it has plans for "after high school" (B to A), has a teacher one would like to have next year also (B to A), and is more meaningful and worthwhile (B to A). At the same time its tempo is such that it deprives some students of the chance for practice they would like (A to C), and it is less interesting to talk about on the "outside" (B to C).

The experimental class appears to see the demands made by the teacher as coming more from the subject and less from the teacher. The frequency of all affective behaviors by the teacher is perceived less: less blaming and criticizing, sympathizing, talking out of turn, becoming upset, and "thinking his ideas are best." His ideas are seen as less influential, but he also seeks fewer compromises. In a sense, it appears that Algebra speaks through him. The frequency of student behaviors reflects to a lesser degree the same reduction of affect. The teacher's value system, established by what the students thinks he approves, is mostly the same in the two groups, with a little more tolerance of student ideas and less blaming and less sympathy in the experimental class. The classroom climate is more "objective," with performance more strongly holding the center of attention than feeling.

The interpersonal relations, as shown in the sociometrics, provide striking confirmation of the above impressions. The teacher strongly prefers his experimental students to his control students, both to work with (E to A) and to chat with (C to A). At the same time, the teacher's greater demands and greater impersonality are reflected in his lower personal attractiveness: the experimental students prefer him less than do the control students (B to C, both work with and chat with). The students in both classes choose each other at a higher level of preference than average—possibly because they have a strongly developed common bond: they are the elite of the eleventh graders. For "chat with," the preference is at the A level in both groups; for "work with," the level is B in the experimental group and A in the control. No confident explanation of this difference suggests itself; it may be that the greater work orientation includes a greater demand for individual effort and mastery, and possibly greater competetiveness and lesser attractiveness of socializing.

In summary, it appears that teacher No. 13 is most centrally concerned with teaching algebra as a "high-level academic course" and the experimental group realized this aim more fully than the control class.

The Teachability Factor

The mean teachability score, $S - U$, is 30.6 in the experimental group and 24.4 in the control group. Both groups, of 19 and 20 students, respectively, were drawn from a population of 76 students, and the percentile ranges of the experimental and control groups as measured against the population are 45–100 and 3–95, respectively. Thus there is considerable overlap between the two groups.

In the face of this overlap and of the similarity of the means in the two groups (even though the difference is statistically significant at $p = 01$), we may expect the teachability factor (obtained from the model children selected by the teacher) to call for more differences than were observed.

The brief analysis to follow is based on the complete data from the assessment batteries of the "model" students.

The clearest, most internally consistent distinctions between S and U students are with respect to values. The S students aspire to self-confidence, service to others, activity, fullness in living, a good society, high ideals, and thrift. The virtues are the traditional ones, centering around an active, productive, and socially constructive life. The S students reject most of the inward life of feelings—self-awareness, personal pleasure, concern with "inner thoughts," or with "deep issues" of their personal lives.

Thus we get the impression of students who wish to accept the social world both as it is and as a stage for their own active striving, and who wish to take themselves for granted as active agents in this world. They wish to avoid being "personal" or "emotional." Their idea is to help, not sympathize. In the classroom, the preferences of the S students are for an active, achievement-oriented class, in which the teacher plays a strong role in setting the stage, providing ideas, giving explanations, and evaluating one's progress. The preference seems to be for activity dominated by impersonal demands and making use of ideas, goals, and materials provided by the teacher. They prefer a teacher who will provide a firm structure and, within that structure, can interact spontaneously with them. They see the teacher as a consultant, and can accept his evaluations of them. They tend, in their emotionality, to be heavily dependent on the teacher's decisions about what ought to be done. The teacher is to set the stage for striving, to help them strive, and is to tell them how well they are doing. But he is not to dictate, crack down, nor operate as an authoritarian.

With respect to peers, we find the same preference for cooperation, activity, and work. They like to communicate with other students, hear their thoughts, get their advice about action. But they strongly draw the line against criticism, evaluation, expression of "negative" emotion, and communication or penetration of "private" feelings and ideas. They tend to reject "unstructured" interactive situations, probably seeing them both as unproductive and somewhat threatening. They like classwork only when its purpose is clear and the activities well defined.

With respect to emotional responses to stress, the S students tend to reject flight and concentrate on work; they recoil at hostility directed at them; and they tend to "pair" when other people get angry with each other.

The S students have more positive feelings about themselves, see work as more adventurous, probably strive for popularity, and their sexual associations conform more closely to the stereotype of "health"—than do the U students.

The U students, the ones seen by teacher No. 13 as "getting little out of class," are in many ways the mirror image of the S students. The U students reject the active, constructive, and social striving of the S students. The U students are much more interested in their own internal life of feeling and emotion. They enjoy criticizing, and evaluating each other; and hearing revelations of personal feelings. They reject the "planning" type of teacher, and they tend to get their behavioral standards from the class, rather than from the teacher or from within themselves.

The Fit between Teacher No. 13 and His Teachable Students

The fit appears to be good. Both the teacher and the students tend to seek the demands of the classroom in the given nature of algebra rather than in the personal wishes of human beings. Both tend to avoid emotion and to act impersonally. What the students expect from the teacher is also for the most part what he expects from himself. The teacher is willing to set the stage and provide the opportunities for striving, and he is delighted with the striving of the students.

At the instrumental level, both teacher and pupils can serve their purposes in the same way of life. At a somewhat deeper level of motivation, however, the teacher and students may have slightly different purposes. We get the impression that the teacher is most deeply involved in conceptual and cognitive matters, that is, logic, explanation, relationships, and information. On the other hand, the students seem mostly to be seeking active participation in interactive activities. The cognitive elements provide the basis for the structure of these activities and are certainly acceptable to the students on this basis, but they provide the occasion and authority for the game rather more than the purpose of the game. It seems that the teacher has developed a style of teaching which can accept and even encourage the students' active participation while channeling it into learning algebra as the teacher understands it.

The teacher was pleased with the teachable class. He felt that his goals were better accomplished, that the class required less of an explanation of principles, and that his class was more cooperative and more committed to learning algebra. It was, he said, the best class he ever had. Its mean IQ, incidentally, was 119.6 as compared to the control class' 119.5. The two ranges, respectively, were 105–159 and 106–160.

TEACHER No. 8:

Classroom Operation

Teacher No. 8 is especially interesting because for him "teachability grouping" was definitely not a success. It is possible that he got what he subconsciously wanted, but, judged by most of the usual criteria of sound classroom operation, his teachable class was inferior to his control class. The question is whether there are some teachers for whom teachability grouping does not work, or, that something went wrong in the process of composing the teachable group.

The summary statement of the team of observers, based on their anecdotal records, presents a rather clear picture of the operation of teacher No. 8.

Observers' Summary: The Style of Teacher No. 8

Re: Teaching Methods

Q-A discussion format in which teacher frequently gets involved in long, rambling discourses as he tries to make a point in the lesson. At times the teacher gives forth with a "sermonette" filled with moralistic platitudes that may or may not have anything to do with the lesson.

Presentation shifts between a tightly structured, technical approach and a highly disorganized, self-concerned approach. Thus the teacher's statements typically fall within levels of descriptive fact-giving and subjective impulsive reactions. The self-concern enters in most frequently when the teacher becomes personally threatened, defensive, self-depreciating and when he feels forced to justify his teaching approach or his personal worth.

Self-concern is made more obvious by the teacher's bid for acceptance by his students as a 'good guy,' a friendly, joking, good-natured fellow who 'understands' the student. In this, he confuses the role of 'counselor' with *his need* for gaining acceptance. Consequently, he makes excuses for student behaviors which admittedly are disturbing to him and others in the class. He tends to over-react in his comments of praise so that these sound like grateful acknowledgments and thanks for students "being with him" on a point. His attempts at being humorous often turn into personally vindictive, smart-alec wisecracks. Generally, humor in this class is nonfacilitative with students and teacher taking joking pot-shots at one another.

Fosters student participation in class discussions. However, the discussions frequently deteriorate to low-level opinionating, impulsive blurt-outs and superficial comments. The teacher's ambivalence about setting clearly defined limits triggers off situations in which the students take control of class away from him.

Displays much more enthusiasm and interest in the literature part of the course than in the grammar and English usage part. Teacher has broad background in the area of literature and likes to demonstrate this. He is somewhat of a pretentious intellectual striving to impress others with depth and breadth of his knowledge. He often gets into college-level materials and uses them as means to impress class members and observers.

Re: Teacher's Expectations for Students

Supposedly, students were to engage in class discussions, do assigned work, etc. Actually, and more precisely, their roles as students were never very clearly defined. Their expectations were vague since the teacher's goals were really hard to predict. They responded to the emotional cues and capricious whims of the teacher with wise-cracking, lack of attention, etc.

Re: Differences between Classes (special note)

Exp. class—girls more prone to go along with teacher and wait out the storm. Passive. Small group of boys took class control away from teacher early in first semester and running battle ensued for rest of year.

X and C boys more prone to engage in the harrassment of teacher—taking class away, dominating discussion, stalling and redirecting class, etc.

The quantitative data, although less colorful, generally tell the same story. Starting with the observations of student behavior, we find that the control class has the largest amount of whispering and emotional episodes (quintile A). The teacher and students both ask few questions (quintile D), and the students volunteer few answers (quintile D). The class is about average for other kinds of student participation. What the figures do not tell us is that there were two sorts of activity. The questions were mostly confined to that part of the time when the teacher was going over the assigned lesson; at such times the students "understood clearly what the class was supposed to do today" (quintile B). At other times, when the teacher had lost his authority, the class became more disorderly, and the teacher more subjective and self-concerned (quintile B). It was during these periods, too, that the teacher expressed a great deal of emotion (quintiles A or B in 11 of the 14 categories). In

general, then, the picture is one of oscillation between the tightly structured question and answer activities and the defensive, self-concerned,
emotional activity.

With the teachable class, the emotional, subjective, impulsive activities become far more dominant. It is as if the whole balance of the class
had been tipped completely to one side. There is almost twice as much
whispering, three times the number of "blow-offs," and more other type
disturbances by the students. The teacher attempts to keep control by
talking 90% of the time (instead of 74%). He "flights" into subject-
matter, but not into work. He presents more ideas, both subjective and
moral ("generalized adult"—0 to 14%). At the same time, the professional and relationship categories both drop from C to D. The emotional categories show the same picture of flight. He now exceeds
average in only five categories. And we see that what he is escaping
(flight) from is interpersonal interaction with the class.

It is possible that to the students the class seems rather pointless.
The control group, more than the experimental, had some sense of purpose associated with the routine lesson coverage. In the control group,
too, the teacher interacted more freely with the students; he could con-
verse back and forth with them, thus giving some guidance to the discussion. In neither class could the students get their guidance from
purposive work or from the demands that must be met consciously in
order to achieve some significant purpose. The experimental group was,
to all intents and purposes, a leaderless and anarchic group. There was
less guidance from lesson demands, and the teacher's flight into continual discursive talk took him out of personal contact with the class.

The students in the experimental class were especially frustrated,
and they reacted with emotional blow-offs: insolence, attacks, rudeness
—some 27 times in a single class period.

The Post-Meeting Reactions Sheets, Guess Who, and Student
Opinion Survey all present the same picture. The PMR's suggest
especially that the technical highly-structured parts of the lesson had
been quite satisfying to the control group but that the other aspects of
the class work were average to unsatisfactory. In the experimental
class, the satisfactions of the highly structured aspects are not present,
and, most emphatically, the value of learning has dropped (C to E)
and rapport with the teacher (helpful and understanding answers) is
down (C to D—).

The sociometric ratings show that the teacher had the same lack
of enthusiasm for both classes ("work with" is D and "chat with" is E
in both). The control class liked him (B and C) more than did the
experimental class (D and D), which is hardly surprising. What is inter-

esting, however, is that the students in both groups have very low preferences for each other (quintile E). This suggests that the classes were actually quite demoralized, and confirms the characterization of the situation as anarchic.

Thus we wind up with the picture of these tenth grade English classes: basically, the teacher does not represent firm authority. He has neither No. 5's authority in interpersonal relations, nor No. 13's authority as an instrument of algebra. He has, at times, the authority of a technician, enforcing certain routine procedures with respect to clearly structured "lessons." In the experimental class, even this authority is almost lacking, and neither the teacher nor the class has anything to fall back on. The teacher runs away from the problem and in doing so he loses contact with the class which reacts with frustration and, at times, violence.

The Teachability Factor

The mean teachability score and ranges are almost identical with those for teacher No. 13. The averages in experimental and control classes respectively are 36.9 and 30.6, with the ranges (compared to the total population of 127 students) being from the 65th to 100th and the 9th to 97th percentile. Thus again we have considerable overlap, and we would again expect the differences between the model S and U students to be considerably greater than the differences between the experimental and control classes. Nevertheless, it is the model children who show us what the teacher wanted. Whether he got what he actually wanted remains to be seen. Both classes contained 14 boys; the experimental had 15 girls; the control had 11.

The S students are obvious. They want serenity, peace, and self-confidence, with personal issues resolved. They want a group which is lively, spontaneous in its expression of feeling, uncritical and nonevaluative; a group in which they are "accepted" as persons quite apart from performance as judged by socially given criteria of merit. They want a teacher who does not play the role of expert and does not hand down rules; they want him to plan activities with the class, and they do not expect to be very comfortable with him. Their central interest is the class as a psychological milieu, and teacher, subject, and work are incidental. Their image of *girl* is a secure and good mother; *boy* is little, cute, and active; *myself* is important, passive, and slightly unsafe. Psychologically they recoil at hostility and seek warm interpersonal relationships. One decides for himself which demands he will meet, and the class or gang decides the standards of conduct in the class.

These students reject work and projects that demand accomplishment; they reject all criticism and advice from each other; and they reject their own sensual impulses. They appear to be primarily other-directed, happy in the anonymity of a conflict-free, personally communicative, group.

The *U* students agree on fewer items than do the *S* students. They seem to want more self-discipline in the control of feeling, and they want critical feedback from each other. They do not seek personal sympathy from each other and they reject self-exposure and value privacy. For the most part, the *U* students contrast with that part of the picture of the *S* students that has to do with undemanding personal acceptance and emotional spontaneity without danger of reprisal.

The Fit between Teacher No. 8 and His Teachable Students

The fact that neither *S* nor *U* students show any distinctive agreements one way or another about the teacher's role as leader or about individual autonomy is in itself suggestive that these are things to which the teacher is most indifferent. If we accept that a teacher would select students whose expectations of him reinforce the teacher's expectations of himself—then teacher No. 8 would appear to have no very clear image of himself as a teacher.

Our description of the *S* students selected by teacher No. 8 seems to us to also be an excellent description of teacher No. 8 himself. In other words, he appears to have selected the students he could best identify with on a personal level. It may be that in his class these are also the students who "get most out of class," since he provides them with very little challenge or raison d'être beyond interacting with him in a pleasant manner.

It seems reasonable to conclude that the teacher taught the sort of students he wanted. And, according to our observers, the experimental class was a better class than the control class (higher morale, better teaching) for the first month or so. But after that, it deteriorated rapidly —a classic example of a group which cannot sustain itself because a vital role is missing: the role of leader. And neither the teacher nor the students he has selected can develop this role.

TEACHER No. 7:

Classroom Operation

Teacher No. 7 is fairly representative of five of the 13 teachers. Her style is "routine-technical," which, in our category system means that she works out her lessons in advance and then the class follows them in order. All lessons are handled the same way, with the advance "preparation," the homework assignment, and the class coverage of the assigned work. The subject is Geometry, tenth grade, and we get the impression that the course is always the same, regardless of the students, the season, or the year. The observers' summary of their anecdotal records conveys the picture.

Observers' Summary: The Style of Teacher No. 7

Re: Teaching Methods

Q-A approach. Teacher normally asks a series of rapid fire questions on the lesson material and homework problems assigned to the students. The teacher sets a highly structured class work situation and takes the students through a swiftly paced lesson. Students move through assigned problems which are done either at their desks or at the blackboard. Usual procedure is to cover the previous day's homework problems and then to take on the next batch assigned.

The presentations which the teacher makes (explanations of steps involved in working a problem, etc.) are highly impersonal and very much concerned with the details of the subject. Her delivery is a soft monotone. She gives the impression of being highly work-oriented—strictly business. While she is working through a lesson with the students there is little or no affect in what she says and does. Yet, if the lesson she had planned is somewhat short of the class period, she is observed to be more relaxed with the students and to get some pleasure out of watching the social interaction which the students engage in after finishing the lesson.

Re: Expectations for Students

Students are expected to answer the teacher's questions. Do problems when called on. Be business-like and pay attention to the work at hand. Most of their responses are subdued in tone and sometimes inaudible. When the students enter into some kind of play or social conversation, the teacher is quick to reprimand and quick to get on with her business.

Re: Differences between Classes

Observers note little difference between the way the teacher handles the classes and little difference in the behavior of the students. The only observable difference in a higher incidence of lack of attention on the part of the control class and the occasional discipline problem in that same class.

The behavioral data support the observers' description. Teacher No. 7 gives more time than most to participation by the students (33%, quintile D). Her questions are somewhat more generally addressed to the class (quintile B), and she gives a great many more procedural instructions (19%, quintile A). She is higher than usual in the straight "descriptive" or informational loading of her comments (quintile B) and lower on pointing out relationships (8%, quintile D). Compare, for example, with the algebra teacher, No. 13, with 19% "relationship" and 19% "professional." Teacher No. 7 has about 7% professional comments. She is typical of the whole group of teachers in expressing very little affect of any kind.

The experimental class differs only slightly insofar as teacher behavior is concerned. There are fewer comments to control the group activity (B to C); fewer personal, that are subjective, and self-concerned; and a few more "professional" comments. Emotion remains at the same level, practically zero.

Observation Schedule No. 2, however, shows some differences. The teacher more than doubles the question-asking tempo, and all voluntary participation by the students is down—including both lesson-oriented and nonwork behaviors. As with the other math teacher, teacher No. 7 drives harder and faster; but unlike teacher No. 13 who also "goes deeper," teacher No. 7 remains on exactly the same level of penetration of the subject matter. Her experimental class is primarily more submissive and more resentful, whereas No. 13's class was more challenged and gained greater satisfaction.

The satisfaction measures show nearly all the changes going the same way: toward less satisfaction in the experimental class. They rate class meetings less satisfying, claim less understanding of what they were supposed to do, and perceive less of the class "really working" on the lesson. They are a little more satisfied with their own roles, however (D to C). They find the class less meaningful, the materials less interesting, the teacher and class less appealing, and contributing less to the development of interests and plans for "after high school."

The students see the teacher as a little more disruptive and tense; and a little less willing to exert herself for the group although she is also seen as more often coming up with useful ideas. The students see themselves as a little more likely to do things to help each other and the group. The students in both groups see the teacher as equally rewarding.

On the sociometrics, the teacher prefers both classes equally, more than most teachers prefer their classes (quintile A). The students in both classes have average preference for the teacher as someone to work with (quintile C) and less preference for her as someone to chat with (quintile D). The students in the control class have average preference (quintile C) for each other; the students in the experimental class prefer each other a little more to work with (quintile B). Thus although the students had somewhat less satisfaction with the classroom operations, they did not translate this into less satisfaction with the teacher.

The Teachability Factor

The mean teachability scores are 46.7 and 37.1 in the experimental and control groups respectively. The ranges, compared to the population of 114 from whom the classes were chosen, are from the 59th to the 100th percentile and the 2nd to 97th percentile respectively. Thus, once more, we have considerable overlap, and the expectation that the differences between the model groups of S and U students should be greater than between the two classes.

In view of the impression that the students in the experimental class must have been considerably more submissive than those in the control group to this subject-oriented teacher, it is interesting that the control class contained 18 boys and 11 girls, whereas the experimental class contained 8 boys and 19 girls. The teachability factor is clearly more typical of girls. (As a matter of fact, *all* the students in the experimental classes of teachers No. 7 and No. 2 would have been girls had we considered only the test scores. But administrators have their rights, too.)

Let us now consider the nature of the teachability factor. The S students are self-confident and positive in their outlook, as shown by their very large number and range of highly positive choices. They accept comfort and popularity as desirable and legitimate, but evaluate *having power* as bad. *Girl* is good and vital; *boy* is loose, dangerous, strong, loud, and big; *myself* is vital, secure, but rather weak. These girls *are* girls.

They prefer a mutual (rather than dominant or submissive) relationship to other students, and they would like to tell and hear opinions and personal feelings. They reject direct criticism of "personality," but enjoy evaluation of behavior and ideas. They respond with work to practically all emotion—trying to remedy the situation rather than being provoked.

They value activity, adequacy, and trustworthiness. They prefer classroom activities very much like those the teacher provided: note taking during lectures, practical exercise assignments, listen to explanations by teacher . . . , have teacher lead a discussion in which principles are explained, begin homework assignments, explain a homework problem to the class, get individual help and instruction from the teacher while doing class work, grade or evaluate their own performance, discuss class material.

They see a "challenging" teacher as the one from whom they can learn the most. The "planning" and "challenging" teachers are most typical; and the "planning" and "traditional-professional" are most comfortable. They tend to reject the "rule giver" or authoritarian teacher as uncomfortable, and they have no particular feelings about the "buddy-buddy" type teacher. In short, they prefer a teacher who is work-oriented, who will provide a firm structure for activities, and who can stimulate them with direct demands. They would like a cooperative relationship to him, and they do not seek a warm personal relationship.

These students expect to work hard under the supervision of adults, they enjoy interactive communication with each other, they are constructive and work-oriented in stress situations, and they have little wish to dominate others.

The Fit between Teacher No. 7 and Her Teachable Students

The fit seems good, and the questions one might raise have to do, not with what happened in class, but with what other things might have been valuable to the students. As for what happened, the students clearly had a strongly work-oriented teacher who kept her distance psychologically, who provided a continual barrage of stimulation in the form of specific demands, who did a good deal of explaining, and who, while not a "planner," nevertheless discussed in detail what the activities would be and how they were to be carried out.

The questions we might raise stem from the impression that the fare offered the students was rather "thin," subdued, and colorless. These are students who tend to be active in work and interactive with each other. For the most part the teacher suppressed interpersonal interaction except when there was time left over after the lesson, and at this time she allowed the students to visit and talk quietly among themselves. The teacher had no objection at all to visiting under such conditions, and it therefore seems reasonable to wonder whether a way could not be found to allow more of the work to be motivated and vitalized by utilizing more of the interactive potentials and interests of the class. To this teacher, having work-oriented students merely meant the opportunity to step up the pace, and to become even more dominant over the class; to another teacher, such a class might be capable of accepting a good deal more responsibility for planning and thinking about its own progress and logically required activities—consequently with greater involvement, motivation, and satisfaction.

TEACHER No. 14:

Classroom Operation

Teacher No. 14, along with No. 6, displays yet another pattern. It is a pattern marked by flexibility and variety, by the day-to-day development of the course through diagnosis of the responses of the students to the work. The course is American Literature, eleventh grade level. The observers' summary of the anecdotal material gives us a beginning impression:

Observers' Summary: The Style of Teacher No. 14

Re: Teaching Methods

Makes use of several different kinds of activities including student-led discussions, individual research projects, play reading and acting, writing skills, lab sessions, etc.

Attempts to develop new interests and critical taste in reading outstanding literature—encourages watching of quality TV shows, movies, plays. Has personal enthusiasm for literature and drama which he tries to communicate to students. At times, he plays the role of literary critic . . . giving rather routine reviews of some literary works.

Spends much time in giving instructions and announcements to do with future assignments. Goes into elaborate detail on this matter.

Strives to be a friendly, good natured fellow while at the same time serving as expert consultant and counsellor. Can be somewhat vindictive when crossed. Sometimes insinuates emotionally charged or seductive statements into class discussion, presumably to get reaction from students; some of his comments reflect and enhance his self-esteem.

When dealing with subject content the teacher's statements range from thought-provoking, inquiry-oriented sort to factual coverage of technical details. His presentations are often much more full than necessary to make his point—resulting in loss of thrust and restlessness among students. When leading class himself he controls things by sheer speed and energy of his detailed presentation and instruction.

Standards of conduct in class tend to be liberal in that students are free to move about, talk with one another during "lab" writing or buzz periods. When noise level or disorder is high, the teacher calls this to the attention of the class, often with little effect. During individual work periods teacher walks around seeking to be useful to students.

Frequently responds to penetrating questions by bringing discussion back to more factual considerations.

Re: Expectations for Students

Work creatively on task (individual projects, etc.) to which they are personally committed.

Engage in class discussions—try to extend beyond factual material.

Student-leaders expected to prepare materials to stimulate discussion and point up important issues.

To be independent workers—assume responsibility for doing things on their own.

To be audience for teacher's commentary and fantasy.

From the behavior ratings, it appears that this teacher searches for meanings more than most. "Relationship" and "professional" are in the A quintile. He directs attention to explanations, themes, and basic characterizations in the literature. He tends to address his comments to particular students (quintile B) and expresses a great deal of encouragement and support to them ("pairing, person," quintile A).

Given the teachable class, his behavior changes in many ways. The students are given twice as much time to talk; the teacher's comments about procedures, group progress, and personal characteristics of the students drop out almost completely, with a corresponding increase in comments related to subject matter. He offers seven times as many personal opinions, reveals himself much more (quintile C to A) in self-concerned statements, and halves the number of moralistic "generalized adult" statements. He expresses a great deal more warmth to the group and there is a small increase in "pairing" with individuals.

The observations thus show us a generally professionally oriented teacher, with increased time spent on subject matter, many more expressions of personal opinion by the teacher, and somewhat more warmth expressed by the teacher to the group.

The student behaviors are quite interesting: the only difference worth noting from Observation Schedule No. 2 is that the experimental class is more orderly (except for whispering, which remains at the same relatively high level (quintile B). The number of questions and comments by the students is about the same, as is the number of questions asked by the teacher. There is no evidence of a change of pace or of increased demands.

Most of the differences in student satisfaction with meetings favor the experimental class, which is higher with respect to the general value of meetings, less frustration, helpful responses by teacher, part of the class seen as work-oriented, and satisfaction with own role. As compared to other classes the students have, the control group rates their class lower than do all other control groups: the student opinion survey shows eight E quintile ratings and three D quintile ratings. The experimental class is higher by one quintile on all but five points: meaningfulness of class (E), wish to work with same students next year (D), further plans after leaving high school (D), development of new interests (E), and enjoyment of activities (E).

The Guess Who shows the teacher nearly average in most of the categories in the control class. In the experimental class, he is seen as less possessive, more critical of students, more worried about his own behavior, less likely to get upset by questions, and less influential with his ideas. The most marked change the students see in themselves is the frequency of worrying about how well they are doing (D to B). The other five changes are small, but add to a lesser perception of responsible, group-oriented behavior. The approval of the teacher is perceived mostly in the same way in both groups. The experimental class shows more approval for concern as to how well one is doing (E to C) and they see the teacher as slightly more permissive in regard to sympathetic and inattentive remarks. What comes through most clearly in the perceptions of the students is the teacher's own greater self-concern, which is reflected in similar concern of the students.

The sociometrics show the teacher preferring both classes alike (quintile B). The students in the control class prefer the teacher at the E quintile level; those in the experimental prefer him at the D quintile level. The students prefer each other a little more for work with in the control group—quintile A; and the same for chat with in both groups —quintile B.

In summary, teacher No. 14 becomes more subject-oriented, freer with opinions, warmer, and more self-concerned in the experimental class. The students respond to him with more satisfaction in those dimensions which are close to the class and its interactive processes.

The Teachability Factor

The mean teachability scores are 38.7 and 26.6 in the experimental and control groups respectively. The ranges, compared to the population of 224 students from whom the classes were chosen, are from the 75th to 100th percentile and from the 6th to 96th percentile. In both classes there were 19 girls; in addition the control class contained 7 boys and the experimental had 9.

The S students regard *myself* as *secure, active,* and *potent. Girl* is *good, boy* is *good, active,* and *potent. Being comfortable* is *good, secure,* and *potent; work* is *potent* and *passive.* It appears that all these concepts are *potent,* that is, matters of importance; and for the most part they are accepted as positive. This same lack of constriction is found in the emotional responses. Unlike teacher No. 7's S students, whom these students resemble in many ways, teacher 14's S students agree on a wide range of spontaneous behaviors; they respond to flight and annoyance with work, but depending on the situation, they also can hit back, express warmth, and be grateful for someone on whom to be dependent. Their values also reflect a wider range of "living;" they wish to be conscientious members of society while being self-realizing, adventurous, and productive. A great range of aspirations seems important to them.

In the classroom, these students are quite positive in their liking for a wide range of activities. They select 7 that are clearly teacher-dominated, 6 that involve cooperative work with other students, and 4 that require working more or less autonomously on one's own. With other students, they enjoy expressing feelings and advice, hearing what the other fellow has to say, evaluating process problems in their groups. The only rejected situations are those in which another student is recounting some event in which the listener did not share (namely, a football game, last year's committee); they also reject "making a spur-of-the-moment speech about himself to the class" and we can see several hypotheses that would explain this rejection.

With regard to the teacher, they seem to prefer an expert who interacts with them; the "subject-expert," "pupil-teacher planner," and "challenging" teacher is nominated for "learn most from," and the "subject expert" and "teacher-pupil planner" types are people they would be "most comfortable with." The fact that they choose the same types for comfort and learning suggests that learning is part of their way of life, not just something imposed on it. (The average correlation between "learn from" and "comfortable with" choices was .30 in the factor analyzed population of 216 students.) Of the 10 decisions agreed to by the S students, 6 are to be made by "you plus the teacher," 2 by a committee, 1 by the teacher, and 1 by the class. It appears that these students tend to prefer cooperation rather than independence when it comes to situations in which they are in fact interdependent with an adult.

The Fit between Teacher No. 14 and His Teachable Students

The S and U items for teacher No. 14 have been analyzed very intensively to see which of his needs might best be met by his teachable students. The research team formulated the conclusions:

1. To be needed by his students. That is, he needs to have his students rely on him and to view him particularly as a "guide" and "wise counsellor" and not as the strict disciplinarian. He needs to be accepted as a *good* person, one whom the students can trust and on whose judgment they can depend;

2. To have feedback from his students. That is, he needs expressive students who will be responsive to him and from whom he can get further stimulation. Thus, he needs to have active participation and the reassurance that his students are "with" him;

3. To be able to demonstrate his capacity and knowledge. The students may serve as audience in this respect or as participants in a discussion on a topic of particular interest to the teacher;

4. To have students who are cooperative, responsible and reasonably self-controlled. With such students support and acceptance is more readily possible for him so that "disciplinary measures" would not have to be used. The teacher,

thereby, can reinforce the image of the "good person" rather than the image of the "punishing person";

5. To avoid the free-wheeling, independent unburdened student as well as the hostile, unwilling, negative student. He needs students who come toward him rather than those who do not need him or who turn against him.

The agreement between these points, the teachability factor as already presented and the observations of the teacher, seems clear enough to require no further comment.

But it is one thing for the students to be able to meet the teacher's needs and another, perhaps, for the teacher to be able to meet the student's needs. Obviously we do not mean to suggest that the teacher should meet all the students' needs, but those needs that most directly influence the educative outcome of classroom experience ought, at least, to be identified and considered.

From this point of view, there does appear to be a conflict of interest between the teacher and students: the students appear to be seeking a cooperative relationship in work with the teacher, whereas the teacher appears more concerned with establishing his role of counselor and "wise man." That is, the teacher has no hesitation about interacting with the students, but the interaction is one of their personalities, not their roles as sudents engaged in work activities. This counseling relationship and accompanying warmth was indeed responded to with greater satisfaction by the students, but it nevertheless very probably failed to meet (or stimulate) their more central needs and capabilities (at least in the classroom) for active, work-oriented, shared, purposive action.

Chapter Nine

CHANGE: One Classroom's Dynamics of Mutual Accommodation

In the Beginning · At the End · Summary of Changes

The five case studies presented in Chapters 7 and 8 give us some of the flavor of the "fit" between teachers and the students chosen for them. Among our 13 teachers, 12 were facilitated and one very definitely was not, and the teacher in this latter case seems to have given, as his model of "teachable" students, individuals he could identify with rather than individuals he had observed to perform effectively in class. (There is, in fact, reason to suspect that he was relatively blind to effectiveness of performance and substituted for this the strength of his private likes and dislikes.) We think it fair to say that the teachers who used effectiveness of performance for their criterion of "getting a lot out of class" did indeed have facilitative experimental classes.

But what happens during the school year? Does the initial advantage continue? Is the initial relationship maintained intact during the year or does it change as a result of shared experience? Is there some image of a mature, "good," or more educable group toward which the experimental group, more than the control group, will tend? Or will the values and attitudes (etc.) of the two classes become more similar because of the strong influence of the teacher over both? And what sort of "growth" happens to the teacher? If he achieves a higher development of his "style" will it show up in changes of his own values and attitudes?

Since we had administered the assessment battery to the classes and teachers both at the beginning and end of the school year, we had in hand the data required to describe some changes that may have occurred. While the principal investigator was away during the first half of 1961, four members of the research team undertook factor analyses of the beginning and end data. They had considerable help from a statistical expert, Alan Herzog; and the chairman of the department provided the additional financing needed to support the computer.

In addition to the questions about what occurred in the "fit" between teacher No. 14 and his classes, the researchers were interested in the utility of factor analysis as an analytical tool. What the analysis does is to summarize that part of the data which represents what several persons or several items have in common. Thus if half a dozen students all mark the same twenty responses, we can say that those particular students, however else they may differ, have in common this pattern of responses. If the class contains 30 students, and the assessment battery contains over 200 items, and the only community that can be found is that of the six students on 20 items, then obviously most of the data must portray highly individual or unique patterns rather than common patterns, and any generalization that can be offered leaves most of the data unaccounted for. The factor analyses through a series of trial and errors identify such communality as the computer can find. In the case of teacher No. 14, the computer found six clusterings of items and students in the beginning data and five in the final data. Among them, the six "factors" at the beginning collect only 28.9% of the relationships between students and items into communalities; and the final factors in similar fashion account for only 25.5% of the "variance." The generalizations that can be reached thus are with reference to only about 30% of the total assessment information, leaving 70% of the data unaccounted for and attributed to unique individual differences. If the factors had accounted for 100% of the data, then they would give a complete picture, but on the basis of 30%, a great deal is left unexplained. If all we had to go on was the partial picture presented by the factors, we would not have any idea how significant the picture was: that is, whether it represented some highly superficial set of manners imposed on the class or it really portrayed very basic dynamics which the other information elaborated but did not extend. But since we have already presented a separate picture of teacher No. 14, we have something against which to compare the factor picture, and we find that the two pictures together give us considerably more understanding than either one by itself.

The plan of this report will be to present first the factors on which the experimental class is significantly high or low as compared to the control class and on which the teacher similarly is significantly high or low. These factors will tell us what teachable students have in common with—and in opposition to—the teacher. Then we shall consider the factors on which the experimental class *or* the teacher (but not both) are significantly high or low; and these factors may suggest the sort of influence the teacher and the class might potentially have on each other. We shall go through both the beginning and final factors in this fashion, and will cite other evidence from time to time to illuminate the discussion. Finally, we shall compare the results from the beginning and final tests, and try to answer our questions about changes—at least with respect to the case of teacher No. 14. Tables 26 to 37 in Appendix L show how many items from each section of the assessment battery are included in each factor.

The factors to be considered are:

	Pretest factors	Posttest factors
1. Teacher and E class both high	I	I'
2. Teacher and E class both low	III	V'
3. Teacher high, E class low	IV	—
4. Teacher low, E class not significant	II	
5. Teacher high, E class not significant		IV'
6. E Class high, teacher not significant		II', III'
7. Neither teacher nor E class significant	V, VI	

IN THE BEGINNING

Factor I of the pretest battery is significantly high for both the teacher and the experimental class. It portrays cooperative work-social interaction. It is composed of variables with highly positive loadings indicating an optimistic, confident approach to school work. Students high in this factor would be characterized by social skills, relaxed confidence in their ability to achieve goals and self-assurance in their ability to compete successfully for the rewards of life. All of this might be summed up as high ego strength.

Among the details are an active imaginative concern for getting things done. A variety of work situations are perceived positively, especially those which allow opportunity for individual initiative and self expression.

There is a consistent preference for engaging in cooperative group activities in a variety of participant roles, both of leader and follower.

There is a positive and constructive attitude toward work and emotionality, and when confronted with stress from task demands or from emotionally charged situations, performance would tend to be adaptive rather than maladaptive.

There is outgoing concern for the welfare and interests of others— a tendency to "accept" persons and to want to get along well with others.

Finally, we see a respectful, somewhat formal attitude toward teachers, with the student seeking to establish a relationship based on work. Teachers are viewed as friendly and cooperative, but not to be relied on for intimate personal-social gratifications.

This socially constructive interaction in connection with tasks has its limits, however, and Factor III provides a very clear picture of things the teacher and his experimental class tend to avoid.

They avoid curiosity about personal, private feelings and motives of others. They do not seek intimacy with others, nor the sort of "groupness" which invites expression of emotional impulses. They avoid interpersonal involvements of the sort that are characteristic of nonwork oriented persons and which originate in self-centered concern over oneself. The good life for the class and teacher is one of self restraint and minimal pleasure seeking.

The first two factors, common to both teacher and class, present a strong picture of cooperative, interactive, work-oriented activity together with avoidance of concern over personalities, either of other persons or of oneself. But Factor IV brings in a note of conflict, for the teacher rates high on it whereas his experimental class rates low or rejects it. The rejection by the class is consistent with the first two factors and adds little to the picture. But it is quite informative about the teacher, for it suggests some of the motivation that may lie behind his active encouragement of rather "free" participation by the students.

Factor IV, then, connotes rebellion against authority and rejection of work structures imposed from "above." Power is evaluated negatively and is perceived as threatening. Close association with the boss in work is seen as unrewarding and uncomfortable. There is rejection of routine work and avoidance of personal responsibility and commitment to work. There are negative and/or neutral attitudes toward all the types of personal values represented in our questionnaire—for example, social restraint and self-control; adventure and initiation of change; withdrawal and self-sufficiency; receptivity and altruism; sensual enjoyment and life of pleasure.

This factor, and the teacher's high score on it corresponds with our observations of the teacher: he tends to place himself in the role of adviser rather than work superintendent, and sets up activities and projects in which he is at least as much a consultant as a director. The lack of a clearly formulated set of personal values adds to the impression of a person who derives stimulation and direction from other people—for example, a counselor who concerns himself primarily with the problems of his clients.

The students, on the other hand, are significantly low on this factor. They are unrebellious, will accept routine work, and are perfectly happy with demands by authorities. We suspect that there may be a struggle between teacher and class over the problem of his right to "structure" activities for the class—with the teacher being somewhat reluctant to do so.

Factor II adds further nuances to the teacher's attitudes toward authority, but the class is indifferent to it. The teacher rejects this factor; to us this means that he rejects impulsive hostility and self-centeredness in favor of acceptance of warm, supportive relationships to others. Any demand imposed by virtue of authority or power is rebelled against. On the other hand, he wishes to trust the persons in authoritative positions, not as demanders, but as protectors—as persons willing to relieve one of the discomforts of self-assessment. In short, it is acceptable to submit to a person in authority but not to impersonal, authoritatively given demands. Here we seem to see the "counselor" image being projected loud and clear.

Factors V and VI are not significant for the teacher or the experimental class. They however, exist in the combined population of control and experimental classes. Although they do not distinguish between the two classes, they do represent sets of attitudes (etc.) that exist, and with whose variability the teacher must contend.

Factor V is composed principally of variables that present a picture of a personal quest for autonomy. There is a high value placed on an active, productive life of pleasure and adventure coupled with an aversion toward restricted freedom imposed through the discipline and control of others. It is as if the desire for personal freedom and independence had resulted in an overreaction against external authority. Work is not perceived as worthwhile or meaningful in itself. It is acceptable when incorporated in interaction with others, but when pursued alone it becomes threatening.

Factor VI is an all-girl factor, and it documents some confusion. Its salient characteristics appear to be: (1) no clear-cut commitment to life goals is present; (2) work is perceived suspiciously and given a higher preference in esteem than it is in pratice; (3) high concern for peer relationships in which expressed aggression toward peers is coupled with professed concern for participating in such interaction; (4) security and risk taking are viewed positively, and both discipline and freedom are desired.

There is a revealed tendency to reject work that demands self confidence or patience with routines; desire for attainment of an easy life of self gratification, conflicting with a need for an active adventuresome life of self denial; positive perception of comfort and power; anxiety when in personal contact with a teacher (preference for teachers who stand aloof and maintain social distance); and a tendency to be aggressive in peer relationships which are, nevertheless, viewed in active, stimulating, and desirable terms.

AT THE END

Factor I' conveys a clear picture of creeping socialization. Both teacher and experimental class rate significantly high.

This factor is characterized by passive acceptance of and conformity to social norms. The normative pattern has been so internalized that rebellious tendencies are apparently nonexistent. Persons rating high on this factor would avoid *any* expressive-impulsive behavior. They would be industrious but work would be done more out of concern for achieving goals set by others than out of consideration for personal goals.

In more detail, there is a consistent acceptance of the normative values of living a productive, useful, and cooperative life guided through self-control and social restraints; emphasis is on discipline and structure rather than on permissiveness and freedom. There is avoidance of any display of emotionality. One holds oneself in check. Expressions of fight and flight are avoided. Sensual enjoyment, adventure, and risk-taking are strongly rejected. The tendency is to be reflective, not impulsive.

There is a sense of being industrious and productive, and an attitude of acceptance of work. The orientation, however, is to work at labor which one is supposed to do rather than as a stimulating activity to be viewed enthusiastically and engaged in creatively. Finally, there is a tendency to define social values in conventional and stereotypic terms.

This factor suggests the development of rather traditional group norms. The "good group member" has developed, with muted emotionality, and he has internalized the social controls through which the group maintains itself as a social order. But the reduction of emotion and the emphasis on the social order has now changed the status of work—from an end to be sought through cooperation to a means of maintaining the social order.

Factor V' shows what the teacher and experimental class both reject: they reject negative attitudes towards peers, teacher, and school work; uncooperativeness, complaining, or resentment of interpersonal relationships; resistance to the authority of the teacher; feeling that the teacher does not help enough; and fight or flight, rather than constructive action, as ways to deal with stress.

Factor V' has much the same flavor as the opposite of Factor I'. It is primarily a negative way of defining a high solidarity group. Factor I' portrays the teacher-sanctioned social controls that developed, whereas Factor V' shows some of the psychological conditions of "climate" that are rejected. Together they show a good deal of "group growth," not all of it necessarily facilitative of educational endeavors.

Factor IV', on which the teacher is significantly high and the class indifferent, may be the result of influences of the group on the teacher. Persons high on this factor tend to be more active than passive, but seem unwilling or unable to take initiative or assume personal responsibility. They seek support from and want to be able to fit into their peer group. The relationship, however, is more that of getting support *from* rather than of actively contributing *to* the group. There is rejection of teacher control and of tasks which are imposed or legitimized by authority of the teacher. There is reflected both the desire to be an active and responsible individual and feelings of being uncertain, uneasy, and cautious. Finally, there is an unformulated personal value orientation. Every life style presented in the battery is rejected or viewed neutrally. The most nearly accepted values depict a highly energetic, forceful mastery of nature. This is coupled with rejection of a comfortable, pleasure-filled life, a conventional-conformistic life, and a receptive-uncomplaining life.

Here we seem to find the teacher's ambivalence between teaching and counseling reflected at the more personal level of the group member. In the developed social groups, which both classes had become after eight months, the teacher finds a supportive milieu; and, as often happens under such conditions, senses the possibilities of greater autonomy and strength. On the other hand, if he follows up these possibilities, he may find himself in a dominant and authoritative position, and this he rejects. Hence he appears somewhat trapped. It is quite possible that the problem is augmented by his identification with students who are facing the same problems in their own development.

We shall now consider Factors II' and III'. On both of these the experimental class is high, whereas the teacher is indifferent. The central theme of Factor II' is a need for structure so strong that it permeates virtually all work and interpersonal situations. Both teacher and school tasks are viewed in positive terms. There is desire for self-sufficiency and for accomplishment. Persons high on the factor would tend to be serious in their work efforts. They would tend to be active, dominant, and task-centered when working with classmates. Interaction with peers would be chiefly in work activities not social activities. Self-sufficiency and autonomy are valued. Work commitment is mingled with aspiration to attain personal strength and to cope with life's exigencies.

Factor III' is composed largely of items which reflect strong characteristics of avoidance and self protection. Tendencies are: to be socially distant and aloof in personal relationships, and this is combined with an unwillingness to make personal sacrifices for the benefit of others; to be critical of social "small talk," indicating some degree of impatience with social amenities; to have a favorable, though possibly unrealistic self image, protected by avoidance of self-criticism; to be unwilling to reveal or share feelings with others or to relax and have fun; to avoid taking initiative and/or assuming responsibility; to be threatened by work especially when it is done under the authority and supervision of the teacher; and to avoid personal contacts with the teacher.

These two factors carry on with the themes which represent final communalities between teacher and class (Factors I' and V'). We now see that at least part of the experimental class went somewhat further than the rest of the class and the teacher. In Factor I' we considered the possibility that work had shifted from an end in its own right to a means by which the new group solidarity and standards could be maintained. Now we see another purpose of work—for another part of the class—as defense against emotional interaction. It is as if these students were "running away" ("flight") from the interactive warmth and emotional freedom of the cohesive group into impersonal, "safe," structured activities which would make no demand for involvement nor for revelation of self.

It is entirely possible that the teacher himself unwittingly brought this change about. For in his role of "counselor," driven by his own need to resolve his own deeper ambivalences, the teacher tended to do a good deal of probing of the feelings and emotions of his students. Both in the context of clarifying their uncertainties about how to carry out his projects and in the elicitation of personal reactions to characters and situations portrayed in novels, the teacher continually invited highly personal reactions and revelations from his students. There is, we think, good reason to suppose that this behavior of the teacher, interacting with some of the less self-assured students, may have created Factor III'.

SUMMARY OF CHANGES

The factor analyses reveal both typical and atypical developments as compared to other, nonfactorial studies of group "growth." The development of greater solidarity and the increasing routineness of work are both part of a generally accepted picture of institutionalization of social controls, shared expectations, and habits within the group. The fact that this happened more completely in the experimental group than in the control group merely shows that the combination of personalities was more compatible or "ready" for interaction.

What happens to personal emotion, however, is very much a matter of leadership, and of the "climate" primarily established through the influence of the leader. The factors and observations suggest that teacher No. 14, with his ambivalences toward independence and authority and his lack of clearly established goal commitments, had arrived at a "counseling" relationship as the one most congenial to his needs. On the whole, this relationship seems reasonably well integrated with his pupil-centered but professional style of teaching. Given the more teachable students, this "counseling" approach very likely facilitated the development of the group's solidarity. We have suggested, however, that this development may have "trapped" the teacher between his group-supported impulses to freedom and independence on the one hand, and his fear that to act on such impulses would alienate him (as teacher) from the group. Under such conditions, his leadership would be from "behind"; that is, he would seek cues from the students (rather than from the requirements of the "subject") to justify or legitimize his ideas of what activities the class should engage in next. The effort to demonstrate these "cues" was what we noticed as "probing" behavior, and the class, which wanted nothing better than to have a strong teacher set up the activities, found that the teacher's originally spontaneous expressions of personal interest were now becoming contaminated with his leadership problems. The students would, we believe, become wary of the probing, and the result would be withdrawal and self-protectiveness.

At the same time, the quality and feel of work would change. Three things would occur. First, the group would develop work norms which would integrate work activities within the maintaining activities of the group—the normal process of institutionalization. Second, since work demands could come only from the students, work would become subordinated to maintenance of the group—which is not at all a necessary consequence of institutionalization as teacher No. 13 showed. Finally, the students' pressure on the teacher to structure activities would be yielded to with respect to only those activities whose need was so self-evident that they would not arouse his anxieties about imposing—these would be the routine technical ones. But they are the least congenial to the teacher, and it seems fair to reason that in an effort to escape them he would redouble his probing—thus setting the vicious circle in motion again.

Chapter Ten

REFLECTIONS: Conclusions and Strategies

Summary of Findings · Discussion of the Rationale and Method of Grouping · Practical Suggestions For Grouping Students

In this chapter we shall attempt to review the most significant findings, discuss the rationale and method of grouping that these findings support, and make a few practical suggestions about how grouping may be done in schools.

SUMMARY OF FINDINGS

Our thirteen teachers tend, on the average, to make use of preparatory presentations, assignments, and class recitations, followed by the teacher's preparation of the next assignment. The students they selected as "getting most out of class" tended, on the average to be more psychologically mature than the students they selected as "getting least out of class." By psychologically mature, we mean more work-oriented, freer emotionally, more secure in the face of expressed emotion, more interactively interdependent, more autonomous, and more able to cooperate with the teacher.

Given classes composed of more "teachable" students, the teachers on the average had more orderly and manageable classes; they tended to like the students better; they gave them better grades. The "teachable" students tended to like the teacher only slightly more than did the control students, they *gained* no more on achievement tests, and they tended to express a higher level of satisfaction with the activities and with the course as a whole. They also tended to like each other better and by and large the teachable classes had greater solidarity than did the control classes.

This general picture, however, covers up a fascinating variety of actual classes and teachers. The general characteristics of teachability gleaned from the 13 comparisons actually represent only about 40% (on the average) of the pattern of differences between high and low teachables selected by each teacher. The other 60% of the differences modify the picture very markedly—so much so that the low teachables of teacher No. 8 bear a decided resemblance to the teachables of teacher No. 7. Further, the "routine-technical" aspects of style, most common to all the teachers, are embedded in a total method which varies all the way from predominantly a bull session, through highly directive non-interactive, to inquiry-oriented cooperative teaching. Finally, the results of all the teaching agree almost completely on the higher grades given to the teachable classes, but every other result has prominent exceptions in at least a few of the cases.

To demonstrate better "what really happened," we offered case studies of the five most different teaching styles. From these studies we concluded that the teachers interpreted the selection criterion in quite different ways, that the teachable students for one teacher may be quite different than for another, that the fit between teacher and teachable students primarily results in better meeting of the teacher's most dominant needs (possibly at the expense of more superficial professional needs), that what happens in class is entirely consistent with our knowledge of the students and of the teacher. Generally speaking, unless the teacher is driven by compelling personal needs, he is able to accomplish his aims more fully with the teachable class than with his other classes.

The supposition we started with now seems to be correct: that successful grouping must take the teacher himself into account. We remain convinced that any grouping which does not in some way attempt to "fit" students and teachers together can have only accidental success.

Nevertheless, the experiment raises a good many issues in our minds, and as we have discussed it with the experimental teachers, workshops, and administrators, we have become aware of a great many implications going way beyond the problem of grouping. We would like to present these further considerations now, and we will organize the discussion around a variety of topics.

DISCUSSION OF THE RATIONALE AND METHOD OF GROUPING

The Problem of Grouping

We believe that some percentage of the students in all schools—regardless of how carefully they may have been screened on entry to the school—will require special personnel arrangements. Public school teachers and guidance workers we have talked with place the figure variously between 10 and 25%. These are students for whom the institutional arrangements, traditions, and expectations simply do not fit at all well. They include both strong "natural" leaders and "problem" children. For them, four possibilities exist: (1) by combing the faculty and program carefully, we can certainly find some particular teachers and courses that will minimize the maladaptation, and we can try to get the students into these situations; (2) by studying the students carefully—both in and out of school—hunches may be arrived at and special arrangements made within the existing school structure; (3) they can be referred to someone else to worry about; (4) they can, under certain conditions, be excluded.

In most cases, especially involving "remedial," passive, and unmotivated students, the most important element in rehabilitation is the interpersonal relations between the students and some staff member, whether he be a teacher, counselor, or coach. For the problem is to "get to" these students, and it has to be done on their own terms. Remarkable results have been reported when the student is finally able to enter into a healthy relationship: gains of two to four years in reading, for example, may occur within a single school year. Yet the "deviate" often is merely the dramatic instance that calls attention to universals. There is every reason to believe and none to doubt that all students will be better off if, at least during some part of the school day, they do have warm and esteem-building personal relationships with some adult. To this extent, "fitting" the teacher to the child should not be confined only to "special cases."

In addition to these "special cases," there is probably another group —maybe 25 to 40% of the student body—who can exist tolerably well within the existing school patterns and procedures, but who could be very greatly assisted (educationally, personally) by small modifications that could be made informally within classes or school activities. For the most part, the most sensible suggestion stimulated by these kids is to attempt to make teaching methods more responsive and adaptable to groups of children in the classrooms. Such teaching would (1) involve student participation under such conditions that the teacher could get enough "feedback" that he could assess much better the effectiveness of his activities; (2) use a great enough variety of activities so that it would be possible for a wide gamut of strengths and capabilities to be demonstrated by the student—thus giving the teacher more avenues for "reaching" the student through capitalizing on his strengths; (3) utilize teacher-pupil planning and evaluation of class and individual progress as a means to develop a commitment to long and short-range goals for the class and for individuals during the course; (4) be reinforced by professional discussion among the faculty for the purpose of aiding each other to implement conditions 1, 2, and 3.

Finally, the remaining 35 to 65% of the students probably find school experiences sufficiently worthwhile and rewarding so that the "average" teaching in the school is satisfactory in the sense that there are no strong cues from the students themselves to stimulate any change in the average teacher himself or his methods of teaching. If all the students were of this sort, then changes in methods and courses would be entirely stimulated by pressures from outside the school: parents, national planners, subject experts, technologists, etc.

If we assume that these statements are substantially true, then there are two courses of action open with respect to grouping. The first course of action is the one most often taken at present: division of the students into categories, separating them in the various subject-fields of study, and dealing with each group in some way appropriate to its nature. Thus we have the "ability" tracks in schools as recommended, for example, in the Conant report on high schools. There are special groupings of "unteachables" in "opportunity" classes, and of the "gifted" in "research" courses; recently the newspapers even carried a story about the development of special courses for the "average" student. We shall refer to this as grouping on the basis of (alleged) characteristics of students.

The chief finding from studies of such groupings is that sometimes they work and sometimes they do not. There is a reason for this: in the classes where homogeneous grouping seems to be advantageous, the teacher is modifying his teaching to "fit" the group. In other words, special grouping makes sense only when the teacher has a clear and accurate idea of what to do with the special group. From this standpoint, the chief difficulty with homogeneous ability grouping is that the guesses about how to deal with the group are often wrong. Thus we find teachers who think "bright" children "ought" to be more self-directing, more interested in the subject, more creative, or more eager to have a continuous, heavy load of work. By and large, however accurate these guesses may be with regard to impressions of bright adults who are successful in the adult world, the guesses are mostly not true —and certainly not *necessarily* true—as applied to most bright children under usual school conditions.

What this experience tells us is that we need facts instead of guesses. What relevant aspects of classroom operations correlate with "ability" —or whatever other selection criterion is used? In view of the way the teacher teaches, what evidence is there that a high IQ would be required for success in the class? Until we know more about these matters, every grouping experiment should be viewed primarily as a "field" experiment designed at least partly to obtain this sort of information.

Grouping students on the basis of characteristics of the students themselves assumes that different "types" of students exist and can be described. To work practically, it must further be assumed that the number of types is relatively small, and that all students can be stereotyped as one type or another. We have recounted our efforts to find such "types;" they have failed. While we think our techniques could be improved considerably, we doubt that better techniques would lead to much different results. The state of affairs seems to us to be as follows:

1. Conceptually, in terms of broad philosophic, cultural, or psychiatric orientations, a limited number of types can be proposed. But very few people are the least bit "pure" with respect to these types; nearly everyone is a blend, and the particular way the blend is organized within the person may be at least as important as the quantity of the ingredients relative to each other.

2. Practically, given a specific situation, there are a limited number of ways to react to it: one can fight, withdraw, become dependent, seek intimacy, analyze, etc. If most or all of the "situations" in the classroom were identical, then students could be "typed" by their most usual mode of reaction. But even the most routine teaching offers much greater variability than this, and most students react differently to different situations.

3. If only one measuring stick, such as IQ, dominance, weight, or strength of grip is used, then all students can be distributed along a scale from highest to lowest scores, and different ranges of scores, obviously more homogeneous than the total range, could be labeled "types." But if two, three or 172 scales are used, the types would have to be defined by *patterns* of responses. And what we found is that the number of patterns is practically infinite. Moreover, such patterns, obtained from all sorts of test situations that are quite unlike classroom situations, offer very involved problems of interpretation; to decide what practical implications any such pattern has for the conduct of the class requires a high degree of clinical sophistication.

4. Finally, we found that teachers recognize four kinds of students: good, bad, indifferent, and sick. But the problem is that each teacher places different students in these categories, so that whatever is being judged is certainly *not* primarily some characteristic of the student.

Thus we conclude that in the present state of the art the concept of dividing students into objectively definable types presents formidable difficulties. And that even if it could be done, the problem of deducing from existing curriculum theory what ought to be done with each type is also a formidable one.

There are, of course, other, noneducational reasons for grouping by characteristics of students. These reasons have to do with the class structure of society. The "top" group, however defined in a particular community, is the elite; the bottom group, the "followers." The purpose of "education" is to teach students their "place," and to prepare them to occupy this place with as much grace as possible. Whether this is called a "recognition of societal facts" or simply the need to have someone to discriminate against, it is at least a widely found element in practically all school programs. This is clearly seen in the fact that achievement in a course is measured by "what the student knows" at the end of the course rather than by "what he has learned" or "gained" during the course. Until tests and other measures are administered *both* at the beginning and end of the course so that we know what children learned during the course, the school will be open to the charge that it is more interested in selecting and creating social structure than in educating children. The problem is especially complicated by the fact that as yet most of the "educational product" cannot be defined conceptually, let alone be measured with much confidence. Certainly it is not measured with much accuracy by teacher-constructed or selected "achievement" tests of the sort most commonly used in school today.

The second course of action is not in theory, at least, antithetical to the first, even though it appears quite different in terms of present practice. This course of action attempts grouping, not on the basis of objectively defined types of students, but on the basis of conditions required for more effective teaching and/or learning. In other words, it starts with the proposition that the particular "personalities" in the group are, in fact, important given conditions which have a great deal of influence over the nature and productivity of classroom experience. It is this method of grouping that we have tested in our experiment. We have called it "teachability" or "facilitative" grouping.

Teachability grouping can be approached from two different directions. One can ask, as we did, "what sort of student can a given teacher teach most effectively"—and then the teacher can be given a classroom full of such students. The second approach would be to ask "what sort of teacher can a given student learn from most effectively"—and then the class group for that teacher would be composed of students for whom this was judged to be the best teacher. Best of all would be to combine these two; to try to answer both questions and then attempt to get groupings such that both criteria were satisfied as well as possible. Our findings suggest that the groupings obtained from the two approaches would not necessarily be the same. In some cases, such as that of teacher No. 13, central education-relevant needs of both teacher and students were met. In the case of teacher No. 5, some needs, much less centrally relevant to most definitions of education, were met by both teacher and students. In the case of teacher No. 7, education-relevant needs of the teacher were met, but at the cost of not meeting some strong needs of the students; and the consequences are of doubtful educational value (as judged by us, not the teacher). In the case of teacher No. 8, the needs of teacher and pupils were met for a short while, and then the situation deteriorated because the role of leader was missing. In this case, however, the teacher apparently did not use the selection criterion we asked him to use.

On the other hand, as a practical matter, it can be argued that if each teacher is teaching more effectively, the school is a better school, and if the condition required for teaching more effectively is that the teacher can meet his needs better, then we are still better off—even if in some or a few classes the students are no better off than they would be if grouping were not attempted.

The Educational Strategy of Teachability Grouping

The central proposition is that a teacher does a better job with some pupils than with others, and that therefore it makes sense to assign him a class composed of the sort of students with whom he has been found to do a better job. An obvious corollary is that the students to assign to each teacher must be determined in some way that takes each teacher into account. Let us consider some implications of this proposition.

One implication is that certain student characteristics, probably not constituting a tight pattern (or "type" as considered above) will be found to be positive indicators for particular teachers. Thus it might turn out that the teachable students for teacher A do, in fact, tend to be "bright." If it also turns out (as seems unlikely) that "brightness" is the only important characteristic of teacher A's techable students, then clearly teacher A should be given a homogeneous "bright" group. In other words, it seems to us that grouping might be done at least partly on the basis of objectively defined student characteristics *once these characteristics have been demonstrated to be important for a certain teacher.* Preliminary experiences with "teachability" grouping might lead in some cases into more objective grouping on the basis of student characteristics. But we insist that the prescription should be written to fit the teacher rather than giving all teachers the same prescription and then studying the mortality rate.

A second implication is that it is time to face up to the fact that most teachers do a better job with some students than with others; and there are some students, different from teacher to teacher, that the teacher simply does not reach at all. Realizing this would immediately (according to the school psychologists we have interviewed) reduce a great deal of anxiety among teachers, and would put them on a more realistic footing vis-a-vis their administrators.

A third implication is that there is no one "right" way to teach, at least not if teaching is defined as a set of specific procedures. Certainly all teaching should be facilitative of inquiry by students, but the practical meaning of this requirement may be very different from one kind of student to the next, and also from one teacher to the next. There are two important consequences that follow: first, within a broad orientation to inquiry, the faculty should be heterogeneous, and each teacher should be encouraged to develop to the hilt his own style of teaching. Only thus can grouping meet a wide range of student characteristics. Second: in-service training and professional discussion within the school should be based first on agreement on the conception of education as inquiry and second on agreement that there is no one set of procedures, kind of materials, particular range of activities, or personality of teacher that is "right." The question should not be, either directly or by implication, "what is the right way to teach." The question should be first, "how do I teach," and second, "for whom and under what conditions is this way of teaching most appropriate." Asking the question this way would open the door for examination by each teacher, with the cooperation of other teachers, of his own teaching— a very rare thing indeed in the schools of today.

A fourth implication is that grouping belongs among the professional responsibilities of the teacher rather than the administrator. Every teacher should be professionally concerned with the problem of defining what sort of student he can best teach, just as a doctor or psychiatrist has the responsibility of deciding what patients he can help. The continual examination of this question could be both a stimulus to "growth" on the part of the teacher and a way to get the really important information required for grouping that will best use the resources of the faculty.

A fifth implication is that teachability grouping may lead to some striking improvement of teaching. We have shown that there are fewer "management" difficulties in the teachable groups. Less of the teacher's efforts are required to "manage" the group, that is, to secure conditions such that he can "teach" the group. (We deplore the distinction between "management" and teaching, but there it is.) The implication is that the teacher should feel more adequate to teach; relieved of some of his anxieties about controlling the group, he should be freer to create and experiment with new procedures and methods. Certainly to the extent that the teacher feels that he "must" teach in a dull, noninteractive, and routine way in order to keep the class under control, the introduction of teachability grouping should result in a considerable improvement of teaching. The general proposition is a commonly understood therapeutic one: when people feel more adequate and less anxious, they then are "freer" to use their intelligence to guide their behavior.

A sixth implication is that, although teachability grouping may support heterogeneity of teaching procedures, it nevertheless may tend to bias all teaching in certain ways. We consider these ways to be good, and to be deducible from sound educational theory. We will organize the discussion of this point around the question: for whom does "teachability" grouping work best.

For Whom Does Teachability Grouping Work Best?

To be able to help himself by telling us what sort of students he can best teach, the teacher must be able to recognize these students with some accuracy. A good many hypotheses stem from this proposition, and we formulated them at the end of the period of observation of the classes.

1. The teacher must realistically select students who "got a lot out of class."

2. To have enough evidence to do that, the teacher must teach interactively, getting plenty of feedback from the kids.

3. To be able to judge this evidence accurately, the teacher must be oriented to the "whole child" and be acceptant of a wide range of needs (that is, the teacher is unanxious).

4. A teacher this realistic, responsive, and willing to provide interactive opportunities would also modify his teaching to fit his class. He should, therefore, show differences between his behavior in the teachable and control groups.

5. The method of teaching which allows for greatest adaptation or flexibility of means employed by the teacher (range of behavior and learning activities) is one whose ends are defined but whose means are left somewhat "open" to be worked out (or emergent) in class. Thus there would be a number of alternative procedures any of which could be used to move the class toward the same desired goal.

6. Given the need to choose among alternative ways of proceeding toward a desired end, the teacher needs criteria to guide this choice. His criteria reflect some combination of the two logical possible policies: "the end justifies the means," which is the justification for "efficiency;" and "the means determine the end," which leads to use of values of process. Clearly the condition under which the two criteria become

identical in practice is when the end of the teaching is the development of inquiry. . . ."

We believe our case studies, in Chapters 7 and 8, throw a good deal of light on the validity and applicability of these hypotheses. Let us review certain features of the case studies with these hypotheses in mind.

Teacher No. 5 appears to have selected students who could co-participate with him in vigorous give-and-take interaction. He was very responsive to them, and felt he accomplished his educational purposes with them. His educational purpose was to teach them how to behave in certain sorts of social situations. His criterion of selection appeared to fit very well his method of teaching and his goals. Hypotheses 1, 2, 3, and 4 appear to fit the case. Hypotheses 5 and 6 are less clear. The teacher's limited goal, involving very little intellectualization and inquiry, rather limited his range of procedures to affective ways of responding during discussion, and in this he was quite flexible, thus substantiating hypothesis 5 as applied to a predominantly non-inquiry situation. Hypothesis 6 says that when the teacher is concerned both with efficiency and process, the result will tend toward inquiry. Teacher No. 5 was concerned hardly at all with "efficiency" in the sense of utilization of student capacity; he was largely concerned with the interaction process itself, and he achieved the values he sought. But this teacher will not move toward inquiry unless and until he is willing to concede a larger measure of intellectual capability and responsibility to the students. There is reason to suppose that this change may be more likely to occur if he has teachable groups—whose need he so far does not appear to recognize—but whether it will occur depends on the teacher achieving some new insights.

Teacher No. 13 is one for whom all the hypotheses fit very well. He selected students who in fact *did* get "a lot out of class." He does have and respond to interaction with them, and he clearly did "go deeper" in the sense of inquiry in his teachable class.

Teacher No. 7 apparently equated the criterion of "getting a lot out of class" with "docile in carrying out my procedures." She got what she wanted. The only significant change in her teaching was a markedly stepped-up pace, to which the students responded satisfactorily in class but with some hidden resentment. She clearly did *not* select students "who got a lot out of class" and there is little reason to suppose she would be able to select them. There is nothing in this picture to suggest that the teacher will move toward more inquiry in her method of teaching. She should, however, continue to bring her students up to the level of test-achievement she has set for them.

Teacher No. 8 also did not use the criterion of "getting a lot out of class." He apparently selected personalities he could identify with. The amount of interaction (as psychological give-and-take) was reduced because there was no leadership capable of structuring activities and the teacher responded to the resulting chaos by withdrawing from contact with the class.

Teacher No. 14 did appear to select students who "got a lot out of class." Hypotheses 1 through 5 are clearly supported by the evidence, and the results are all the more striking because the teacher was "against" the experiment from the start. On the other hand, hypothesis 6 was not borne out because the teacher was unable to integrate his "educational" goals with his "counseling" goals. His bases for decisions in the classroom remained somewhat incompatible. Presumably, this teacher may bring these two goals together as he rationalizes the relationships between individual "psychological health" and engagement in classroom activities. The theory that would result would be oriented to inquiry.

On the whole, then, we are inclined to think our hypotheses are too rigidly cast, although it seems to be true that the more nearly the teacher selected students who "got a lot out of class" the greater the number of hypotheses that seem to be supported.

The most reasonable statement is that in all cases what later happened in the classes is compatible with the way the teacher selected his students, and both appear to be compatible with the teacher's "actual" purposes. But "actual" purposes are not necessarily conscious purposes, and they are not necessarily educational purposes. And to the extent that there is conflict among "actual" purposes, as in the case of teacher No. 8 and, to a lesser extent, teacher No. 14, the teacher may get the group he wants, proceed more effectively than usual to satisfy certain purposes, and then discover that it is at the cost of other purposes whose desirability becomes clear only at the point of denial. Thus if the teacher's deep purposes are primarily self-serving, then the teachable group tends to seduce him into even greater exploitation of students and at some point the students, especially if his need is for vigorous and active students, may rebel. Having this sort of experience could, of course, be the start of some excellent soul-searching.

What Can Reasonably be Expected of Grouping?

Apart from the variety of good things that might be occasioned by the effort to group students, we conclude the following:

Teachability Grouping facilitates the accomplishment of some or most of the teacher's purposes, and in most cases, makes him more effective with whatever methods of teaching he has developed. Such facilitation, however, has educative outcomes only to the extent that the teacher's purposes are predominantly educative. In short, grouping can increase the teacher's effectiveness, but no amount of grouping will turn him into an educator, even though it may provide conditions such that he is more likely to grow in that direction.

In our experiment all but teacher No. 8 accomplished his goals, and all but teacher No. 12—as judged by teacher marks—"educated" the teachable children better. It seems quite clear that, by and large, teachers equate their purposes, whatever they are, to educating students. The teacher may be seeking comfort, self-aggrandizement, more extensive "coverage" of the text, deeper insights from his students, more exciting interaction, etc. He is more likely to get this in his teachable group, and he will give them higher grades if he does. Some of these purposes (given a particular sort of student) may lead to higher achievement gains on tests, but there is no reason to think they all will. Some of these purposes (given a particular sort of student) may lead to greater liking between students and teacher, but, again, there is no reason to expect that universally. Therefore we view the failures of achievement to be not failures of grouping but rather failures of purpose. And this calls for re-thinking on the part of the teacher.

We believe that the experience by the faculty of finding out these things for themselves would be a first-rate inquiry which would contain all the elements of the most effective possible "in-service" (or, better, "professional") training.

PRACTICAL SUGGESTIONS FOR GROUPING STUDENTS

The method requires: (1) identifying students to serve as models for the students to be selected for each teacher; (2) describing these models well enough that one can recognize other students who are like them; (3) screening the students available for each teacher's classes and selecting those who are most like the models. We will consider these steps separately.

The selection of model "teachable" children has to be made by the teacher for whom the grouping is to be done. Note that he is *not* asked to describe or characterize these students. He is asked merely to point them out. In our experiment, the teachers, after seven months of teaching, could for the most part point out such students (and their opposites) with very little thought—possibly, in some cases, too little thought. We suggest that teachers be asked to take a month, along about April, to decide which of their students they really feel are "getting a lot out of class" and which they feel are "getting very little out of class."

The next step is to compare these high and low teachables in order to arrive at prescriptions for the students to give the teacher next fall. In the experiment, we administered a very long test and then arrived at the prescription by item-counting all the responses and selecting those that were significantly different between the two groups of students. (Incidentally, the particular tests used for this purpose do not matter; all that is required is that there is enough to choose so that a few responses are bound to be significant. We do not think this was a very good way to do it; it was all right for research purposes, but it denied the teachers a valuable experience.)

Our suggestion is that the lists of names be given to a group of teachers who have the same children in their classes. This group now becomes a diagnostic conference group, whose purpose is to study the lists and attempt to define recognizable characteristics of the students who should be earmarked for the teacher in question. Note that the prescription or set of earmarks is by no means a clinical diagnosis, and note that it has nothing to do, so far as the conference group is concerned, with knowledge of how the teacher runs his class. This undoubtedly will enter the discussion when the teachers are ready to discuss it, but it does not have to.

Can a conference group of teachers furnish these prescriptions? We think so, but until some experiments now under way in three schools in California and Illinois are a little further along, we cannot say for sure. Our idea is that if the teachers realize how simple the job is, they can do it. Suppose, for example, that we are trying to compose groups for four teachers all of whom will be teaching eleventh grade English. The practical decision that has to be made is which students should be given to each of these four teachers. The conference group examines the lists of names given to them by each of the four teachers. The members of the group have these students in their classes, too, and they suggest hypotheses about how the students differ among the various lists. The end result is four descriptions in the form: "If the student is like this (short description) he goes to Miss A; if like this (another short description) he goes to Mr. B, etc."

The third step is to send these descriptions to the teachers in the grade below who presently have in class the students who will be in next year's classes of Miss A, Mr. B, etc. These teachers each rate all of their present students with respect to how well they fit each prescription. What we expect is that each teacher will be quite certain about how to rate some of the children, will be less sure of others, and will be unable to rate still others. If this is the case, they should so indicate. The ratings, made separately by each teacher, can now be pooled. The best way to do this would be to have the teachers who made the ratings argue out their differences of opinion.

The result of these deliberations would be a list of students who should be given next year to Miss A, Mr. B, etc. The list for each teacher will contain a few names that the teachers "below" are certain about. There will be some further students they feel uncertain about, and there will be some more they cannot decide about at all. What this means is that in making up the class lists, the administration should definitely accept the "certain" recommendations, try reasonably hard to meet the more doubtful recommendations, and use the other students, as convenient, to round out the classes of Miss A, Mr. B, etc.

It is possible that experience will show that fitting the students to teachers may be reduced to the problem of fitting only the "standout" children—possibly a quarter of the students; and the rest may be filled in more or less at random. In other words, certain "strong" students and certain "weak" students should be very carefully placed; but the others may not matter so much. The defect in this reasoning is that the list of strong and weak students, as judged by the teachers in the grade below, may miss a good many who, it will turn out, should have been considered. Hence we think it wiser to consider all the students, at least for the first few times.

This method, as just described, would be the equivalent of the research procedure we followed. There is another method which may be even better, although we must confess that the administrators we have discussed it with seem singularly unenthusiastic about it. The alternative method is as follows:

We assume that the first two weeks of school are part of a shake-down period and might well be sacrificed if the time lost could guarantee better teaching during the rest of the year. On this assumption, our proposal is that the four eleventh grade English classes be scheduled at the same period of the day, and that the division of the students among the four teachers be done more or less at random. During the first two weeks, let the four teachers rotate among the classes, and at the end of each class period, let each teacher note on the seating chart the students he thinks he would like to have in class. In addition, let the students fill in a Post-Meeting Reaction Sheet (such as the one in the appendix) at the end of each class period. Finally, let each teacher exert himself to put each class through selected representative kinds of activities which the teacher feels are important to him.

At the end of two weeks, the teacher's choices and the students' satisfaction ratings can be pooled and the classes reconstituted in such a way as to satisfy the teachers and students as well as possible.

This plan has further advantage that since all the eleventh grade English classes meet during the same period, students can be shifted from one to the other at any time. The plan has an advantage (or disadvantage) in that it eliminates the need for much of the discussion that the first plan requires. It also substitutes first impressions of the teachers who will teach the children for more reasoned judgments of those who really know the children. But there is enough evidence of the accuracy of first impressions in groups that it seems worth chancing. The use of information from the students themselves to help compose the groups is advantageous and we now believe that this is far more important than it seemed at the start of the experiment.

A variation of this plan would be to have the trial teaching occur during the last two weeks of the school year. In this case, each teacher would be rotated through the classes in the grade below. We do not know whether this is a better plan or not. The teachers would be "taking over" classes that have already been shaken down and been molded by another teacher, and many of the problems that plague "substitute" teaching might exert a baleful influence. And, of course, if the students are coming from lower schools, it would be difficult to arrange. On the whole we like the plan better than this variant.

There is a third plan which we think is best of all, but it would work well only with a mature faculty. This plan has been tried in some elementary schools, and the testimony is encouraging; the plan is also very simple:

Let the teachers in the grade below confer with each other and decide to which teacher each child should be sent.*

Obviously such a plan would work only if the teachers in the grade below know a good deal about how each teacher deals with the class; this is information which is not only hard to come by, it is usually strongly and defensively protected. Thus the plan would require a good deal of trust among the teachers. It would also require that teachers visit each other's classes, and, hopefully, discuss teaching with each other. We would have a good deal of confidence in any faculty that made this plan work!

* If there is only one teacher teaching the course, then there is no grouping problem because there is no choice. If, at present, one teacher has all five eleventh grade English classes and another has all five twelfth grade classes, then each could be asked to take half the classes for both grades. This would give each teacher two "preparations" instead of one. In return for this, each teacher may have somewhat better classes, and a greater range of students can be accommodated.

Appendix A. ASSESSMENT BATTERY
Items Keyed to Categories and Sections

The following is a brief description of the nine instruments composing the assessment battery. As an aid to anyone who might be interested in using one or more of these questionnaires we have included where necessary the original categories employed in the design of the instrument. Assessment battery item numbers for those items composing the category are also listed.

1. *Classroom Activities.* On this questionnaire the students were asked to indicate frequency and worthwhileness preferences for described activities of four sorts. The activity category and the assessment battery item numbers composing each are:

Class-as-a-Whole activities	1, 6, 7, 12, 18, 22, 26, 29, 32, 39
Small Group activities	2, 8, 13, 20, 25, 30, 34, 36, 38, 40
Teacher Directed activities	4, 5, 9, 11, 16, 19, 23, 28, 31, 35
Alone activities	3, 10, 14, 15, 17, 21, 24, 27, 33, 37

2. *Participation.* This instrument attempts to ascertain relative preferences for working under five social conditions where, in each instance, five kinds of interaction are possible and the participant can react either actively or passively. The five social conditions and the assessment battery items representing each are:

As member of a Committee	47, 54, 60, 75, 82, 83, 89, 92, 94, 95
As a Class Member	46, 50, 51, 55, 62, 66, 68, 72, 80, 87
With Friends	49, 53, 58, 61, 63, 70, 73, 76, 78, 85
With Interpersonal emphasis	52, 56, 64, 67, 69, 78, 84, 86, 90, 93
By the student Alone	48, 57, 59, 65, 71, 74, 77, 81, 88, 91

The five kinds of interaction and the items representing each are:

Mutual (cooperation with common purpose)	46, 47, 48, 49, 52, 71, 73, 75, 80, 86
Neutral (emotionally uninvolved)	60, 65, 67, 72, 77, 78, 85, 91, 93, 95
Role (influence by or on others)	58, 59, 61, 66, 68, 69, 82, 84, 89, 92
Threatening (exposure of private feelings)	51, 53, 54, 55, 57, 62, 64, 76, 88, 90
Evaluative (criticism of self or others)	50, 56, 63, 70, 74, 79, 81, 83, 87, 94

The active-or passive aspect (usually "listening" or "telling") is self-evident in the item. Each of the 25 combinations of conditions and interactions is represented by one listening and one telling item.

3. *Teacher Descriptions.* On this instrument the students rated six "types" of teachers with respect to: (*a*) "typicality"—judging the paragraph according to their impression of the typical teacher; (*b*) "learn most from"—judging the paragraph in accord with their impression of the teacher they would learn most from; (*c*) "comfortable with"—giving their impression of the teacher—type with whom they would be comfortable.

4. *Who Should Decide?* The test measures the individual student's attitude toward decision making and his relationship to authority. The instrument is self-explanatory consisting of five categories based on the student's opinion about the proper locus of authority in a variety of classroom decisions. The five categories (locus of decision) are: (*a*) the student alone; (*b*) the teacher alone; (*c*) the class-as-a-whole; (*d*) the student and a few other pupils; (*e*) the student plus the teacher.

5. *Situations.* This is a forced choice questionnaire assessing tendencies toward work, fight, flight, pairing, and dependency in social stress situations. These categories were derived from the theorizing of W. R. Bion. A coded copy of the instrument will be gladly forwarded on request.

6. *Reactions to Groups.* This instrument presents the student with 15 group work and emotionality situations on which he is asked to check behaviors he would or would not do, whether a boy, girl, or either a boy or girl would do it, and whether he would approve or disapprove the other person doing it.

7. *Ways of Doing Things.* This questionnaire rates the extent to which advantages and disadvantages are perceived in four types of work-social conditions where, in each instance, the characteristic of the activity can focus on one of four basic concerns. The work-social involvements and the assessment battery items representing each are as follows:

Involving Teacher	92, 96, 101, 104, 108, 112, 117, 120, 124, 128, 133, 136
Involving Class-as-a-Whole	91, 94, 98, 102, 107, 110, 114, 118, 123, 126, 130, 134
Involving a Small Group	93, 97, 100, 105, 109, 113, 116, 121, 125, 129, 132, 137
Involving a Student Alone	95, 99, 103, 106, 111, 115, 119, 122, 127, 131, 135, 138

The four foci of concern and the assessment battery items representing each are:

Focus on Work	93, 95, 98, 101, 109, 111, 114, 117, 125, 127, 130, 133
Focus on Others	92, 94, 100, 106, 108, 110, 116, 122, 124, 126, 132, 138
Focus on Self	97, 99, 102, 104, 113, 115, 118, 120, 129, 131, 134, 136
Focus on Ideas	91, 96, 103, 105, 107, 112, 119, 121, 123, 128, 135, 137

8. *Values.* This questionnaire requires the subjects to rate 60 items related to personal values. The items are keyed to a category system developed by Charles Morris. The six categories and the assessment battery items assigned to each are:

Category I represents a way of life that emphasizes social restraint and self-control. See items 16, 24, 26, 42, 44, 47, 2, 8, 13, 22.

Category II presents a value-orientation accenting delight in vigorous action and the overcoming of obstacles. See items 30, 31, 41, 45, 46, 48, 3, 6, 12, 18.

Category III is concerned with a life of withdrawal and self-sufficiency. See items 18, 23, 27, 34, 38, 49, 4, 9, 15, 19.

Category IV deals with values that emphasize receptivity to life accompanied by sympathetic concern for others. See items 19, 21, 29, 35, 39, 43, 10, 20, 23, 24.

Category V stresses self-indulgence and sensual enjoyment. See items 20, 25, 28, 33, 40, 1, 7, 11, 17, 21.

Category VI is an accumulation of items discarded from the above categories because they were rated with overwhelmingly high positivity by the subjects in our pilot study. They have been included as a category of stereotypic value statements, and are interesting as an indicator of nonconformity to social stereotypes. See items 17, 22, 32, 36, 37, 50, 5, 14, 16, 25.

9. *Words! Words! Words!* This is a semantic differential test associating 10 word-pair continua to 7 goal and person concepts. The same word-pairs were used to rate each concept. The word-pairs were themselves broken down into five categories supplying qualitative information about the student's perception of the concept. The word-pairs and the category to which they are assigned are:

Word-pair	*Category*
Tight	Loose–Rigidity
Ugly	Pretty–Evaluative
Safe	Dangerous–Security
Weak	Strong–Potency
Old	New–Activity
Thin	Fat–Activity
Dry	Wet–Rigidity
Loud	Soft–Security
Good	Bad–Evaluative
Little	Big–Potency

Appendix B. ASSESSMENT BATTERY
Symbols for Each Category
(See teachability items, tables, Appendixes K and L)

Listed below are the codes that identify each item according to its assessment battery section and its particular test category.

Classroom Activities

Teacher directed activity . . . . T
Class-as-a-whole activity CL
Small group activity . . . . G
Activity done alone . . . . A

Participation. Each item has a 3 part coding involving one of:

Five Qualities		Five Social Conditions	
Mutual	MU	Alone	A
Neutral	NEUT	Friends	FR
Evaluative	EV	Interpersonal	IP
Threatening	TH	Committee	CO
Role	ROLE	Class	CL

Listening L
Telling . . . . T

Thus, an item might be coded in the following way: MU IP T

Teacher Descriptions. Test requires the ranking of 6 paragraph descriptions of teachers with respect to "learn most from," "be most comfortable with," and most "typical" of teachers in general. The central theme of each paragraph is expressed by the terms:

Paragraph

Subject Expert . . . . A
Planning . . . . B
Rules C
Independent Self Starting . . . . . . D
Buddy . . . . E
Traditional-Professional . . . . F

The codes for the items are the words *Typical, Learnmost,* or *Comfort.*

Situations Test. Code abbreviations represent Work-Emotionality categories. Each item contains a stem and two alternative response choices. Thus, the code will show, for example, W P D (Meaning stem is keyed to *Work;* first alternative is keyed to *Pairing;* second alternative is keyed to *Dependency*).

Work............W
Fight............F
Pairing..........P
Flight............FL
Dependency......D

Ways of doing Things. Each item has a two part coding involving one of the following:

Four Working Conditions	Four Kinds of Content
Alone.............A	Self........S
Group............G	Others......O
With Teacher......T	Ideas.......I
With Class........CL	Work.......W

Thus, an item might be coded in the following way: I G (which concerns working with *ideas* in a *group*)

Reaction to groups test. Items, in this instance, will have codings indicating three types of alternatives:

Step I.
I *would* do this.........WD
I *would not* do this......WN

Step II.
I think a girl would do this...................G
I think a boy would do this...................B
I think either a boy or a girl would do this......E

Step III.
I would feel *good* if someone else did this......GOOD
I would feel *bad* if someone else did this.......BAD

Values test. This section of the battery contains statements keyed to the five categories of value orientations developed by Charles Morris. A sixth category has been included to cover stereotypic responses. The categories are listed as:

Social Restraint and Self-Control........V 1
Adventure and Initiation of Change......V 2
Withdrawal and Self-Sufficiency.........V 3
Altruism and Concern for Others........V 4
Sensual Enjoyment and Pleasure.........V 5
Stereotypic Response Category..........V 6

Thus, an item might be coded as V 1 (meaning that the statement is keyed to the category of Social Restraint and Self-Control).

Words! Words! Words! A semantic differential test, associating 10 word-pair continua to 7 goal and person concepts. Each item for each concept is keyed to one of 5 dimensions.

Security . . . . SE
Rigidity . . . . RI
Potency . . . . PO
Evaluation . . . . . . EV
Activity . . . . AC

Who should decide? The items have been grouped according to 5 possible authority agents who might make decisions involving progress, materials, conduct, and standards in the classroom. The agents are:

You alone . . . . Y
Teacher alone . . . . T
Class-as-a-whole . . . . Class
You plus Others, group . . . . . . Y and O
You plus Teacher . . . . Y and T

Appendix C. THE REVISED
ASSESSMENT BATTERY (405 items)
Classroom Dynamics: A Questionnaire*

Here is a list of activities that occur in the classroom. We have found that students have differing opinions as to which of these activities are the most meaningful and worthwhile. We would like you to indicate on the Response Sheet which of these activities mean most to you. There is no "right way" to respond to any of these items, so simply give your personal opinion about each one. Read all the items carefully and mark each in the appropriate space provided on the response sheet.

For each item (1–40) mark space:

1. If for you the activity is *worthless—a waste of time*
2. If for you the activity is *not so good—slightly dull*
3. If for you the activity is *about average—neither exciting nor dull*
4. If for you the activity is *quite good—rather interesting*
5. If for you the activity is *highly worthwhile—get a good deal from it*

(Be sure to start with Response Sheet I)

1. Have planning sessions in which the whole class is involved.
2. Work with a committee on a written report.
3. Take a test or quiz.
4. Take notes while the teacher lectures.
5. Review a test and correct mistakes.
6. Have a general class discussion led by another student.
7. Go on a field trip.
8. Work with a committee to prepare a lesson to present to the class.
9. Have teacher assign exercises for practice.
10. Work independently on a project you choose yourself.
11. Get individual help and instruction from the teacher while doing class work.
12. Listen to other students recite on assigned homework.
13. Be a member of a panel discussion
14. Grade or evaluate your own performance in an activity.
15. Do research in the library for your term paper.

* Developed by the Staff of the "Grouping Project," under the auspices of the U. S. Office of Education; *Teaching-Learning Laboratory; School Improvement Program,* University of Chicago, 1959.

16. Have teacher lead a discussion in which basic principles are explained.
17. Take notes on a movie or film strip.
18. Have a class discussion on a topic suggested by the teacher.
19. Discuss with the teacher possible activities you could do.
20. Organize a group activity with a few other students.
21. Explain a homework problem to the class.
22. Engage in class discussion of a movie or filmstrip.
23. Have a conference with the teacher concerning your progress in class.
24. Perform a demonstration or experiment for the class.
25. Discuss class material with a group of other students.
26. Have a spelling bee or some type of quiz game.
27. Prepare, on your own, to make a report to the class.
28. Listen to the teacher explain or demonstrate a lesson.
29. Participate in a class drill on fundamentals.
30. Work with other students in designing and completing a project.
31. Have teacher "crack down" on class order and discipline.
32. Watch as problems are put on the board by another student.
33. Study by yourself to prepare for a test.
34. Go to the library with your committee to do research.
35. Have teacher give specific instructions on how to do something.
36. Study basic course content as a member of a small group of students.
37. Begin homework assignments.
38. Be a member of a committee that plans a special event for the class.
39. Have teacher make it clear what is expected of the class.
40. Evaluate the quality of committee work with other group members.

* * * * * * *

Some things are really very enjoyable to do. Others are less pleasant, and still others are most unpleasant. How pleasant or unpleasant for you is each of the following?

Indicate your preference for each item (46–95) by blackening space:

1. If doing this is indeed very unpleasant for you.
2. If doing this is, on the whole, rather unpleasant for you.
3. If doing this is neither pleasant nor unpleasant.
4. If doing this is, on the whole, rather pleasant for you.
5. If doing this is very enjoyable for you.

Sample:

	1	2	3	4	5
45. Hearing the teacher read a story to the class. 45.	‖	**▌**	‖	‖	‖

(The black mark says that this activity, number 45, is, on the whole, rather unpleasant.)

(Be sure to skip to item 46 on Response Sheet I)

46. Hearing the ideas of other students during class discussion of some topic.

47. Listening to others on a student committee discuss a topic on the agenda.

48. Reading a book and deciding what the author is really trying to say to you.

49. Telling a group of your friends your ideas and feelings about the plans they are discussing.

50. Pointing out good ideas and attacking bad ideas offered during class discussion.

51. Hearing another student make a spur-of-the-moment speech about himself to the class.

52. Listening to another student explain his ideas about a topic you both are familiar with.

53. Telling a group of friends your most intimate and personal feelings.

54. Listening to other members of a student committee talking about the anxieties and pleasures they experience in the committee.

55. Giving a prepared report to the class.

56. Being told by another student just what are your good and bad points.

57. Reading a story in which the author describes the innermost private feelings of the characters.

58. Having one of your friends give advice to the whole gang.

59. Thinking about an argument you might have used to persuade others.

60. Listening to another member of a student committee to which you belong explain about parliamentary rules.

61. Explaining to a group of friends how they ought to go about doing their job.

62. Making a speech to the class about your personal experience.

63. Telling a group of friends what is good or bad about their ideas and behaviors.

64. Telling another student your secret thoughts and hopes.

65. Thinking about all the things you have to do today.

66. Keeping class discussion on the beam by bringing the others back to the problem.

67. Telling a visiting student from another school about the program of courses taught in your school.

68. Having the teacher call on individual students by name to answer his questions during class discussion.

69. Hearing another student tell you what he would do if he were you.

70. Listening to a group of your friends very frankly criticizing each other's behavior and appearance.

71. Reading a book in order to learn all about some topic.

72. Listening to other students giving carefully prepared and detailed reports to the class.

73. Listening to others in a group of your friends discuss their ideas and beliefs about some problem you all have.

74. Critically comparing yourself to one of the characters in a TV show or play.

75. Telling a student committee your views about the project they are discussing.

76. Hearing others in a group of your friends tell their innermost feelings about their private problems.

77. Sitting by yourself remembering things that happened today.

78. Reporting to a group of your friends all about an article you read recently.

79. Giving another student your opinion of his strengths and weaknesses.

80. Being one of the more active persons during a lively class discussion.

81. Evaluating a TV program and criticizing the parts that are dull, silly, etc.

82. Telling a student committee what to do next when they appear mixed up or confused.

83. Having a student committee you belong to appraise the performances of the various members.

84. Trying to interest another student in some hobby or interest of yours.

85. Listening to a group of your friends discuss some event such as a football game they went to.

86. Telling another student your ideas about a problem you both have.

87. Hearing the class give opinions about the quality of their own discussion.

88. Writing a letter in which you explain your deepest feelings.

89. Having the chairman of a student committee explain exactly what everyone must do.

90. Hearing the private experiences of another student.

91. Sitting by yourself quietly thinking about things that interest or puzzle you.

92. Pointing out to a student committee in what ways its members are being helpful or making trouble.

93. Hearing a student from another school talk about his school.

94. Telling a student committee quite frankly how you feel about the various members.

95. Describing to a student committee what a similar committee did last year.

* * * * * * *

Most students have a general impression of what teachers are like; that is, they can describe a *"typical"* teacher. Students also have ideas about the sort of teacher from whom they *can learn most,* and the sort of teacher in whose class they *feel most comfortable.* In this section, you are asked to decide how well each of the six paragraphs describes your impression of the typical teacher, the one from whom you would learn most, and the one you are most comfortable with.

Thus, you will judge each paragraph *three* times. In each case blacken answer space numbered:

1. If the paragraph best fits your impression.

2. If the paragraph generally fits your impression, even though it is not quite accurate in some respects.

3. If the paragraph talks about other things so that you can't tell whether or not the teacher would fit your impression.

4. If the paragraph clearly is out of line with your impression.

5. If the paragraph contradicts your impression or describes the opposite of your impression.

On the IBM response sheet, use items numbered 106–111 to judge the paragraphs according to your impression of the typical teacher.

Use items numbered 112–117 to judge the paragraphs according to your impression of the teacher you would learn most from.

Use items numbered 118–123 to judge the paragraphs according to your impression of the teacher you would be most comfortable with.

(Be sure to skip to item 106, on Response Sheet I)

	For *typical* teacher use item	For *learn* *most* use item	For *feel* *comfortable* use item
A. This teacher really knows his subject. He keeps informed on the new ideas in his field. He likes to have students know about these things and he brings new ideas and information into his course. He spends extra time with students who show a particular interest in his subject.	106	112	118
B. This teacher plans learning activities with the students. He takes time to get suggestions from the students and tries to help them work out a plan with which they all are satisfied. He allows students a good deal of freedom in choosing people with whom to work and in deciding on what topics they will work within the plan.	107	113	119
C. This teacher makes sure that rules are clear from the start so that students will know what is expected of them. He reminds the students of the rules when he thinks they have forgotten them. He tries to help the students become aware of the necessity of meeting requirements.	108	114	120
D. This teacher expects students to work independently and to take responsibility for seeing tasks through to the finish. He tries to challenge them to tackle problems that call for imagination and resourcefulness. He encourages students to search for possible solutions on their own and to try out ideas that seem worthwhile to them.	109	115	121

	For *typical* teacher use item	For *learn most* use item	For *feel comfortable* use item
E. This teacher wants students to feel that he can be one of them. He knows a lot about what teen-agers like to do. He plans the work of the class around these things and enjoys discussing them in class.	110	116	122
F. This teacher makes use of a variety of materials and activities which he has worked out and tested in previous classes. He plans the work that the students are to do and tries to make it interesting to them. He expects them to be successful in their work and is interested to know how much they have gotten from it when it is finished.	111	117	123

* * * * * * *

There is an amazingly large number of decisions that seem to affect learning. One way or another, each decision in the classroom is made by:

A—You alone
B—Teacher alone
C—Class-as-a-whole
D—You plus one or a few other students, as a small group
E—You plus the teacher

The purpose of this questionnaire is to find out from both students and teachers, their opinions about who should make certain decisions. We are not asking what these decisions should be, but only who should decide.

Read each sentence. When you have decided which person or groups (A, B, C, D, or E) should make the decision, blacken the corresponding space (A, B, C, D or E) on Response Sheet II.

Sample:
1. What questions should be on a test?   A B C D E
(If you feel the teacher should make this decision, then   ‖ ▌ ‖ ‖ ‖
you would blacken the space under column B for item 1.)
(Be sure to use Response Sheet II)

---

1. Whether your project group should meet after school.
2. Whether, and under what conditions, you will work alone.
3. How much help you should accept from another student.

4. With whom you will work on a project.

5. How worthwhile was your contribution to the class discussion.

6. Where you "went wrong" in working a problem.

7. To what extent the teacher should give you his personal opinion of yourself.

8. What conclusions you should reach from a discussion of current-events.

9. When a committee should ask one of its disturbing members to leave.

10. How good a job the teacher did today.

11. Whether the teacher should tell you an answer, or expect you to dig it out for yourself.

12. To what extent is the behavior of another student "out of line."

13. How worthwhile was the class discussion today.

14. How hard will you work on an assignment that you consider "stupid."

15. Whether the committee you were on did a good job or not.

16. Whether it is a good idea to see the school counselor about a personal problem.

17. What type of project you will work on next.

18. When you will come in for a conference with the teacher.

19. Whether you will do extra-credit work.

20. Who you should sit next to in class.

21. Whether you are making satisfactory progress.

22. When you need to go the library.

23. When your skit or report is ready to present to the class.

24. Whether it is all right to ask questions to end someone's boring report.

* * * * * * *

You will be presented with one-sentence descriptions of a lot of incidents of the kind that frequently occur in classrooms.

Each of these descriptions is given in an incomplete sentence that can be finished in either of two ways, A or B. *Decide which way you prefer* to finish each sentence. On the separate response sheet, either A or B (not both) should be marked opposite the number of the sentence, to complete the sentence.

Make your selections quickly. Don't linger over the items—your first impression is good enough.

Please do not leave out any items.

(Be sure you skip to item 31, on Response Sheet II)

---

31. When I wanted to work with Frank, I . . .

    A. felt we could do well together.

    B. asked if it would be all right with him.

32. When the group wanted his views about the task, Sam . . .

    A. wondered why they wanted his views.

    B. thought of what he might tell them.

33. When the leader made no comment, I . . .
    A. offered a suggestion of what to do.
    B. wondered what to do next.
34. When Don said he felt closest to me, I . . .
    A. was glad.
    B. was suspicious.
35. When I felt helpless, I . . .
    A. wished that the leader would help me.
    B. found a friend to tell how I felt.
36. When Henry was annoyed, Ray . . .
    A. thought of a way to explain the situation to him.
    B. realized just how he felt.
37. When Ned felt eager to go to work, he . . .
    A. got mad at the late-comers.
    B. wanted to team up with Jim.
38. When Glenn bawled me out, I . . .
    A. lost interest in what we were supposed to be doing.
    B. thought that some of his ideas would be useful.
39. When the leader lost interest, Mort . . .
    A. suggested a way to get everybody working.
    B. started talking with his neighbors.
40. When Phil felt warm and friendly, he . . .
    A. accomplished a lot more.
    B. liked just about everyone.
41. When the leader was unsure of himself, Norm . . .
    A. wanted to leave the group.
    B. didn't know what to do.
42. When the group just couldn't seem to get ahead, I . . .
    A. felt like dozing off.
    B. became annoyed with them.
43. When the group wasn't interested, I . . .
    A. just didn't feel like working.
    B. thought that the leader should do something about it.
44. When the leader said he felt the same way I did, I . . .
    A. was glad that I had his approval.
    B. thought we would probably begin to make progress now.
45. When I became angry at Jack, I . . .
    A. felt like dozing off.
    B. ridiculed his comments.
46. When the leader wanted me to tell the class about my plan, I . . .
    A. wished I could get out of it.
    B. wished that he would introduce it for me.
47. When Art criticized Bert, I . . .
    A. wished that the teacher would help Bert.
    B. felt grateful to Art for really expressing what we both felt.
48. When Henry and Mary enjoyed each other's company so much, I . . .

A. thought that I'd like to leave the room.

B. felt angry.

49. When the leader changed the subject, Al . . .

    A. suggested that they stick to the original topic.

    B. felt glad that the leader was finally taking over.

50. When the others became so keen on really working hard, I . . .

    A. made an effort to make really good suggestions.

    B. felt much more warmly toward them.

51. When I felt angry enough to boil, I . . .

    A. wanted to throw something.

    B. wished that the leader would do something about it.

52. When Lee was not paying attention, I . . .

    A. did not know what to do.

    B. wanted to tell him he was wasting our time.

53. When Harry thought that he needed a lot of help, Martin . . .

    A. warmly encouraged him to get it.

    B. helped him analyze the problem.

54. When Jack reported his results so far, I . . .

    A. laughed at him.

    B. was bored.

55. When everyone felt angry, I . . .

    A. suggested that they stop and evaluate the situation.

    B. was glad that the leader stepped in.

56. When no one was sticking to the point, I . . .

    A. got bored with the whole thing.

    B. called for clarification of the topic.

57. When Herb said he felt especially friendly toward me, I . . .

    A. wanted to escape.

    B. wanted to ask his advice.

58. When the group agreed that it needed more information about how members felt, I . . .

    A. described my feelings to the group.

    B. wasn't sure I wanted to discuss my feelings.

59. When the leader offered to help Carl, Joe . . .

    A. wanted help too.

    B. resented the leader's offer.

60. When Dave and Lou argued, I . . .

    A. asked Hank how he felt about them.

    B. hoped they would slug it out.

61. When Chuck felt especially close to Steve, he . . .

    A. let him know it.

    B. hoped he could turn to him for assistance.

62. When several members dropped out of the discussion, Henry . . .

    A. thought it was time to find out where the group was going.

    B. got sore at what he thought was their discourtesy.

63. When Stan told me he felt uncertain about what should be done, I . . .

    A. suggested that he wait awhile before making any decisions.

    B. suggested that he get more information.

64. When Jim realized that quite a few people were taking digs at each other, he . . .

    A. wanted to call the group to order.

    B. got angry at the stupidity of their behavior.

65. When the group suggested a procedure, I . . .

    A. thought the teacher ought to express his approval or disapproval of it.

    B. thought we ought to decide whether to carry it out.

66. When Ed seemed to be daydreaming, Bill . . .

    A. winked at Joe.

    B. felt freer to doodle.

67. When Tom and Mary arrived twenty minutes late for the meeting, the group . . .

    A. went right on working.

    B. was very annoyed.

68. During the argument, Roy's opposition caused Earl to . . .

    A. withdraw from the discussion.

    B. look to the teacher for support.

69. When Marvin suggested we evaluate how well we were working as a group, I . . .

    A. was glad that the period was almost over.

    B. gladly backed him up.

70. When the group seemed to be losing interest, Pat . . .

    A. became angry with the other members.

    B. thought it might just as well adjourn.

71. Together John and Fred . . .

    A. wasted the group's time.

    B. supported one another's arguments.

72. When Mal offered to help me, I . . .

    A. said I was sorry, but I had something else to do.

    B. was pleased that we would be partners.

73. When the other group became so interested in their work, George . . .

    A. wanted to ask their leader if he could join them.

    B. felt resentful that his group was so dull.

74. When Art left the meeting early, Dick . . .

    A. and Michael told each other what they felt about Art.

    B. was glad that he had gone.

75. When Lou turned to me, I . . .

    A. wished that he would mind his own business.

    B. asked him for help.

76. When Hal felt hostile to the group, he . . .

    A. wished he would not have to come to the meeting.

    B. was glad that Bob felt the same way.

77. While Dan was helping me, I . . .

    A. became annoyed with his superior attitude.

B. felt good about being with him.
78. When I lost track of what Paul was saying, I . . .
    A. asked the teacher to explain Paul's idea to me.
    B. was pleased that it was Mike who explained Paul's idea to me.
79. While the group was expressing friendly feelings toward Bill, Ken . . .
    A. thought that now Bill would be able to work.
    B. opened a book and started to read.
80. When the leader offered to help him, Pete . . .
    A. said that he did not want any help.
    B. realized that he did need help from someone.

* * * * * * *

We have classified activities as being *Ways of Doing Things:* with a teacher, in a class, with a few others, or by yourself. As students participate in activities of these kinds they are often aware of certain disadvantages. On the next two pages you will find a number of disadvantages that various students have told us about. To some extent, each kind of activity may have some of these disadvantages for you too. Please indicate, in your opinion, how often each of the following disadvantages is likely to occur. The ratings to be used are as follows:

A—almost always
B— frequently
C— often as not
D— occasionally
E— almost never

Read each sentence. When you have decided how often each disadvantage occurs for you, blacken the space under the appropriate letter on the answer sheet.

(Be sure to skip to Item 91 on Response Sheet II)
91. When doing things in a class I forget ideas that have been explained previously.
    92. When talking with a teacher I lose the thread of conversation.
    93. When doing things with a few other students I get confused in my work.
    94. When doing things as a member of the class I get into trouble with others.
    95. When doing things by myself I delay getting started on work.
    96. When discussing things with a teacher I lose interest in ideas.
    97. When doing things with a few other students I become upset easily.
    98. When doing things as a member of a class I get distracted from my work.
    99. When doing things alone I find it hard to think clearly about myself.
    100. When doing things with a few other students I get into trouble.
    101. When I have work to do with a teacher I don't feel like getting started.
    102. When doing things as a member of the class I become upset easily.
    103. When doing things by myself I lose interest in ideas.

104. When doing things with a teacher I feel very little enjoyment.

105. While doing things with a few other students I forget ideas that have been explained.

106. When doing things by myself I think about things I want to say to others.

107. When doing things in a class I find it hard to consider ideas.

108. When doing something with a teacher I have difficulty talking.

109. When doing things with a few other students I waste time.

110. When doing things in a class I lose interest in what others say.

111. When doing things by myself I get distracted from work easily.

112. When discussing things with a teacher I find it hard to consider ideas.

113. When doing things with a few other students I feel very little enjoyment.

114. When doing things as a member of a class I get confused in my work.

115. When doing things by myself I become upset easily.

116. When doing things with a few other students I have difficulty talking.

117. When I do something with a teacher I get confused in my work.

118. When doing things as a member of the class I feel very little enjoyment.

119. When doing things by myself I have difficulty understanding ideas.

120. When doing things with a teacher I find it hard to think clearly about myself.

121. When doing things with a few other students I find it hard to consider ideas.

122. When doing things by myself I think about people I dislike.

123. When doing things as a member of a class I get confused in my thinking.

124. When doing something with a teacher I feel difficulty in asking for help.

125. When doing things with a few other students I learn very little for my work efforts.

126. When discussing things in a class I have difficulty talking to others.

127. When doing things by myself I get confused in my work.

128. When doing something with a teacher I get confused in my thinking.

129. When doing things with a few other students I have difficulty expressing my feelings.

130. When doing things as a member of a class I learn very little for my work efforts.

131. I feel very little enjoyment when doing things by myself.

132. When doing things with a few other students I feel difficulty in getting help as needed.

133. When doing something with a teacher I waste time.

134. When doing things as a member of the class I have trouble expressing my feelings.

135. When doing things by myself I find it hard to consider ideas.

136. When doing something with a teacher I become upset easily.

137. When doing things with a few other students I get confused in my thinking.

138. When doing things by myself I feel difficulty in not being able to get help as needed.

* * * * * * *

In any situation there are a number of ways of acting which you or any other person might choose. You are being asked to choose some of these ways of acting.

Following is a description of a situation and fifteen possible ways of acting. These ways are numbered 1–15, corresponding to items 1–15 on Response Sheet III. You will deal with these ways of acting in three steps.

Step I. For *each* way of acting (1–15), blacken space:

  1. If you would act this way   or   2. If you would not act this way
    in this situation.   in this situation.

Step II. Now picture all the ways of acting being done by someone else. Then, for each way of acting (1–15), blacken space:

  3. If you think a girl would   4. If you think a boy would
    act this way.   act this way.
  or
  5. If you find it impossible to see any difference between a boy or a girl acting in this way.

Step III. Now think how you would feel if someone else were to do these things. Then, for each way of acting (1–15) blacken space:

  6. If you would feel *good*.   or   7. If you would feel *bad*.

(Be sure to use Response Sheet III)

Situation: You are a member of a small group which is trying to think up a project which they will work on together and present to the class. Quite a few ideas have been offered and there is strong disagreement among the group members about which of the ideas is the best.

Items:

1. Suggest some aims that the project should have.
2. Tell the group to stop acting like babies.
3. Excuse yourself politely and leave the discussion.
4. Show your friendly support to the ideas of others.
5. Tell the group to select a leader to tell them what to do next.
6. Think to yourself about the different ideas the group has to choose from.
7. Insist that each person show exactly how his idea will work.
8. Just wait quietly for the group to settle its differences and reach some agreement.
9. Whisper to a neighbor the way you feel.
10. Decide for yourself which idea most of the others think will work, in order to make up your own mind.
11. Get the group to look calmly at the fact that they are showing a lot of personal feeling.
12. Strongly defend your own point of view against the attack of others.
13. Suggest a completely new topic that would be easier for the group to discuss.

14. Agree in a friendly way with the feelings of others that are like your own.
15. Go and ask the teacher what he would do if he were you.

* * * * * * *

The following questionnaire is concerned with personal values. It contains a list of sixty statements all of which describe an important and desirable approach to life. We want you to rate them according to how important you think each is *for your own personal life*.

Read each statement carefully. If the statement describes an approach to life which for you is of extreme importance, then fill in space 9 on the response sheet; if you feel the statement is of average importance then fill in space 5; or if for you the statement is of little importance, then fill in space 1. The spaces numbered 2–4 and 6–8 should be used to rate statements which you think fall somewhere between these points.

Remember you are to rate the statements to the degree you think they describe ways of living which will help you get the most out of life. A 1 rating does not mean that you consider the statement to be unimportant. It simply means that in your opinion, for your own personal life, it is of *little* importance. Likewsie, the 9 rating should be given to statements which you think are of *extreme* importance for your own personal life. Probably everyone will consider some statements to be of extreme importance for his personal life, while at the same time he will see others as being of little importance. Think carefully about each statement and use the whole range of responses 1 through 9.

This diagram shows the location of the spaces on the Response Sheet.

of little importance for my life				of average importance				of extreme importance for my life		
1	2	3	4	5	6	7	8	9	10	15
										to
::::	::::	::::	::::	::::	::::	::::	::::	::::	::::	::::

(Disregard spaces 10 to 15)

To get the most out of life I think it is important to . . .

16. hold my feelings in check and live a life of self-control
17. have confidence in my personal strength and ability to do things on my own
18. cherish personal privacy and the chance it affords to simply be myself
19. live a life of service to others.
20. relax and enjoy every possible moment
21. live a life in which the interests of others are put ahead of my own
22. do things actively and with enthusiasm
23. find the center or real meaning for life within myself, e.g., self-awareness
24 use the wisdom of the past in order to make a better future

25. experience simple physical pleasure to the fullest
26. behave in a self-disciplined manner
27. have time to think about the deep issues of my personal life
28. be at ease both physically and mentally without being too ambitious
29. live in close relationship with others sharing their joys and sorrows
30. live an adventuresome, daring life
31. plunge courageously into the challenges of life
32. become a responsible, conscientious citizen
33. enjoy good food and drink with a group of friends
34. be aware of and understand my innermost thoughts
35. be grateful and undemanding in my acceptance of life experiences
36. live in a reasonable and intelligent way
37. develop and maintain my bodily strength and health to the fullest
38. develop understanding of others through self-awareness
39. be sensitive and responsive to life without trying to change things
40. be able to find pleasure in new experiences at any time
41. overcome, dominate, or conquer obstacles that hinder human progress
42. live a well-organized and productive life
43. be willing to make sacrifices for the welfare of others
44. realize that attaining future goals is more important than present pleasure
45. have much freedom at home, school and work
46. actively compete for the rewards of life
47. try always to act in a socially acceptable manner
48. be able to do things that are new and interesting even if they are risky
49. realize that though the world is disappointing I can find happiness in me
50. learn that affection and love for others is one of the main joys in life

---

Turn to Response Sheet IV and continue

1. be able to enjoy things as they are
2. live a refined and well-mannered life
3. work hard on my own and pioneer some endeavor
4. find the most enduring satisfactions within myself
5. live in harmony with nature and other men
6. tackle the job of changing society and making a better world
7. fully experience present pleasure and not worry about the past or future
8. live a moral life of high ideas
9. live a quiet, unassuming life that allows time for thought and meditation
10. have a sympathetic appreciation for the feelings of other people
11. be able to enjoy life without working too hard
12. master the world I live in by use of science, tools, and bodily energy
13. cultivate a wide circle of useful acquaintances
14. be the kind of person in whom others will want to put their trust
15. "go it alone," for the most part, and not be dependent on others
16. work hard to attain the good things of life honestly

17. be able to let oneself go and really enjoy life

18. get out and do things and not merely be a thinker or spectator

19. find inner peace and contentment through self-understanding and independence

20. have confidence in other people and the world in general

21. free myself from the burdens of care and worry and simply enjoy life

22. be thrifty and plan for tomorrow

23. live by the rule of loving my neighbor as myself

24. trust in the goodness of nature and life in general

25. be a credit to my family and community

* * * * * * *

Words or ideas mean different things to different people.

On the following pages you will find several words written in capital letters and underlined. Below each such word, you will find 10 descriptive scales, like this:

13. Fair   1   2   3   4   5   6   Unfair

Describe the underlined idea by selecting where it fits along each of the scales, locations 1–6. Opposite the number of the scale on Response Sheet IV blacken the space, 1, 2, 3, 4, 5, or 6 corresponding to the place where the word fits along the scale.

Sample:

```
        1    2    3    4    5    6    7    8    9    10   11
13.                                                              etc. to 15
      ::::  ::::  ::::  ::::  ▬▬   ::::  ::::  ::::  ::::  ::::  ::::
```

(Disregard spaces 7 to 15)

By blackening space 5, scale 13, we have indicated that some idea was somewhat "unfair."

Please do not omit any of the scales, and please indicate only one position per scale.

Sometimes it may seem to you that a scale is not related to a meaning or feeling you have about the underlined idea; nevertheless we would like to have you rate it anyway . . . It is your first impressions, the immediate "feelings" about the words, that we want. On the other hand, please do not be careless because we want your true impressions.

(Be sure to skip to item 31, Response Sheet IV)

Being Popular is

31. Tight	1	2	3	4	5	6	Loose
32. Safe	1	2	3	4	5	6	Dangerous
33. Ugly	1	2	3	4	5	6	Pretty

34. Weak	1	2	3	4	5	6	Strong
35. Old	1	2	3	4	5	6	New
36. Thin	1	2	3	4	5	6	Fat
37. Dry	1	2	3	4	5	6	Wet
38. Loud	1	2	3	4	5	6	Soft
39. Good	1	2	3	4	5	6	Bad
40. Little	1	2	3	4	5	6	Big

Girl is

41. Tight	1	2	3	4	5	6	Loose
42. Safe	1	2	3	4	5	6	Dangerous
43. Ugly	1	2	3	4	5	6	Pretty
44. Weak	1	2	3	4	5	6	Strong
45. Old	1	2	3	4	5	6	New
46. Thin	1	2	3	4	5	6	Fat
47. Dry	1	2	3	4	5	6	Wet
48. Loud	1	2	3	4	5	6	Soft
49. Good	1	2	3	4	5	6	Bad
50. Little	1	2	3	4	5	6	Big

(Go on to Response Sheet V, item 1)

Being Comfortable is

1. Tight	1	2	3	4	5	6	Loose
2. Safe	1	2	3	4	5	6	Dangerous
3. Ugly	1	2	3	4	5	6	Pretty
4. Weak	1	2	3	4	5	6	Strong
5. Old	1	2	3	4	5	6	New
6. Thin	1	2	3	4	5	6	Fat
7. Dry	1	2	3	4	5	6	Wet
8. Loud	1	2	3	4	5	6	Soft
9. Good	1	2	3	4	5	6	Bad
10. Little	1	2	3	4	5	6	Big

Having Power is

11. Tight	1	2	3	4	5	6	Loose
12. Safe	1	2	3	4	5	6	Dangerous
13. Ugly	1	2	3	4	5	6	Pretty
14. Weak	1	2	3	4	5	6	Strong
15. Old	1	2	3	4	5	6	New
16. Thin	1	2	3	4	5	6	Fat
17. Dry	1	2	3	4	5	6	Wet
18. Loud	1	2	3	4	5	6	Soft
19. Good	1	2	3	4	5	6	Bad
20. Little	1	2	3	4	5	6	Big

Boy is

21.	Tight	1	2	3	4	5	6	Loose
22.	Safe	1	2	3	4	5	6	Dangerous
23.	Ugly	1	2	3	4	5	6	Pretty
24.	Weak	1	2	3	4	5	6	Strong
25.	Old	1	2	3	4	5	6	New
26.	Thin	1	2	3	4	5	6	Fat
27.	Dry	1	2	3	4	5	6	Wet
28.	Loud	1	2	3	4	5	6	Soft
29.	Good	1	2	3	4	5	6	Bad
30.	Little	1	2	3	4	5	6	Big

Work is

31.	Tight	1	2	3	4	5	6	Loose
32.	Safe	1	2	3	4	5	6	Dangerous
33.	Ugly	1	2	3	4	5	6	Pretty
34.	Weak	1	2	3	4	5	6	Strong
35.	Old	1	2	3	4	5	6	New
36.	Thin	1	2	3	4	5	6	Fat
37.	Dry	1	2	3	4	5	6	Wet
38.	Loud	1	2	3	4	5	6	Soft
39.	Good	1	2	3	4	5	6	Bad
40.	Little	1	2	3	4	5	6	Big

Myself is

41.	Tight	1	2	3	4	5	6	Loose
42.	Safe	1	2	3	4	5	6	Dangerous
43.	Ugly	1	2	3	4	5	6	Pretty
44.	Weak	1	2	3	4	5	6	Strong
45.	Old	1	2	3	4	5	6	New
46.	Thin	1	2	3	4	5	6	Fat
47.	Dry	1	2	3	4	5	6	Wet
48.	Loud	1	2	3	4	5	6	Soft
49.	Good	1	2	3	4	5	6	Bad
50.	Little	1	2	3	4	5	6	Big

OBSERVATION SCHEDULE No. 1
Categories and Rationale

SUMMARY OF CATEGORIES EMPLOYED IN OBSERVATION

A. Statements by: Teacher
       Students

B. Statements addressed to: Teacher
          Students
          Class-as-a-whole

1. *Topic of Discussion*

  I— *idea-centered;* subject matter, opinions about experiences and ideas of phenomena outside the classroom.

  A— *Activity-centered;* instructions, work demands, rationale, reactions to learning activities.

  G— *Group-centered;* group standards, morale, organization, roles.

  P— *Person-centered;* needs, values, personality of individual qua person.

2. *Concern; relation to inquiry: operations*

  R— *Relationships* among concepts; interpretative, explanatory.

  D— *Data,* facts, quoted statements, part of culture; descriptive, remembered.

  S— *Subjective opinion;* awareness of own experience; fantasy, hunch, opinion.

  I— *Impulsive,* spontaneous acting out; exclamation, attack.

3. *Frame of Reference*

  P— *Professional;* behavior determined by reality factors; involves making of choices; inquiry-oriented.

  T— *Technical;* behavior determined by rules and prior considerations such as defined procedures, ground to be covered; achievement-oriented.

  S— *Self-concerned,* personal; behavior determined by own feelings, desire to promote and maintain personal role. Self-oriented.

  G— *Generalized, adult;* behavior is effort to socialize child within community stereotypic values of respect, tolerance, hard work, etc.

4. *Emotionality*

  a. *Fight:*

   T— By teacher; *threatening,* punitive, directed at class; affects climate.

   D— By teacher; *defensive,* usually directed at class.

b. *Dependency:*

S— *Submissive;* "tell me what *you want* me to do."

W—*Weak* or inadequate; I'm weak; be sympathetic; don't hit me."

R— *Rules;* "what is the right way; what does the book say; what is the procedure we agreed on."

c. *Flight:*

I— *Irrelevant;* off the point, wandering, withdrawn, nonpurposive, lost.

E— *Escape;* tension release through changing subject, humor, adjournment.

B— *Breakdown;* disorganized, incoherent, repetitious, fighting for time.

d. *Pairing:*

P—With *person.*

G—With *group.*

e. *Unidentifiable affect: A*

f. *Usefulness of humor:* + +, +, —, — —.

1. TOPIC OF DISCUSSION

In the classroom, conversation may be about ideas, activities, group organization and standards, or persons. Often it is about two of these at the same time. Topic of discussion is to be judged *entirely apart* from all the other categories such as how it is discussed, what sort of emotionality it contains, whether it is opinion and not fact, etc. The question for the observer is, "What is this statement talking about?" In most cases it is expected that this will be obvious; in some cases not. In an obvious case both the intent and the content agree; in non-obvious cases, it is likely that the intent belies the surface appearance of the content.

Ideas (I)

"Subject matter," presentation of ideas or opinions, reporting of relevant experiences, working on problems and thought questions. This category is confined to subject-related discussion, and specifically excludes discussion of group standards, giving of instructions, etc. But it does *include* evaluative reactions to ideas (so long as it is the idea that is being evaluated with little or no regard for who said it). It includes things one is reminded of—free associations—so long as they refer to experiences which extend, illuminate, contrast, etc. with the material under discussion. *Ideas* does not include any of the material defined in the other three categories, although they may appear along with such material. Examples:

That idea is incorrect. You have the wrong answer.

I agree with that idea. What do you think about this? (idea)

That's an easy mistake to make.

If wages go up, so will prices; what good is it to raise wages?

What problem arises over and over in this connection?

How many of the class have ever been on a ranch?

What do you girls admire about the heroine in the story?

All descriptions, explanations and interpretations of experiences related to course content.

(*Note:* The predominant element being reacted to is the ideational content. In some cases, the teacher's questions are also implicitly instructions, and might be confused with Activity; let us agree that questions simply to get more facts or opinions, or to clarify meanings belong in the category of ideas; the distinction is between doing (activity) and procedures and purposes consciously and explicity sought through a sequence of actions *versus* thoughts presented with no particular consciousness of a method of inquiry or of self as actor.)

Activity (A)

Learning activities, jobs to be done, assignments, are the subjects of discussion. The activity may be individual, subgroup or group. It is planned, has purposes, requires consciousness of procedures, has a set of reasons which justify the procedures. Note that the topic is some aspect of action one engages in or is thinking about engaging in. *Substantive* assumptions and propositions are *ideas,* but assumptions about how to proceed come under *activity.* Examples:

May we (pupils) play the racing game today?

If nobody has further questions (about the proposed test) you should all be able to get A's.

There's a TV show this weekend that you would enjoy.

Let's have volunteers to put problems on the board.

We won't be able to finish at this rate, so I'll take over.

Everybody write down the assignment so there will be no confusion tomorrow.

Draw our lines in diagramming exactly as shown in the book.

Read the question from the sheet and then give your answer.

Who would like to prepare and give a report on gerrymandering?

Group (G)

The topic of conversation is the group, its culture, values, generalized expectations of members, needs, etc. Comments in this category are likely to have a long-range influence on climate and culture. A very frequent kind of teacher comment is primarily to reinforce the values or standards of punctuality, work, accuracy and expenditure of effort. These comments are meant to be for the group to hear, even though they may be occasioned by and addressed to one person. The reactions of members to the group as an organization fits here, as well as comments evaluating the group (we are a good group, we did well). Comments about its specific performance *on tasks,* however, belong under *activity.* Comments about what will have to be done in order to carry out an activity belong under *activity,* but comments about who is going to do each of these things come under *group.* Examples:

Mike did a good job, even though he did not follow the outlined procedure. (originality)

I feel very bad about a theme turned in without thought.

Going to the basketball game won't get you into college—mastering algebra possibly will.

Nobody likes to work hard, but you'll thank me someday for making you work.

When you got to the board, write large enough for everyone to read. (rules)

If you haven't the material with you, why come to class? (preparation)

Quiet down, now!

The class showed up badly on that test.

Personal (P)

The topic of conversation is the individual—his personality, needs, values, attitudes, etc. His ideas and performance fit only to the extent that it matters that *he* is the one who uttered them; not for this category are ideas reacted to as data for the group to use to reach a conclusion or to solve a problem, nor ideas reacted to as expressing a feeling of the group. Ideas in this category are reacted to as an extension of the self of the individual. Those aspects of interpersonal exchange that are oblivious to the rest of the class fit *here;* those aspects designed to be over-heard by the class fit under *group*. Evaluative comments fit here to the extent they evaluate the person rather than the validity of his ideas or the perfection of his performance. (Thus "Good idea!" fits under ideas, but "Good idea, Carol!" fits under both ideas and personal, since it gives explicit recognition to the person.) Examples:

Why don't you stay home?

Stop whispering, John.

I agree with that, Jack.

Mike did a good job . . .

Doggone, get your hand *up*—you make me sleepy.

I'm glad to hear you didn't finish for once, Mitch.

Jack be quiet. We've heard enough from you.

Karen surprised even me by doing so well. Ha Ha.

Dual Ratings

Many sentences have components of two or more of the above categories. If they were broken down phrase by phrase, a single category might be assigned to each phrase. But if the unit being rated is the entire sentence—or the entire con-tribution—then it is enough to note only the dominant category.

2. LEVEL OF CONCERN

There are five categories: universals; reasons; objective data; subjective data; impulses. The categories make several continua: abstract to specific; contemplative to emotional; "outer" to "inner." They are arrived at by quite different mental activities: significant generalizations of ideas or values; interpretation and explanation; citing of written or authoritatively presented ideas; giving one's opinion about specific elements in a situation; "popping off " spontaneously and affectively.

They express different concerns:

P—A philosophical interest in the nature of man and the universe.

R—A concern with finding relationships among concepts or variables.

D—An effort to describe the world in objective terms.

S—A concern with one's own (subjective) awareness of his experience.

I—A spontaneous "acting out" of impulses to relieve tension.

In our model of inquiry, we tend to think of impulses, subjective data and objective data as information to help know or describe the situation; and of the reasons and universals as useful to understand, account for, and find significance in the situation. We should expect to find some movement between and among these levels; and would tend to think of such movement as the way to find "meaning."

The thing to be rated is the *concern* of the comment. Generally speaking, we conceive the category D, an effort simply to describe the world, as the teaching mode called "covering the ground." "Critical thinking" would certainly involve category R. Reflective thinking on "broad meanings" and tendencies would be category P. Concern with how students react to the other three categories would be category S. Responses unmediated by consciousness would be category I.

There is one tricky aspect to category D, covering the ground. The "ground" may include broad generalizations, reasons, etc., which are to be memorized and which operate primarily as cliches or stereotypes in the student's mind. In this case, although the comments take the form of P or R statements, they are still actually D statements—simply a part of the objective information the kid learns without internalizing. In other words, the concern is to discover what has already been formulated by others and put into books and lectures rather than to find significance or develop skills of interpretation, explanation and prediction.

Thus, the "level of concern" can also be thought of as the kind of mental operation signified by the statement. The reason for thinking of these categories as concerns rather than as operations is to make room for questions. Thus, the teacher may inquire about the "broad view of man implied in this incident"; this expresses a concern for the P level but is not itself a result of P level mental operation.

Reactions to statements at these different levels will not necessarily be on the same level as the statement. Thus the P statement, "The purpose of life is to get ready for death" could be reacted to at all five levels: "Baloney" (I); "that idea makes me uncomfortable" (S); "the author of that idea is Grobnitz" (D); "in that case I don't see how you would explain the development of arts and sciences" (R); "This idea expresses a feeling that all men have" (P). Examples:

P level (Philosophical)

What does Pearl symbolize? (character in story)

What do you think about Descartes' "I think, therefore I am."—what is he trying to get at?

What basis for the necessity of nations getting along together do you see in modern developments of communication, travel and warfare?

The theme is the struggle of man against nature . . . an epic theme.

R *level* (Relationships)

Does war make a country prosperous?

Who sets production rates in manufacturing?

Do you believe it (this explanation) and why or why not?

Show how international relations is influenced by trade and production.

Compare the treatment of superstition by Poe and Melville.

What were the differences between Silas Marner and Ebeneezer Scrooge as misers?

All right, class, how will we apply this formula to plotting our graph?

What interpretation shall we make of these test scores?

D *level* (Information, givens; descriptive, mundane orders)

How long do you want the themes to be?

An extraneous root is defined as follows . . .

The line separating subject from predicate should go straight up and down.

Let's have some volunteers who have completed the assignment to put it on the board.

Who was in the first cabinet? How did political parties get started in the U. S.? (Book)

Who will give a sketch of Melville?

Read the question from the sheet and then give your answer.

What are the three kinds of Federal powers indicated by the U. S. Constitution?

S *level* (Subjective)

That's fun and not a learning experience. I don't care about the people in the problem.

You should all get A's tomorrow.

A class can drive a teacher crazy.

How can you spell a word right 25 times one day and misspell it the next day?

Well, I'm glad to hear that you didn't finish for once, Mitch.

I feel very bad about a theme turned in without thought.

Nobody likes to work hard.

Note: Some comments could be either R or S level depending on what quality of mental operations produced them. Thus the following could be asking for interpretations from data already presented (R level) or they could be inviting unthoughtout opinion:

The U. S. was not very prosperous at the close of the Revolution. Why do you suppose this was so?

How could it occur that rural state populations dominate the legislature even though most people live in the cities?

Similarly, a theory might be offered as the rationale for some practice under consideration (R level) or it might be used as a subjective rationalization for one's own attitudinal bias (S level).

Latest educational theory says that the best education takes place when the student's are following their own interests, thus exploiting a "natural" educational opportunity.

You can't get anything out of reading unless you concentrate; and this requires effort.

I level (Impulsive)

Doggone, get your hand up. You make me sleepy.

Jack be quiet. We've had enough from you.

Karen surprised even me by doing well. Ha Ha.

Bruce, What's your trouble? (irritated)

Think you will have any cookies left for lunch?

If it fails we'll all bow our heads in shame.

3. TEACHER ROLE

A role is a set of expectations consistently held with respect to the performance of a function. Each teacher develops a set of expectations about how he shall teach; and these expectations appear to be held both by himself and by others. Underlying these expectations is the philosophy or point of view about the nature and method of teaching. Each behavior of the teacher is more or less consistent with his expectations.

Since, however, life in the classroom and the teacher-pupil relationship comprehends much more than the function of teaching, one might suppose that teachers at different times take several different roles, only one of which is primarily a "teaching" role. Thus the teacher is also a representative of the opinion of the adult community, a surrogate for authority, a counselor, a friend or enemy of particular children, an administrator, etc. His enactment of those other roles should, of course, not conflict with his role as teacher or guide of learning.

The categories to be described now lie beneath the details of role enactment; they are basically frames of reference within which the role-performance is understandable. Those frames of reference imply a philosophy about teaching as well as identification with a particular reference group.

P (Professional)

The frame of reference of a professional is organized around these basic postulates: that choices of behavior and procedure must be partly dependent on the realities in each situation (flexibility); that the demands to be met are to be deduced from an idea of "what needs to be done" rather than from the purpose of simply maintaining a procedure or relieving the teacher's anxiety; that there is a "discipline" to be learned, and this discipline is important. In the "professional" category we find teacher behaviors that recognize realities (individual differences, feelings); that signify efforts to diagnose; that show awareness of alternative ways of doing things; that encourage the learner to practice and understand the knowledge-discipline; that help encourage the group to see what roles are needed for different learning activities. This frame of reference can be summed up as inquiry-oriented. Examples:

Mike did a good job even though he changed the procedure.

A person can know "the facts" and still not act in accordance with them. Grading (giving marks) in social studies is hard. Should we grade on behavior?

To understand the background is more complex, though in the end more understanding than confusion will occur.

I agree with that, Jack, and think it would be worth discussing further.

There's a TV show this weekend dealing with Mayan culture.

Wars often make for prosperity, but the U. S. was not very prosperous at the close of the Revolution. Why do you suppose this was so?

How did I arrive at this formula?

Having gotten this far, what do you think we as a group need to plan to do next?

Can you develop a proof for this notion?

T (Technical)

The frame of reference of the technician is organized around these basic postulates: a complex function may be logically broken down into a sequence of steps; all instances of each step are identical; there is a "best" procedure to be employed for accomplishing each step. The technician works by formula more than purpose; his diagnosis goes no further than deciding on the step the group is involved in. He sees the classroom as a processing plant, and his job is to maintain a set of policies dictated by inflexible and unchangeable requirements; he sees the need for some accommodation or adjustment of individuals to the requirements and procedures; but he does not see individual differences as data to use in creating new procedures or in re-interpreting policies. Procedures are ends in themselves, and knowledge is defined as the organized information in the textbook. This frame of reference can be summed up as "achievement" rather than inquiry-oriented. Examples:

There need be *no* talking while handing in papers.

Write large enough for everyone to read. Now do it right.

I don't care about the details; get to the problem.

We won't have time to finish the story at this rate, so I'll read it to you myself.

I don't know what extraneous means, but an extraneous root is defined as follows.

The line separating subject from predicate should be straight up and down.

Everybody write this down so there will be no confusion.

S (Self-concerned, personal)

The frame of reference of the self-concerned teacher is his own personal comfort. His purposes are to meet his own needs for power, love, etc.; and such need-meeting is the route to comfort. Withall's categories of self-justification, capricious criticism, and steam-rollering fit here. Also attempts to be a good guy. The sort of teacher who is usually considered "inadequate" is likely to show a blend of self-concern and technical, for the rigid procedures may be fallen back on since he hasn't the ego strength to think on his feet in the face of shifting classroom conditions. On the other hand, there may be a complete absence of technical, since the rigid demands generated by fixed procedures tend to reduce the potency of the demands coming from an insatiable personality. Generally speaking, the self-concerned or personal behaviors of the teacher tend to carry a load of affect.

I never watch TV quiz shows, they are a waste of time.

Did you learn anything today, class? (bid for reassurance)

I don't know if I care to go over more of these questions—I don't know if its worth the trouble. (self-pity)

That's a silly error.

A class can drive a teacher crazy.

Captain Ahab would make a fine cheerleader.

I don't know how to explain what I mean. (defensive)

G (Generalized—Adult)

The frame of reference here is primarily that of an adult concerned with conditioning the child to accept the value-system of the general community or that group with which he personally identifies. The comments have a quality of indoctrination, and very generally sound like cliches or platitudes. The values involved are such things as the "importance" of education, the proper "respect" to be shown the teacher, the virtues of punctuality, hard work, concentration, tolerance, etc.—all left floating in the air and not operationally connected to on-going classroom activity. They are sentiments rather than policies or criteria for performance. Examples:

Unless you want to be dumb you have to study.

Dope addicts are not to be cast off as worthless.

You can't get anything out of reading unless you learn to concentrate; concentration is vital and requires effort; learn to concentrate.

Nobody likes to work hard, but someday you'll thank me for making you.

Going to a basketball game won't get you into college; doing algebra possibly will.

4. EMOTIONALITY

This is judged from the affect one hears in the statement. This affect engenders emotional response in the observer. Only statements arousing feeling in the observer can be rated as having emotionality. More than one quality of affect may be attributed to the statement; if the particular affect cannot be categorized with the code given below, then the symbol A (unidentifiable affect) is used. The categories for coding are:

a. *Fight*

T—Any fight statement addressed to the class or an individual student with the intent to punish or *threaten* the class. They affect the climate.

D—Any defensive statement by the teacher which has the quality of weakly lashing out at the class or defending himself from real or fancied attack. These statements might be directed at one kid, but ordinarily (if not always) will be directed at the class.

Examples—T statements:

Jack be quiet. We've had enough from you.

You are from a good middle class family and read the Tribune; and you don't know who Taft was?—(tempered hostility)

Next time your homework better be good! (to class—threat, direct)

Come on, you people know—lets have more people talking, not just four of us. (cajoling)

Examples—D statements:

I don't know if I care to go over these questions—I don't know if its worth it. —(hurt feelings, intrapunitive, guilt-provoking, but also weak)

Nobody likes to work hard—someday you'll thank me—(defensive)

Such drill is necessary for acquiring basic communication skills demanded in our society. Unless you want to be dumb, you have to study. (defensive, conditionally hostile)

I don't care what your other teacher says, spelling comes before extra-curric. activities. (defensive justification plus hostility at other teacher and his supporters)

b. *Dependency*

S—*Submissive.* Direct appeal to stronger *person,* giving up one's own self-determination. (I just want to do what you want me to do)

W—*Weak, inadequate.* (I am weak and muddled and want your *support,* not necessarily your direction.

R—*Rules.* (We give up our self-direction and power to choose because some extraneous authority must be obeyed.)

Examples—W statements:

If it fails, we'll all hold our heads in shame—

A class can drive a teacher crazy—

Did you learn anything? (seeking reassurance)

I don't know how to explain what I mean—(seeking sympathy)

I can't agree with that, but what do some of you others think? (seeking support, fearful of taking stand)

Examples—S statements:

What do you want me to do?

Professor Smith says this is the best way to do it.

Examples—R statements:

Lets draw our lines in diagramming in exactly the same way they are in the text—(unquestioned acceptance of "outside," apparently arbitrary authority)

I don't know what extraneous means, but an extraneous root is defined as . . .

You voted for more drill on sentences.

It is expected that we as a class learn this material at this time.

Read the question from the sheet and then give your answers—(this depends on how arbitrary the instruction is, that is, on how far it *feels* like a reasonable obvious thing to do)

c. *Flight*

I—irrelevant, off the point, out of field, free association, etc.
E—escape, in the sense of *tension reduction,* change of subject, humor.
B—breakdown, repititious, incoherent, rambling, intellecturalizing. Indicates a disorganization under stress. Fighting to gain time, etc.

Examples—I statements (irrelevant):

TV heroes never die . . . what happened to Kookie (free association)

Examples—E statements (escape):

Quiz shows in this room will not be rigged. (presumably a response to a legitimate concern or tension)

Examples—B statements (breakdown):

Long rambling illustration from a story, ending lamely with the point that "Don't look for greener pastures and let the present slip by" (which is also disorganized as a metaphor)

d. *Pairing*

P—Personal (agreement, support, warmth expressed to person)

G—Group (agreement, support, warmth expressed to group)

Examples—P statements (personal):

Yes, this is a universal theme . . . monumental (ego-building to student).

Think you will have any cookies left after lunch? (tempered with some hostility?)

That's an easy mistake to make.

Very good, that's excellent, Carol.

I would like to hear more of your good ideas, Jack—you think so clearly.

Examples—G Statements (group):

Now we are really getting some place. That's good.

This is a very pleasant class to work with.

Let's try for the jackpot.

These are really very good ideas we have on the board.

e. Unidentifiable affect: (A or a)

f. Usefulness of humor: $++$, $+$, $-$, $--$

TYPESCRIPTS CATEGORIZED
BY OBSERVATION
Schedule No. 1

TEACHER NO. 1

		Topic of Discussion	Level of Concern	Frame of Reference	Emotion-ality
T	In fact, now that I think of it, didn't he say this on the program?	I	D	P	
	Let them do whatever they want to in Europe and Asia. We just want to lookout for ourselves.	I	D	P	
	Why is this a silly, stupid point of view? Steve.	I	R	G	a
T	Do we need trade? Can't . . . can't we just get along by ourselves.	I	R	P	
T	Well lets say, Steve, that we have everything . . . Right? Sell your stuff.	I	R	P	
	We can't possibly keep being prosperous unless we build up overseas markets.	I	R	P	
	This is an economic fact.	I	D	P	
	You should have learned this from your geography in 6th and 7th grades.	I	D	T	
	To be a prosperous country, more has to go out than comes in. You have to sell the surplus	I	D	T	
	Just like if you were a farmer and had a family and lived on a farm, would you make any money				

TEACHER NO. 1

	Topic of Discussion	Level of Concern	Frame of Reference	Emotion-ality
and be getting ahead in the world if you just raised what your family needed? Maybe you wouldn't have to go to town to buy anything from the store, but unless you had a cash crop which you could sell, you couldn't, unless you could make, for example, your own automobile and your own records and that sort of thing. You wouldn't have many of the nice things in life.	I	R	P	
T (laugh) Well you can barter for a lot of things, but the point is that you always have something left over to sell.	I	D	T	
This is how you make money.	I	R	P	
T That's true.	I	D	T	p
Mike!				
T Yes.				
T That man! That ridiculous man, polishing his ridiculous car, saying they can do anything they want to over there, but we're going to look out for ourselves.	I	S	G	a
Well how long is it going to take that intercontinental B.M. to get here, if it's set off	I	R	P	
T 15 minutes!				
Steve.	I	D	T	
T Drop the bomb?	I	D	T	
Well I think everybody in here is bright enough to realize that wouldn't solve any problem at all.	I	S	P	1
T Well he was doing it with such reverence too. You could just				

TEACHER NO. 1

		Topic of Discussion	Level of Concern	Frame of Reference	Emotion-ality
	see that this was what he worshipped—a big powerful car.	I	D	G	
T	I don't know that. It doesn't matter.	I	S	T	
	The point was that his job, working with this steel god, (laugh), the great big car.	I	S	G	
T	It probably meant that too.	I	D	T	p
	It probably meant that too, that he couldn't think a little better—perhaps, that if he had a better education.	I	S	P	
	You see a better education would have told him that things just don't stay the same.	I	S	G	
	He should have been able to have seen the writing on the wall that might tell that we are on the downgrade . . .	I	S	T	
	that many people can tell today.	I	S	G	

TEACHER NO. 2

		Topic of Discussion	Level of Concern	Frame of Reference	Emotion-ality
T	Just like saying, Jack Lindstrom—we'd put Jack and Lindstrom on the same line. Wouldn't we?	I	D	T	p
T	A noun clause?	I	D	T	
	Not all the time, no!	I	D	T	
T	No!	I	D	T	a
T	No more than there is any set word that you start a sentence with.	I	D	T	
T	Nancy				
T	I marked it incorrect.	I	D	T	
T	For two reasons—for two reasons	I	D	G	d

TEACHER NO. 2

		Topic of Discussion	Level of Concern	Frame of Reference	Emotion-ality
	The first reason because you were told to write me a noun clause using a predicate nomina- tive, I believe, and that wasn't . . .	I	D	T	r
	Second reason. You were told not to give me back examples that I had given you.	I	D	T	r
	See you used it as an object of a preposition in that sentence.	I	D	T	
	All right, any others?	I	D	T	
	If you would draw the drape over there you wouldn't have the glare in your eyes.	P	S	T	
T	You people don't think for yourselves, huh?	G	I	G	
T	Barbara.				
T	No, because we won't say all of them are(were) adjective.	I	D	T	
	A non-restrictive clause is an adjective clause. Isn't it?	I	D	T	
	Weren't you—When you are talking about a non-restrictive clause and a restrictive clause you are talking about an adjective clause.	I	D	T	
	If you remember reading in that— in the English book back there on your parenthetical expressions, it classified a parenthetical expression as neither.	I	D	T	r
	It didn't classify it as an adjective or an adverb. Did it?	I	D	T	r
T	Yes.				
T	No!				
T	You are trying to complicate matters again. But they are not because a restrictive or non-restrictive	P	I	T	l

TEACHER NO. 2

		Topic of Discussion	Level of Concern	Frame of Reference	Emotion-ality
	clause must be adjective and adjective only.	I	D	T	
T	They are a part of your sentence.	I	D	T	
	A restrictive clause is an important part of that sentence, a parenthetical expression is not.	I	D	T	
T	All right, a nonrestrictive clause?	I	D	T	
	Now you diagram it as a part of that sentence—do you not?	I	D	T	
	Whereas if you remember diagrams of parenthetical expression in the book, they were diagrammed as being separate entirely from the sentence . . . weren't they?	I	D	T	r
T	A restrictive clause is not set off by comma.	I	D	T	

Appendix F.

OBSERVATION SCHEDULE No. 2

Observers equipped with seating charts employed the following shorthand symbols to record every perceived instance of teacher questions and student work and non-work behavior during a class hour.

On each occasion when the teacher asked a question, a number 1, 2, 3, ... etc., was recorded in a special cell on the seating chart assigned to the teacher. A reply by a student was given the same number as the question to which he replied.

Work behaviors:

Raise hand	1
Volunteer answer	1, 2, 3, . . . , etc.
Conscripted answer	$1_c, 2_c, \ldots$, etc.
Impulsive (spoken-out) answer	$1_s, 2_s, \ldots$, etc.
Lesson participation—apart from questions asked by teacher	X, X, . . . , etc.
Questions asked by student	$X_q, X_q, \ldots$, etc.
Comments made by students	$X_c, X_c, \ldots$, etc.

Non-work behaviors

private play	P, P, . . . , etc.
study, not related to class	S, S, . . . , etc.
disturb other students	D, D, . . . , etc.
blow off to class—loud, impulsive remark	B, B, . . . , etc.
receive a reprimand from the teacher	R, R, . . . , etc.
whisper with his neighbor	$\longrightarrow$ (link linking cells on seating chart with arrow point indicating recipient of whisper.)

Appendix G.
POST MEETING REACTION OPINIONNAIRE

OPINIONNAIRE

Teacher_____ Period_____ Date_____ Name or Code_____

1. How did you feel this class meeting was today?

•	•	•	•	•
no good	poor	all right	good	excellent

2. How often did you find yourself wanting to say things to the class, but for one reason or another you did not actually say them?

•	•	•	•	•
never	a few times	fairly often	frequently	very frequently

3. How worthwhile to you was what you learned in class today?

•	•	•	•
worthless; waste of time	rather pointless now possibly useful someday	quite useful and interesting	highly meaningful, most worthwhile

4. How often were the questions and comments of the students really understood and replied to fairly and helpfully?

•	•	•	•	•
never	a few times	fairly often	frequently	very frequently

5. How clearly did you understand exactly what the class was supposed to do today?

•	•	•	•
not at all	vaguely	pretty well	perfectly

6. How difficult was the lesson today?

•	•	•	•
too simple; baby stuff	fairly easy	rather hard	very difficult over my head

7. What part of the class was really working on the lesson today?

•	•	•	•
almost nobody	a few students	most of the class	everybody

8. How satisfied were you with the part you played in class today?

•	•	•	•
really disappointed or discouraged	rather disappointed	fairly well satisfied	really delighted and pleased

9. Toward how many students did you feel uncomfortable today? Give number_____

10. Whose actions and behavior concerned you *most* in class today? Check one.

yours_____ teacher's_____ a few others'_____ whole class'_____

STUDENT OPINION SURVEY

Name_____   School_____

STUDENT OPINION SURVEY

Students differ in feelings about the classes they are taking in school. We would like to know how you feel about the classes that you have.

Begin by listing all the classes you are taking by writing the specific subject name under the general heading that is provided below. The letter symbol that is underlined will be used to represent the subject throughout the remainder of the questionnaire. For instance, if you are taking American Literature you would write the course title "American Literature" under the general heading English, and this course would be represented by the letter *E*. At this point fill in the names of all the courses you are now taking in the appropriate spaces below.

E̲ English   S̲S̲ Social Studies   M̲a Mathematics

_____   _____   _____

F̲ Foreign Language   P̲E Physical Education   S̲c Science

_____   _____   _____

B̲ Business Courses   M̲u Music   H̲ Home Economics

_____   _____   _____

I̲ Industrial Courses (shops)   A̲ Art   O̲ Other

_____   _____   _____

The next thing to do is for you to write the specific course names and the letter symbols, underlined above, in the spaces provided at the top of the next page. Do this and then return to the remainder of the instructions on this page.

_____

From here on the task is for you to rate all of your classes on the list of items on the next page. Read each statement carefully. Then place the letter symbol for each course in the space on the scale that best represents your opinion about this course. For instance, a student taking E̲ American Literature, S̲S̲ World

245

History, PE Physical Education, Ma Algebra, and Sc Biology rated these courses on the following statement in this manner:

"To what extent do each of your classes consist of students whom you admire?"

• Ma • Sc • • • PE • • E • • • SS •

not   completely
at all

Notice that this student placed the letters SS at the extreme right of the scale. This indicates that he admires all the students in his World History class. The letters Ma are placed on the extreme left of the scale indicating that there are no students in Algebra that he admires. In his opinion the other courses fall between these extremes and are rated accordingly. This student spaced his ratings over the entire length of the scale. However, another student might have placed his ratings all on the left end of the scale, while still another student would want to use only the right end. From this you can see that you should feel free to use that part of the scale that best represents your opinion about the statement. Finally, as in the example, you are to use the spaces provided between the points on the scale. Please do not place any ratings above the points themselves.

Remember you are to rate all of your classes on an item before you proceed to the next item.

Letter Symbol	Course Title		Letter Symbol	Course Title
___	_____		___	_____
___	_____		___	_____
___	_____		___	_____

1. In general, how meaningful and rewarding is each of your classes?

• • • • • • • • • • •

not   completely
at all

2. To what extent does each class make use of subject materials of the sort you would like to study or work with next year?

• • • • • • • • • • •

not   completely
at all

3. To what extent does each of your classes deal with things that are interesting to talk about outside of class?

• • • • • • • • • • •

hardly   most of
ever   the time

4. To what extent is each of your classes a group of students you would like to work with again next year?

• • • • • • • • • • •

not   completely
at all

5. To what extent are you willing to do the work required in each of your classes?

• • • • • • • • • • •

not   completely
at all

6. To what extent does each class further your plans for things you want to do after you leave high school?

• • • • • • • • • • •

not   completely
at all

7. In what ways have each of these classes opened new interests or things for you to do?

• • • • • • • • • • •

no ways   lots
  at all   of ways

8. What per cent of the time in each class is spent on activities which personally you enjoy?

• • • • • • • • • • •

none of   all of
the time   the time

9. To what extent does each class have a teacher with whom you would like to work again next year?

• • • • • • • • • • •

would not   would like
like at all   completely

10. To what extent do you look forward to going to each of these classes?

• • • • • • • • • • •

not   completely
at all

11. To what extent have each of the classes given you opportunity to practice or try out some special skill or talent which you have?

• • • • • • • • • • •

little or   lots of
no opportunity   opportunity

Appendix I.

GUESS WHO

I. How often is each behavior done by you, and by the teacher?

In the columns below, indicate how often each behavior is done by *yourself,* and by the *teacher.*

In each box in each column, write in one of these numbers:

1. *Always*—seems to happen every day.
2. *Usually*—this is done nearly every day.
3. *Occasionally*—occurs once every week or two.
4. *Rarely*—this has been done a few times.
5. *Never*—I can't remember this being done.

II. To what extent do you think that the teacher approves of these behaviors?

In the boxes below, place the number which you feel indicates the extent to which the teacher approves or disapproves of these behaviors or actions.

1. Is *really glad* when a student does this.
2. *Shows approval* when this is done.
3. *Neither approves nor disapproves* of this behavior.
4. *Barely tolerates this behavior.*
5. *Tries not to let this happen again.*

I. How often?

I Do It	Teacher Does It	WHO:	II. How approving is teacher?
Example: 1	4	a. talks about himself	4
		1. suggests new ideas when the group seems to be stuck? 2. continually asks questions in class? 3. talks the most? 4. usually comes up with the answers? 5. does not pay attention in class? 6. brings in a lot of extra work that he or she has done on things relating to this class? 7. usually thinks his or her idea is best? 8. gets things done when most of the class is confused? 9. never breaks the rules?* 10. offers compromises, when there are several sides being taken on a topic? 11. usually criticizes and blames other peoples' actions or ideas? 12. disrupts the work of the class by clowning and fooling around? 13. goes along with the class, and just accepts the ideas of others?* 14. worries about how well he or she is doing? 15. sympathizes with others when this is needed most? 16. usually talks out of turn? 17. seems to get upset when unable to answer questions? 18. presents ideas which influence the class?	

*Dropped from analysis as subjects were confused by item wording.

SOCIOMETRIC QUESTIONNAIRE

INTRODUCTORY PAGE

We choose to be with different people for a variety of purposes. We may seek one person to work with and another person with whom to just chat about personal experiences and interests.

Consider each of your classmates and teacher and how you feel about them. On the following pages you are asked to choose which ones you would prefer to work with, and which ones you would prefer to sit and chat with.

* * * * * *

Name _____

Period_____

School_____

WORK

Whom would you choose to work with?

Opposite each person's name, enter the appropriate number as follows:

1. If you *really would be very pleased* to work with this person.
2. If you would *like* to work with this person.
3. If you would *be willing* to work with this person.
4. If you *don't know how you feel* about working with this person.
5. If you would *rather not* work with this person.

Robert Blumberg	_____	Ronald Fagorske	_____
Clifford Brickman	_____	Michael Graham	_____
Mr. Brunner	_____	Kathrine Kaestner	_____
Joe Cheesebrough	_____	John King	_____
Anne Collins	_____	Ruth Mosner	_____
Richard Engberg	_____	Susan Mulrine	_____

CHAT WITH

Whom would you choose to sit and chat with?

Opposite each person's name enter the appropriate number:

1. If you *really would be very pleased* to sit and chat with this person.
2. If you would *like* to chat with this person.
3. If you would *be willing* to chat with this person.
4. If you *don't know how you feel* about chatting with this person.
5. If you would *rather not* chat with this person.

Robert Blumberg	_____	Ruth Mosner	_____
Clifford Brickman	_____	Susan Mulrine	_____
Mr. Brunner	_____	Bruce Nahrath	_____
Joe Cheesebrough	_____	Donna Olsen	_____
Anne Collins	_____	Sandra Peck	_____
Richard Engberg	_____	Diane Rosenberg	_____
Ronald Fagorske	_____	James Schaefer	_____
Michael Graham	_____	Mark Stein	_____
Kathrine Kaestner	_____	Charles Theune	_____
John King	_____	Richard Weisel	_____

Appendix K.

TABLES TO ACCOMPANY CHAPTER 7

TABLE 22

S Students, Positive Responses, Teacher No. 5

Classroom Activities

A	3.	Take a test or quiz. (5)
CW	6.	Have a general class discussion led by another student. (4)
SG	8.	Work with a committee to prepare a lesson to present to the class. (4)
A	10.	Work independently on a project you choose yourself. (5)
TD	11.	Get individual help and instruction from the teacher while doing class work. (5)
CW	12.	Listen to other students recite on assigned homework. (4)
SG	13.	Be a member of a panel discussion. (5)
A	15.	Do research in the library for your term paper. (4)
CW	18.	Have a class discussion on a topic suggested by the teacher. (4)
TD	19.	Discuss with the teacher possible activities you could do. (4)
A	21.	Explain a homework problem to the class. (4)
CW	22.	Engage in class discussion of a movie or filmstrip. (5)
TD	23.	Have a conference with the teacher concerning your progress in class. (5)
A	24.	Perform a demonstration or experiment for the class. (5)
SG	25.	Discuss class material with a group of other students. (5)
A	27.	Prepare, on your own, to make a report to the class. (5)
TD	28.	Listen to the teacher explain or demonstrate a lesson. (5)
CW	29.	Participate in a class drill on fundamentals. (5)
SG	30.	Work with other students in designing and completing a project. (5)
A	33.	Study by yourself to prepare for a test. (5)
A	37.	Begin homework assignments. (5)
TD	39.	Have teacher make it clear what is expected of the class. (5)
SG	40.	Evaluate the quality of committee work with other group members. (4)

Participation

Mu	Cl (L)	46.	Hearing the ideas of other students during class discussion of some topic. (5)
Mu	Co (L)	47.	Listening to others on a student committee discuss a topic on the agenda. (4)

252

Mu	A (T)	49.	Telling a group of your friends your ideas and feelings about the plans they are discussing. (5)
Eval	Cl (T)	50.	Pointing out good ideas and attacking bad ideas offered during class discussion. (5)
Mu	IP (L)	52.	Listening to another student explain his ideas about a topic you both are familiar with. (5)
Threat	Fr (T)	53.	Telling a group of friends your most intimate and personal feelings. (3)
Threat	A (L)	57.	Reading a story in which the author describes the inner-most private feelings of the characters. (5)
Role	A (T)	59.	Thinking about an argument you might have used to persuade others. (4)
Role	Cl (T)	66.	Keeping class discussion on the beam by bringing the others back to the problem. (4)
Neut	IP (T)	67.	Telling a visiting student from another school about the program of courses taught in your school. (5)
Role	Cl (L)	68.	Having the teacher call on individual students by name to answer his questions during class discussion. (5)
Mu	Fr (L)	73.	Listening to others in a group of your friends discuss their ideas and beliefs about some problem you all have. (5)
Neut	A (L)	77.	Sitting by yourself remembering things that happened today. (5)
Neut	Fr (T)	78.	Reporting to a group of your friends all about an article you read recently. (4)
Mu	Cl (T)	80.	Being one of the more active persons during a lively class discussion. (5)
Eval	A (T)	81.	Evaluating a TV program and criticizing the parts that are dull, silly, etc. (5)
Role	Co (T)	82.	Telling a student committee what to do next when they appear mixed up or confused. (5)
Role	IP (T)	84.	Trying to interest another student in some hobby or interest of yours. (5)
Neut	Fr (L)	85.	Listening to a group of your friends discuss some event such as a football game they went to. (4)
Mu	IP (T)	86.	Telling another student your ideas about a problem you both have. (5)
Role	Co (L)	89.	Having the chairman of a student committee explain exactly what everyone must do. (4)
Neut	A (T)	91.	Sitting by yourself quietly thinking about things that interest or puzzle you. (5)
Neut	IP (L)	93.	Hearing a student from another school talk about his school. (5)
Threat	Co (T)	94.	Telling a student committee quite frankly how you feel about the various members. (3)
Neut	Co (T)	95.	Describing to a student committee what a similar committee did last year. (4)

Teacher Description

109. "Challenging" type fostering independence best fits impression of typical teacher. (1)
111. "Traditional-professional" type best fits impression of typical teacher.   (1)
123. "Traditional-professional" type best fits impression of teacher with whom one is most comfortable. (1)
106. "Subject expert" type best fits impression of typical teacher. (2)

Who Should Decide?

T–Class	2.	Whether and under what conditions you will work alone.
Y–Comm	3.	How much help you should accept from another student.
T	5.	How worthwhile was your contribution to the class discussion.
Comm	9.	When a committee should ask one of its disturbing members to leave.
Y–T	10.	How good a job the teacher did today.
Y & T	15.	Whether the committee you were on did a good job or not.
T–Y	20.	Who you should sit next to in class.
Y & T	23.	When your skit or report is ready to present to the class.
T–Class	24.	Whether it is all right to ask questions to end someone's boring report.

Situations

56. When no one was sticking to the point, I . . . (Flight)
   A. got bored with the whole thing. (Flight)
   B. called for clarification of the topic. (Work)
58. When the group agreed that it needed more information about how members felt, I . . . (Work)
   A. described my feelings to the group. (Work)
   B. wasn't sure I wanted to discuss my feelings. (Flight)

Ways of Doing Things

T–S	92.	When talking with a teacher I lose the thread of conversation. (E)
G–W	93.	When doing things with a few other students I get confused in my work. (E)
C–O	94.	When doing things as a member of the class I get into trouble with others. (E)
T–I	96.	When discussing things with a teacher I lose interest in ideas. (E)
C–S	98.	When doing things as a member of a class I get distracted from my work. (E)
A–S	99.	When doing things alone I find it hard to think clearly about myself. (E)
A–I	103.	When doing things by myself I lose interest in ideas. (D)
T–S	104.	When doing things with a teacher I feel very little enjoyment. (D)
G–I	105.	While doing things with a few other students I forget ideas that have been explained. (E)

C–I   107. When doing things in a class I find it hard to consider ideas.   (D)

T–C   108. When doing something with a teacher I have difficulty talking.   (E)

C–O   110. When doing things in a class I lose interest in what others say.   (D)

A–W   111. When doing things by myself I get distracted from work easily.   (C)

T–I   112. When discussing things with a teacher I find it hard to consider ideas.   (E)

C–W   114. When doing things as a member of a class I get confused in my work.   (E)

G–O   116. When doing things with a few other students I have difficulty talking.   (E)

T–W   117. When I do something with a teacher I get confused in my work.   (E)

G–I   121. When doing things with a few other students I find it hard to consider ideas.   (E)

C–I   123. When doing things as a member of a class I get confused in my thinking.   (D)

G–W   125. When doing things with a few other students I learn very little for my work efforts.   (E)

C–O   126. When discussing things in a class I have difficulty talking to others.   (E)

A–S   127. When doing things by myself I get confused in my work.   (E)

T–I   128. When doing something with a teacher I get confused in my thinking.   (E)

G–S   129. When doing things with other students I have difficulty expressing my feelings.   (E)

C–W   130. When doing things as a member of a class I learn very little for my work efforts.   (D)

A–S   131. I feel very little enjoyment when doing things by myself.   (E)

G–O   132. When doing things with a few other students I feel difficulty in getting help as needed.   (D)

T–W   133. When doing something with a teacher I waste time.   (E)

C–S   134. When doing things as a member of the class I have trouble expressing my feelings.   (E)

A–I   135. When doing things by myself I find it hard to consider ideas.   (D)

T–S   136. When doing something with a teacher I become upset easily.   (E)

Values

V4   19. Live a life of service to others.   (9)

V6   22. Do things actively and with enthusiasm.   (9)

V3   23. Find the center of real meaning for life within myself, e.g., self-assurance.   (9)

V1   26. Behave in a self-disciplined manner.   (9)

V4   29. Live in close relationship with others sharing their joys and sorrows.   (8)

V2   31. Plunge courageously into the challenges of life.   (9)

V6   32. Become a responsible, conscientious citizen.   (9)

V3   34. Be aware of and understand my innermost thoughts.   (8)
V6   36. Live in a reasonable and intelligent way.   (9)
V2   41. Overcome, dominate, or conquer obstacles that hinder human progress.   (9)
V4   43. Be willing to make sacrifices for the welfare of others.   (9)
V2   46. Actively compete for the rewards of life.   (9)
V1   47. Try always to act in a socially acceptable manner.   (9)
V3   4. Find the most enduring satisfactions within myself.   (8)
V1   8. Live a moral life of high ideas.   (9)
V2   12. Master the world I live in by use of science, tools, and bodily energy.   (9)
V3   15. "Go it alone," for the most part, and not be dependent on others.   (9)
V2   18. Get out and do things and not merely be a thinker or spectator.   (9)
V4   20. Have confidence in other people and the world in general.   (8)
V6   22. Be thrifty and plan for tomorrow.   (9)
V6   25. Be a credit to my family and community.   (9)

Words, Words, Words

Being Popular is:

Ri.   More *tight* than loose   (2)
Po.   More *weak* than strong   (2)
Ac.   Somewhat more *old* than new   (3)
Ri.   Somewha*t* more *dry* than wet   (3)

Girl is:

Ri.   Somewhat more *tight* than loose (3)
Ri.   Somewhat more *wet* than dry   (4)
Po.   Somewhat more *little* than big   (3)

Being Comfortable is:

Ac.   Somewhat more *new* than old   (4)
Ac.   Somewhat more *thin* than fat   (3)

Having Power is:

Po.   More *strong* than weak   (5)
Ri.   More *dry* than wet   (2)
Po.   More *big* than little   (5)

Boy is:

Se.   More *loud* than soft   (2)

Work is:

Ac.   More *fat* than thin   (5)

Myself is:

Se.   More *safe* than dangerous   (2)
Ri.   More *wet* than dry   (5)
Ev.   More *good* than bad   (2)

TABLE 23

S Students, Negative Responses, Teacher No. 5

Participation

Eval   IP (L)   56. Being told by another student just what are your good and bad points.   (3)

Role   FR(L)   58. Having one of your friends give advice to the whole gang.   (3)

Ways of Doing Things

A–I   106. When doing things by myself I think about things I want to say to others.   (B)

TABLE 24

U Students, Negative Responses, Teacher No. 5

Classroom Activities

CW   1. Have planning sessions in which the whole class is involved.   (2)

SG   8. Work with a committee to prepare a lesson to present to the class.   (2)

A   14. Grade or evaluate your own performance in an activity.   (2)

A   15. Do research in the library for your term paper.   (3)

TD   19. Discuss with the teacher possible activities you could do.   (3)

SG   20. Organize a group activity with a few other students.   (2)

TD   23. Have a conference with the teacher concerning your progress in class.   (3)

SG   25. Discuss class material with a group of other students.   (2)

A   27. Prepare, on your own, to make a report to the class.   (3)

TD   28. Listen to the teacher explain or demonstrate a lesson.   (3)

CW   29. Participate in a class drill on fundamentals.   (3)

CW   32. Watch as problems are put on the board by another student.   (2)

A   33. Study by yourself to prepare for a test.   (2)

SG   36. Study basic course content as a member of a small group of students.   (3)

A   37. Begin homework assignments.   (2)

TD   39. Have teacher make it clear what is expected of the class.   (3)

SG   40. Evaluate the quality of committee work with other group members.   (2)

Participation

Mu   Cl (L)   46. Hearing the ideas of other students during class discussion of some topic.   (3)

Threat   Fr (T)   53. Telling a group of friends your most intimate and personal feelings.   (1)

Threat   A (L)   57. Reading a story in which the author describes the innermost private feelings of the characters.   (2)

Threat   Cl (T)   62. Making a speech to the class about your personal experience.   (2)

Eval   Fr (T)   63. Telling a group of friends what is good or bad about their ideas and behaviors. (1)

Role   Co (T)   66. Keeping class discussion on the beam by bringing the others back to the problem. (2)

Neut   IP (T)   67. Telling a visiting student from another school about the program of courses taught in your school. (3)

Neut   Cl (L)   72. Listening to other students giving carefully prepared and detailed reports to the class. (2)

Mu   Fr (L)   73. Listening to others in a group of your friends discuss their ideas and beliefs about some problem you all have. (2)

Eval   A (L)   74. Critically comparing yourself to one of the characters in a TV show or play. (1)

Mu   Co (T)   75. Telling a student committee your views about the project they are discussing.

Neut   A (L)   77. Sitting by yourself remembering things that happened today. (3)

Neut   Fr (T)   78. Reporting to a group of your friends all about an article you read recently. (2)

Mu   Cl (T)   80. Being one of the more active persons during a lively class discussion. (2)

Eval   A (T)   81. Evaluating a TV program and criticizing the parts that are dull, silly, etc. (2)

Role   IP (T)   84. Trying to interest another student in some hobby or interest of yours. (2)

Mu   IP (T)   86. Telling another student your ideas about a problem you both have. (3)

Eval   Cl (L)   87. Hearing the class give opinions about the quality of their own discussion. (2)

Threat   IP (L)   90. Hearing the private experiences of another student. (1)

Neut   A (T)   91. Sitting by yourself quietly thinking about things that interest or puzzle you. (3)

Teacher Description

114. The "rules"type is out of line with the students impression of best teacher for learning. (4)

119. The "pupil-teacher planning" type is out of line with students impression of best teacher for comfort. (4)

Ways of Doing Things

C–I   91. When doing things in a class I forget ideas that have been explained previously. (B)

T–O   92. When talking with a teacher I lose the thread of conversation. (A)

G–W   93. When doing things with a few other students I get confused in my work. (C)

T–I   96. When discussing things with a teacher I lose interest in ideas. (C)

C–S   98. When doing things as a member of a class I get distracted from my work.   (C)

A–S   99. When doing things alone I find it hard to think clearly about myself.   (B)

T–W   101. When I have work to do with a teacher I don't feel like getting started.   (C)

A–I   103. When doing things by myself I lose interest in ideas.   (B)

T–S   104. When doing things with a teacher I feel very little enjoyment.   (A)

G–I   105. While doing things with a few other students I forget ideas that have been explained.   (B)

G–I   107. When doing things in a class I find it hard to consider ideas.   (B)

G–W   109. When doing things with a few other students I waste time.   (B)

C–O   110. When doing things in a class I lose interest in what others say.   (C)

A–W   111. When doing things by myself I get distracted from work easily.   (A)

G–S   113. When doing things with a few other students I feel very little enjoyment.   (C)

C–W   114. When doing things as a member of a class I get confused in my work.   (B)

G–O   116. When doing things with a few other students I have difficulty talking.   (B)

T–W   117. When I do something with a teacher I get confused in my work.   (B)

A–I   119. When doing things by myself I have difficulty understanding ideas.   (B)

G–I   121. When doing things with a few other students I find it hard to consider ideas.   (C)

C–I   123. When doing things as a member of a class I get confused in my thinking.   (C)

G–W   125. When doing things with a few other students I learn very little for my work efforts.   (B)

C–O   126. When discussing things in a class I have difficulty talking to others.   (B)

A–S   127. When doing things by myself I get confused in my work.   (B)

T–I   128. When doing something with a teacher I get confused in my thinking.   (C)

C–W   130. When doing things as a member of a class I learn very little for my work efforts.   (C)

G–O   132. When doing things with a few other students I feel difficulty in getting help as needed.   (B)

C–S   134. When doing things as a member of the class I have trouble expressing my feelings.   (C)

A–I   135. When doing things by myself I find it hard to consider ideas.   (B)

Values

V5   28. Be at ease both physically and mentally without being too ambitious.   (1)

V5   33. Enjoy good food and drink with a group of friends.   (1)

V1   42. Live a well-organized and productive life.   (5)

V2   3. Work hard on my own and pioneer some endeavor.   (5)

V6   5. Live in harmony with nature and other men.   (5)

Words, Words, Words

Being comfortable is:

Ac.	*New* rather than old	(6)
Ev.	*Bad* rather than good	(4, 5)

Having power is:

Po.	Somewhat *big* rather than little	(4)

Boy is:

Ri.	Somewhat more *loose* than tight	(4)
Ac.	*Fat* rather than thin	(6)
Se.	Somewhat more *soft* than loud	(4)

Work is:

Ev.	More *pretty* than ugly	(5)
Ac.	More *new* than old	(5)
Ac.	Somewhat more *fat* than thin	(4)
Ev.	Somewhat more *good* than bad	(3)

Myself is:

Se.	Somewhat more *dangerous* than safe	(4)
Po.	*Strong* rather than weak	(6)
Ev.	More *bad* than good	(4)
Po.	*Big* rather than little	(6)

Being popular is:

Po.	*Strong* rather than weak	(6)
Ri.	*Wet* rather than dry	(6)

Girl is:

Ac.	*New* rather than old	(6)

TABLE 25

U Students, Positive Responses, Teacher No. 5

Teacher Descriptions

122. The "Buddy" type generally fits the student impression of teacher with whom they would be comfortable.   (2)

Who Should Decide?

Class	2.	Whether and under what conditions you will work alone.
Comm	3.	How much help you should accept from another student.
Comm	8.	What conclusions you should reach from a discussion of current events.
T	10.	How good a job the teacher did today.
Class	12.	To what extent is the behavior of another student out of line.
Y & T	16.	Whether it is a good idea to see the school counselor about a personal problem.
Y	20.	Whom you should sit next to in class.
Y & T	23.	When your report or skit is ready to present to the class.
Class	24.	Whether it is allright to ask questions to end someone's boring report.

Situations

32. When the group wanted his views about the task, Sam . . . (Work)
    A. wondered why they wanted his views. (Fight)
    B. thought of what he might tell them. (Work)
34. When Don said he felt closest to me, I . . . (Pairing)
    A. was glad. (Pairing)
    B. was suspicious. (Fight)
43. When the group wasn't interested, I . . . (Flight)
    A. just didn't feel like working. (Flight)
    B. thought that the leader should do something about it. (Depend)
45. When I became angry at Jack, I . . . (Fight)
    A. felt like dozing off. (Flight)
    B. ridiculed his comments. (Fight)
47. When Art criticized Bert, I . . . (Fight)
    A. wished that the teacher would help Bert. (Depend)
    B. felt grateful to Art for really expressing what we both felt. (Pairing)
53. When Harry thought that he needed a lot of help, Martin . . . (Depend)
    A. warmly encouraged him to get it. (Pairing)
    B. helped him analyze the problem. (Depend)
56. When no one was sticking to the point, I . . . (Flight)
    A. got bored with the whole thing. (Flight)
    B. called for clarification of the topic. (Work)
58. When the group agreed that it needed more information about how members felt, I . . . (Work)
    A. describe my feelings to the group. (Work)
    B. wasn't sure I wanted to discuss my feelings. (Fight)
59. When the leader offered to help Carl, Joe . . . (Pairing)
    A. wanted help too. (Depend)
    B. resented the leader's offer. (Fight)
60. When Dave and Lou argued, I . . . (Fight)
    A. asked Hank how he felt about them. (Pairing)
    B. hoped they would slug it out. (Fight)
71. Together John and Fred . . . (Pairing)
    A. wasted the group's time. (Flight)
    B. supported one another's arguments. (Pairing)
72. When Mal offered to help me, I . . . (Pairing)
    A. said I was sorry, but I had something else to do. (Flight)
    B. was pleased that we would be partners. (Pairing)
75. When Lou turned to me, I . . . (Pairing)
    A. wished that he would mind his own business. (Fight)
    B. asked him for help. (Depend)

Ways of Doing Things

A–I   106. When doing things by myself I think about things I want to say to others. (D)

Values

V4   24. Trust in the goodness of nature and life in general. (9)

TABLES OF ITEMS INCLUDED IN THE FACTORS DISCUSSED IN CHAPTER 9

Table 26. Numbers of Items Contributing to the Dimensions of Factor I

Sections of the Assessment Battery

Dimensions:	Cl. Ac. +	−	Ptcp. +	−	T.D. +	−	Who? +	−	Sit. +	−	Ways +	−	R.G. +	−	Val. +	−	Words +	−
A	4		6								1		2	2	4			
B	11		6								3							
C	3		9						3		4		2	1	2			
D			1						1		2				3		2	
E	1		1		4		1				1							

Table 27. Numbers of Items Contributing to the Dimensions of Factor III

Sections of the Assessment Battery

Dimensions:	Cl. Ac. +	−	Ptcp. +	−	T.D. +	−	Who? +	−	Sit. +	−	Ways +	−	R.G. +	−	Val. +	−	Words +	−
A	1		13		1				2	6	1				3		2	7
B		4	1		1				2	3	7	3			1	2	2	
C											1				6	1	2	
D			8								1				3			

Table 28. Numbers of Items Contributing to the Dimensions of Factor IV

Sections of the Assessment Battery

Dimensions:	Cl. Ac. +	−	Ptcp. +	−	T.D. +	−	Who? +	−	Sit. +	−	Ways +	−	R.G. +	−	Val. +	−	Words +	−
A		3	2		4				1		2		2					4
B		8	2						1		2		4					
C				1					5		1						2	2
D																25		

Table 29. Numbers of Items Contributing to the Dimensions of Factor II

Sections of the Assessment Battery

Dimensions:	Cl. Ac.		Ptcp.		T.D.		Who?		Sit.		Ways		R.G.		Val.		Words	
	+	−	+	−	+	−	+	−	+	−	+	−	+	−	+	−	+	−
A		13							3		2		2					1
B		6				1		2	3		2		2					3
C			1						6		2		2	2				5
D			1												7	1		4

Table 30. Numbers of Items Contributing to the Dimensions of Factor V

Sections of the Assessment Battery

Dimensions:	Cl. Ac.		Ptcp.		T.D.		Who?		Sit.		Ways		R.G.		Val.		Words	
	+	−	+	−	+	−	+	−	+	−	+	−	+	−	+	−	+	−
A													1		15	1	1	
B	1		6	1							1		4		1		2	
C		2		1	4						3		1					1
D		3								2			1		2			2
E				2				1	4						2	1		

Table 31. Numbers of Items Contributing to the Dimensions of Factor VI

Sections of the Assessment Battery

Dimensions:	Cl. Ac.		Ptcp.		T.D.		Who?		Sit.		Ways		R.G.		Val.		Words	
	+	−	+	−	+	−	+	−	+	−	+	−	+	−	+	−	+	−
A				5						1	2							2
B													1		9		8	
C	4							1					4					
D						3		1			4		1					
E				1					5	2	1		5	1	1		8	1

Table 32. Numbers of Items Contributing to the Dimensions of Factor 1'

Sections of the Assessment Battery

Dimensions:	Cl. Ac.		Ptcp.		T.D.		Who?		Sit.		Ways		R.G.		Val.		Words	
	+	−	+	−	+	−	+	−	+	−	+	−	+	−	+	−	+	−
A									1		1				10	4	3	1
B				4					4						5	9	9	
C	3								3				1		2	2	3	
D																	9	

Table 33. Numbers of Items Contributing to Factor V'

Sections of the Assessment Battery

Dimensions:	Cl. Ac. +	Cl. Ac. −	Ptcp. +	Ptcp. −	T.D. +	T.D. −	Who? +	Who? −	Sit. +	Sit. −	Ways +	Ways −	R.G. +	R.G. −	Val. +	Val. −	Words +	Words −
A				4					3		2							7
B		4	1		3						3		2					
C		5		3					1		6		2					
D		1		5					7		3	1	2		2			5
E															2	7		

Table 34. Numbers of Items Contributing to Factor IV'

Sections of the Assessment Battery

Dimensions:	Cl. Ac. +	Cl. Ac. −	Ptcp. +	Ptcp. −	T.D. +	T.D. −	Who? +	Who? −	Sit. +	Sit. −	Ways +	Ways −	R.G. +	R.G. −	Val. +	Val. −	Words +	Words −
A			2	2			1		2				2			1	5	
B		6		1	4				3		1							2
C	1	3		2			1				1				2		3	6
D															2	19		

Table 35. Numbers of Items Contributing to Factor II'

Sections of the Assessment Battery

Dimensions:	Cl. Ac. +	Cl. Ac. −	Ptcp. +	Ptcp. −	T.D. +	T.D. −	Who? +	Who? −	Sit. +	Sit. −	Ways +	Ways −	R.G. +	R.G. −	Val. +	Val. −	Words +	Words −
A	10	4													1			
B		2							7		1		5		1		5	
C	6				2										1			
D	1	2													7		1	3
E		3							9				6			1	1	1
F					2										10			

Table 36. Numbers of Items Contributing to Factor III'

Sections of the Assessment Battery

Dimensions:	Cl. Ac. +	Cl. Ac. −	Ptcp. +	Ptcp. −	T.D. +	T.D. −	Who? +	Who? −	Sit. +	Sit. −	Ways +	Ways −	R.G. +	R.G. −	Val. +	Val. −	Words +	Words −
A			12		1				3		2	1				7	2	
B			14				3				2		2			4	8	
C			1				1		1				1	1	1			
D		1	2		1				1		1		2					2

Table 37. Numbers of Items Contributing to Factor VI'

Sections of the Assessment Battery

Dimensions:	Cl. +	Cl. −	Ac. +	Ac. −	Ptcp. +	Ptcp. −	T.D. +	T.D. −	Who? +	Who? −	Sit. +	Sit. −	Ways +	Ways −	R.G. +	R.G. −	Val. +	Val. −	Words +	Words −
A	5						1	2	1	1							1			
B						1	2					3					3			3
C												1			1	4	2		1	1
D																	11			3
E				1	1						1	4					10	3		
F	3										3	1				4				

Appendix M.
RESUME: SUMMARY OF
PROCEDURES AND FINDINGS*

Background

The recent rapid increases in the number of students to be educated, in the "amount" of knowledge to be learned, and in the difficulties of preparing and maintaining an adequate teaching force have focused interest on the problem of "better utilization" of human resources, both of teachers and students, in schools. One result of this concern is the effort to discover better ways to "group" students and select them into more educationally productive classes.

Objectives

1. To discover a sound basis for grouping of students.
2. To test experimentally the usefulness of such a basis by trying it out in practice under research conditions.
3. To formulate practical and theoretical implications for education in schools.

Procedure

1. Collection of descriptions of "types" of students as perceived by teacher; classification of these descriptions. The descriptions were collected from 25 teachers working with the School Improvement Program, University of Chicago, and from 70 teachers attending a workshop in the Oklahoma Public Schools, Oklahoma City, during 1958.

2. Description by teachers of the "sort of students they liked best to have in class on the grounds that they would have the best educational experience." The description was presented by throwing 44 Q-sort cards which we had formulated from the written descriptions. Forty Midwest high school teachers sorted the Q cards for us during the fall of 1959.

3. Construction of an Assessment Battery to measure those aspects of personality that we considered, on the basis of theoretical analysis, to have most to do with determining how the student would be likely to participate in groups. The Battery contained nine sections, consisted of 724 items, took three hours to administer, and yielded 172 scores. The sections of the battery were tried out and validated against interviews with teachers and classes associated with the School Improvement Project.

4. Administration of the Assessment Battery to 750 students in nine Midwest high schools and in two junior high schools. A sample of 216 was composed in

* Reported to cooperative Research Branch, U. S. Office of Education, June, 1961.

266

such a way that there were equal numbers of students in grades 8 to 11, equal numbers of boys and girls, and equal distribution of three ranges of socioeconomic "background" throughout each sex-grade subsample.

5. Factor analysis of the test papers of the 216 students. This was done on the Univac at the University of Chicago. Twenty factors were "pulled out."

6. Revision and shortening of the Assessment Battery to 405 items.

7. Selection of 15 "experimental" teachers in eight Midwest high schools, to teach a "teachable" class that we would compose for them and a control class that their administrators, following their regular practices, would compose for them.

8. Nomination by each of the 15 teachers of students who "got a lot out of class" and who "got very little out of class"—during the spring of 1959.

9. Administration of the Assessment Battery to all students thus nominated, and counting of all the responses made by the groups of "successful" and "unsuccessful" students nominated by each teacher. From these counts, a "teachability" key was constructed for each teacher.

10. Administration of the Assessment Battery to all the students, 1640 of them, available to be in each of the 15 teachers' classes during the next school year. The papers were then scored with the "teachability" key for each teacher, as appropriate, and the highest scoring students were designated to be that teacher's "teachable" class.

11. Development of observation schedules to use in observing the classes; also Post-Meeting Reaction Sheets, Guess Who tests, Opinion surveys, Sociometric questionnaires, "projective" achievement tests for each course, and objective achievement tests for each course.

12. Administration of all achievement tests to all 30 classes at the beginning of the school year. Regular observation of all classes by observer teams, four to six times during the year. Tape recording of one session in each class, and line-by-line analysis and coding of all remarks. Administration of the post-meeting reaction sheets at the end of 10 to 50 meetings in each class. Administration of the other instruments, including final achievement tests, during the spring of 1960. Also, readministration of the Assessment Battery to all students and teachers.

13. Tabulation of all data, summer 1960 to December 1960.

14. In addition, factor analysis of the pre- and post-assessment batteries of two teachers and all the students in their classes, January 1961 to June 1961.

15. Elimination of two teachers for whom the data were incomplete.

Results

1. The 300 "types" of students described by the 95 teachers revealed four basic categories: "good" (teacher-facilitative), "bad" (teacher hindering or obstructing), "indifferent but nontoxic" (hardly noticed), and "sick" (anxiety-arousing).

2. The teacher's Q-sort descriptions of "the sort of student they liked best to have in class on the grounds they would have the best educational experience" varied markedly and drastically from teacher to teacher, with entirely different emphases on critical thinking, personal adequacy, and social skills and values.

3. The factor analysis of the assessment batteries of 216 students was shut off

after 20 factors had been teased out of the test data. The largest factor, representing 11% of the total variance in the data, portrays optimistic, dependent, and teacher-submissive pupils. The other factors were smaller, accounting for from two and a half to seven percent of the variance.

4. Of the 13 teachable classes, 11 received higher marks from the teacher, 1 received lower marks, and 1 received the same marks—as compared to the corresponding control classes.

5. Of the 13 teachable classes, 5 showed superior gains on achievement tests and 8 showed inferior gains—as compared to the corresponding control classes.

6. Comparing the half of the class with the highest teachability scores with the half of the class receiving the lowest teachability scores, in the 26 classes, three-quarters of the "top half" groups received higher marks from the teacher. The same number of top and bottom half groups gained more on achievement tests.

7. Each of the 8 items on the Post-Meeting Reaction questionnaire was preferred more often by teachable classes than by control classes. Eight of the teachable classes preferred, on the average, more of the 8 items than did their corresponding control classes.

8. Nine of the 13 teachers preferred the students in the experimental class to "work with" or to "chat with." Six of the 13 teachers preferred the experimental students for both purposes.

9. The correlation between the amount of the teacher's mean preference for his classes and the mean achievement gain of the students in the classes was zero.

10. The students in 9 of the control classes preferred the teacher to "chat with" and to "work with" more than did the students in the corresponding experimental classes.

11. The students in 11 experimental classes preferred each other more than did the students in the corresponding control classes to "chat with;" and 8 experimental classes showed a similar preference with respect to "work with."

12. In general, the experimental students rated their classes no higher as compared to the other classes they were taking than did the control classes. Thus preferences seemed to be for activities and persons but not necessarily for the "course."

13. Sixty-six items on the Assessment Battery were found to contribute significantly to teachability among the 13 teachers. These items portray a high degree of personal adequacy, striving to realize one's capabilities, uneasy control over this striving, and effort to develop such control through: acceptance of social values, development of cooperative ways of working, adoption of a strong orientation to "work," and preference for a "firm" teacher with whom one can identify.

14. On the other hand, there is great variability in the make-up of the teachability factor from teacher to teacher. The 66 items account for an average of only 47% to the teachability items for each teacher; and the various sections of the Assessment Battery are represented very differently by the teachability items for each teacher.

15. Of the 95 categories of observation by observers and students, 36% discriminated significantly among the 13 experimental and control classes. These

core items portray the teachability classes as classes with higher solidarity. The 5 themes that emerge are: a more work-oriented, less inattentive, less distractable class; more work-solidarity among the students; more enthusiasm in the teacher's approval of work; less rigidity, more flexibility in the teaching; greater permissiveness with respect to disruptive behavior which, however, occurs very much less frequently. The teacher "gives more of himself," and is "more of a person" in the teachable classes. The differences in the behavior of the teacher seem mostly to be more or less involuntary changes in the way he responds to the higher solidarity, more manageable class.

16. There is, however, great variability in this pattern of difference from one teacher to the next. The categories, significant for the 13 teachers as a group, represent on the average only 41% of the significant categories for any particular teacher; and the various kinds of observations contribute very differently to the pattern.

17. One long case study and four short case studies, based on all the data for five teachers and their classes, show that the teachers wanted and got very different things in their "teachability" classes. (a) One teacher appeared to want more vigorous, personally involving interaction with his students; (b) another wanted a class that could penetrate deeper into principles of algebra; (c) another wanted a class she could go faster with; (d) another wanted a pleasant, friendly, nonwork oriented class that would make him feel more adequate; (e) another wanted a class in which he could combine "counseling" with teaching. In these five situations, varying in the extent of their psychological exploitation of students, all except (d) were successful in the eyes of the teacher. In case (d) the teachable class started off better but rapidly deteriorated because neither the teacher nor the students he selected as teachable were able to give the group the leadership it needed.

18. The case study of changes in factors during the year showed a gradual shift on the part of teacher and experimental students toward less personal enthusiasm and uniqueness, more social control and conformity. The changes were consistent with observations of this teacher.

Conclusions

1. "Teachability" grouping, which gives each teacher a classful of students "like" those whom he believes have in the past "got a lot out of class," results in more "manageable" classes and in higher attainment of the teacher's purposes.

2. The teacher tends to be more satisfied with his teachable class, to like the students better and to give them higher grades. The students tend to be more orderly and manageable, more cooperative, and more satisfied with the activities. They do not necessarily like the teacher better as a person, nor do they tend to rate the course as a whole higher (as compared to other courses). They do tend to like each other better, and their class appears to be more cohesive than the control class.

3. The changed behavior of the teacher in his teachable group seems to be mostly due to his responding differently to his class. He does not consciously plan differently nor execute different strategies.

4. The students, although operating more to give the teacher what he seeks, may gain less satisfaction in the teachable class. This appears to be the case when the teacher is primarily concerned with meeting his own psychological needs rather than with educating the class. The resulting exploitative situation may be reacted to negatively by the students—even though they still perform better in the teacher's eyes.

5. If the personal need of the teacher is strongly dominant and is antithetical to group development, then his teachable class may in fact deteriorate rapidly and become chaotic. This is the one exception to conclusions 1 and 2.

6. Teacher grades appear to reflect attainment of the purposes of the teacher. They reflect "achievement" insofar as "achievement" is central among the teacher's purposes. In half of the cases we studied, achievement, while sought through procedures presumably planned for it, was not very central as compared to such things as enabling the teacher to play some role he wanted or developing a particular quality of interaction among the students.

7. We conclude that the teachable class facilitates the execution, through teaching, of the teacher's purposes, but teachability grouping as such does not make him a different or better educator. That is a different problem and will have to be approached through tactics of training and re-education of the teacher.

8. For teachability grouping to be possible, there must be a choice of teachers available to teach a subject. The more differences exist among the styles of these teachers, the greater range of students can be accommodated.

9. This implies, too, that beyond a general orientation to inquiry, the teachers should be selected to have quite different styles of teaching. The further implication is that, defined procedurally, there is no one "right" way to teach.

10. It is further seen that the teacher has to help by selecting the children who are models for the teachable students. This is pushed further to the conclusion that grouping ought to be counted among the professional responsibilities of the faculty, and should not be left solely in the hands of the administration.

11. Three ways of getting teachable groups, none of which involves tests or consultants, are suggested.

INDEX

WESTMAR COLLEGE LIBRARY